Greenhill Books

LUFTWAFFE VICTORIOUS

Other Greenhill books on World War II include:

BOMBER HARRIS
His Life and Times
Air Commodore Henry Probert
ISBN 1-85367-555-5

GOERING
Roger Manvell and Heinrich Fraenkel
ISBN 1-85367-612-8

LUFTWAFFE OVER AMERICA
The Secret Plans to Bomb the United States in World War II
Manfred Griehl
ISBN 1-86267-608-X

LUFTWAFFE X-PLANES
German Experimental and Prototype Planes of World War II
Manfred Griehl
ISBN 1-85367-577-7

THE RECONSTRUCTION OF WARRIORS
Archibald McIndoe, the Royal Air Force and the Guinea Pig Club
E. R. Mayhew
ISBN 1-85367-610-1

Other Greenhill Alternate History books include:

BATTLE OF THE BULGE
Hitler's Alternate Scenarios
Edited by Peter G. Tsouras
ISBN 1-85267-607-1

DISASTER AT D-DAY
The Germans Defeat the Allies, June 1944
Peter G. Tsouras
ISBN 1-85367-603-9

THE HITLER OPTIONS
Alternate Decisions of World War II
Edited by Kenneth Macksey
ISBN 1-85367-312-9

THIRD REICH VICTORIOUS
The Alternate History of how the Germans Won the War
Edited by Peter G. Tsouras
ISBN 1-85367-492-3

Greenhill offer a ten per cent discount on any books ordered directly from them.
Please call (0044) (0)208 458 6314 or email sales@greenhillbooks.com.

For information on other Greenhill books, please visit www.greenhillbooks.com.
You can write to Greenhill at Park House, 1 Russell Gardens, London NW11 9NN

LUFTWAFFE VICTORIOUS

AN ALTERNATE HISTORY

Mike Spick

GREENHILL BOOKS LONDON
STACKPOLE BOOKS PENNSYLVANIA

Greenhill Books

Luftwaffe Victorious: An Alternate History
first published 2005 by
Greenhill Books, Lionel Leventhal Limited, Park House,
1 Russell Gardens, London NW11 9NN
www.greenhillbooks.com
and
Stackpole Books, 5067 Ritter Road, Mechanicsburg,
PA 17055, USA

British Library Cataloguing in Publication Data
Mike Spick
Luftwaffe victorious : an alternate history
1. Germany. Luftwaffe
2. World War, 1939–1945 – Aerial operations, German
3. Imaginary wars and battles
I. Title
940.5′44943

ISBN 1-85367-611-X

Library of Congress Cataloging-in-Publication Data available

Edited, designed and typeset by Roger Chesneau

Maps drawn by John Richards

Printed and bound in Great Britain by
Creative Print and Design (Wales), Ebbw Vale

Contents

Illustrations

The Me 410A-1, the best Luftwaffe intruder of the war
The Mosquito NF.XII— a superb night fighter and intruder
The Heinkel He 177 Greif
The Heinkel He 277, a rehash of the deeply flawed He 177
Republic P-47 Thunderbolts
A straggling B-17G under attack by an Me 262
The Grumman F6F Hellcat carrier fighter
A Focke-Wulf FW 190G, with an underslung BV 246 glide bomb
The rocket-propelled Me 163 short-range point-defence interceptor
An Me 262A-1a of II./JG 7
The Sturmvogel, the Jabo variant of the Me 262
The two-seater Me 262B, produced to aid conversion training
An Me 262B fitted with radar — the world's first jet night fighter
The Arado Ar 234B Blitz — the world's first jet bomber to enter service
The four-engine Arado Ar 234C, built in small numbers
A Lockheed P-80A Shooting Star returns to base
The de Havilland Vampire, the first jet able to operate from grass fields
The Amerikabomber — the Messerschmitt Me 264A
A specially modified Boeing B-29

Maps and Diagrams

Preface

ADMIRED by the few; feared by the many. That was the German Luftwaffe even before the outbreak of war in 1939. By June 1940 the proud boast of its Commander-in-Chief, Great War fighter ace Hermann Göring — 'lightning speed and undreamed-of might' — seemed justified. The Luftwaffe had spearheaded the Blitzkrieg, which, in a mere ten months, had subjugated Poland, occupied Denmark and Norway and then swept across the Low Countries and France. With the Heer (Army) halted by the English Channel, the Luftwaffe prepared to carry the fight to Great Britain alone.

Few gave the British a chance of survival — certainly not Joseph Kennedy, the American Ambassador to the Court of St James, who predicted that the British government would capitulate in a matter of weeks. He was in error. In the summer of 1940 the apparently invincible Luftwaffe met its first defeat. It was the first crack in the legend — a legend that ended more than four years later with the once-vaunted German Air Force reduced to a pitiable rump, unable even to mount an effective defence of its homeland.

Could the Luftwaffe have done better? Could it have exerted a greater influence on the course of the war? Could it even have been decisive? The answer to the first two questions must be a resounding 'yes', although whether it could have been decisive is open to doubt. Air warfare does not exist in a vacuum: the outcome depends equally, or more so, on events on land and sea.

One thing is certain. The Luftwaffe High Command (OKL) made many grave errors. Priorities were all too often wrong and corners were all too frequently cut, all of which impacted on war-fighting capability. Perhaps worst of all, the Luftwaffe found itself fighting a long war on three fronts when it had been equipped for a series of short campaigns.

If blame for Luftwaffe's shortcomings must be apportioned, then the Commander-in-Chief, Hermann Göring, must take the lion's share, Although extremely able in many respects, he was a political appointee with neither the background nor training for high command. His monstrous ego often made him impervious to reason. His appointments were either cronies like Udet or younger, more malleable men such as Jeschonnek, both of whom he eventually drove to suicide. His method of leadership was to cajole those who pleased him but shout at the rest. To be fair, this was so strongly ingrained in German culture that there was even a special word for it—*Anschnauzen*. Although himself a bully, however, Göring was unable to stand up to Hitler, even on issues of the utmost importance.

As there was no believable way in which Göring's character could be modified to allow him to provide effective leadership, there was no alternative other than to remove him from the scene at an early stage, in a fairly credible manner. With Göring safely in Valhalla, he could be replaced by a hard-nosed commander-in-chief, willing and able to stand up to the Führer as the need arose. The selection process was far from easy. Various candidates were considered but rejected, for reasons as stated. Nor was it credible for Göring's immediate replacement to last the entire war. Two more commanders-in-chief follow the first.

Command changes provided the opportunity to dump some of the dead wood. The playboy Udet was eased from a technical position to which he was totally unsuited, to become (for the second time) General der Jagdflieger. Still later, his failing health forced his retirement. Therefore he did not commit suicide. Nor did the able but inexperienced Jeschonnek shoot himself: just one of a succession of Chiefs of Staff, he was humanely promoted sideways.

Adolf Galland, the most charismatic Luftwaffe leader of the war, suffered because of the historical tinkering. As Udet did not commit suicide, Mölders could not have been killed in an air accident while flying to his state funeral and therefore Galland could not succeed Mölders as General der Jagdflieger. Yet Galland could not simply be ignored; still less could such an iconic figure be bumped off. The solution adopted was for him to be taken prisoner.

Hitler has been portrayed as rather less meddlesome than was in fact the case. The rationale for this is that, as the war was going better than was in fact the case, he had more incentive to trust his generals and less motivation to intervene in operational matters. For this reason, there is no bomb plot in July 1944.

Apart from removing Göring, one massive historical liberty has been taken. Generalleutnant Walther Wever did not die in an air crash in 1936. Instead, he survived to oversee the production of a true strategic bomber, which entered service during 1940 and which influenced events on all fronts throughout the war. He was also mainly responsible for the formation of a dedicated transport fleet, rather than having to 'borrow' aircraft and crews from the multi-engine training units.

A professional and far-sighted Luftwaffe commander-in-chief influenced three major decisions. The first was to allow control of the long-range maritime reconnaissance bomber force to pass to the Kriegsmarine, thus aiding the Atlantic campaign. The second was to get Hitler to reverse his decision, taken in late 1941, to discontinue intruder operations over England. This had far-reaching effects. Large RAF Bomber Command raids were very susceptible to disruption. Over the next three years, Luftwaffe intruders truly proved their worth. Equally important was the C-in-C's refusal to attempt to air supply the Sixth Army at Stalingrad in the middle of winter. Hitler sacked the incumbent, only to find that his replacement was equally adamant. General von Paulus was then allowed to break out, and his quarter of a million men survived to fight another day. This had incalculable consequences for the war in the East.

The importance of a German strategic bomber force is hard to overstate. There were two contenders, and the selection of the Do 19 over the Ju 89 has been based on the sound technical and economic reasons listed. While such a force could hardly have been decisive, it would certainly have posed grave problems for the Western Allies and even worse ones for the

Soviet Union. It is reasonable to suppose that development would have been continued with the Do 219.

Another area which is not historically accurate concerns the development of German jet engines. This section is just plausible, but the scenario is unlikely. It is based on the invaluable help and advice of my good friend Dr Alfred Price, who also suggested jamming 'Pip-Squeak' in 1940. The latter was so simple that one wonders why it was not done in real life.

The greatest divergence from historical fact is the German A-bomb project, which never came close to being realised. However, had it been ignored or glossed over, readers who aware of the 'Germany First' agreement might have regarded the outcome as a foregone conclusion, thus destroying any suspense.

Also explored is the potential of German aircraft carriers. Although these were quite rightly abandoned at an early stage, the concept certainly merited a closer look. Two Schlachtgruppen loose in the Atlantic would have been the stuff of nightmares.

While the Austrian former corporal has often been criticised for poor judgement, he was not always wrong. His decision to use the Me 262 as a Jabo against the invasion beaches was sounder than is usually credited. Given its overwhelming speed, the jet Jabo could certainly have penetrated the Allied fighter umbrella. The impossibility of accurately aiming a couple of conventional bombs could have been overcome by using area weapons such as the readily available cluster bomb. Scattering death and destruction over a wide area, these would have been very effective against a crowded beach-head.

It would, of course, been unrealistic for the British, then later the Russians and Americans, to have sat back and done nothing in the face of the changing German threats. Therefore the more obvious responses and countermeasures have been assumed. A major problem was to prevent the Russian 'steamroller' from gathering momentum. Three devices were used. The first was of course the Uralbomber. The second was the survival of the German Sixth Army, already mentioned. The third was the capture of the Caucasus oilfields. This last would have largely nullified the 1944 Allied air offensive against German fuel production.

The narrative follows the historical record as closely as possible, only gradually diverging as new factors are introduced. At first the results of these are given in detail, but, as the war continues, a broader brush is needed. By 1945, there seemed little point in pursuing an Italian campaign, the need for which has been glossed over.

Because air warfare does not exist in isolation, the text has on occasion had to stray into the domains of the Army and Navy. As the narrative concerns the Luftwaffe, the temptation to stray into the minds of the enemy has been, in the main, resisted.

As the nuclear strike against Germany could have run to a book on its own, a few comments are in order. Munich was chosen for several reasons. It had strong Nazi connections, and it had not been too heavily bombed previously — the better to demonstrate the destructive power of the new weapon. If approached from the south it involved only a short penetration of Reich air space, giving the defenders little time to react. The other problem was where to base the unit of B-29s which had been formed for this very special mission. For security reasons, a base 'in the boonies' was needed. Surrounded by miles and miles of Libyan desert, Castel Benito, about fifteen miles south of Tripoli, met all the requirements. Now read on.

Mike Spick
Morton, Lincolnshire

Prologue

FOR the observer in the leading bomber, making his first war flight over England, things could hardly be better. On each side of him were four huge bombers, stepped back and up in a perfect vic. Close astern were two more identical vics—27 bombers in all. Trailing them were four Gruppen of Heinkel He 111s, black smoke coming from their exhausts as they attempted to maintain station, with two Gruppen of fast Junkers Ju 88s bringing up the rear. Nor was this all. Ahead and on each side, small specks high above betrayed the presence of escort fighters while, closer at hand, Schwärme of Bf 109 fighters criss-crossed incessantly, weaving to avoid overshooting the bombers.

Great banks of cumulus obstructed the view to either side, but the view of the Thames estuary below was unimpeded. Ahead, blurred by industrial haze, was London, with Tower Bridge just visible, although a thin layer of cloud shrouded the City of London itself. The West India Docks, the main target of today's raid, were in the clear, and dead ahead.

The huge column of bombers rumbled majestically on its way, as inexorable as a steamroller. Fired with adrenaline, the observer mused that all that was needed was a sound track—Wagner's *Ride of the Valkyries* for preference. The shield-maidens riding out to bring the heroic slain to Valhalla! That was it! That was what was missing! So far, no battle, no slain! It was all too quiet. Could it be true, as that halfwit Chief of Luftwaffe Intelligence Josef 'Beppo' Schmid alleged, that the English really were down to their last fifty Spitfires?

He had no means of knowing that this first all-out assault on London had wrong-footed RAF Fighter Command, which, expecting a continuation of attacks on its airfields, had deployed to defend them, leaving the German raiders an almost clear run to the capital. So far, the only sign of opposition had been a few desultory flak bursts staining the sky out on their left, but none close enough to be really dangerous. Nonetheless, the formation opened out, and individual aircraft started to snake across the sky in what was called the 'Flak Waltz'.

'Where the hell are the Lords?' he asked pilot Erwin Wims, using the expression for English flyers popularised by Great War fighter ace Theo Osterkamp. Before Wims could reply, over the intercom came a shout of *'Achtung, Spitfeuer, links hoch!'* punctuated by a brief burst of machine-gun fire at an enemy fighter far out of range, the sole effect of which was to fill the cabin with exciting-smelling cordite smoke. From the south-west, a dozen small black dots approached. As they grew rapidly in size, 109s converged from all directions to cut them off. The observer stared left, eager for his first sight of a Spitfire.

'Schwachkopf!' he said scornfully. 'They're Hurricanes!' Jochen Krebs, the dorsal turret gunner who had given the warning, relapsed into a hurt silence. The observer peered avidly at the distant fighters as they wheeled and swung, but was unable to make out any significant details of the action. A pity!

By now the Gruppe was approaching its primary target. A small alteration of course put them nose-on into the forecast wind. Bomb-aimer Egbert Karvola, crouched over the Lotfe 7 sight, fed instructions back to Wims. After what seemed an eternity, a cry of *'Los!'* came from Karvola and the aircraft lifted slightly as the deadly cargo was released and fell away.

The seconds ticked by, and then, some 4,000m (13,124ft) below, evil grey chrysanthemums flowered across the dock area as the bombs detonated, their thunder unheard by the aircraft high above. Wims began a gentle turn to the left, with the remaining 26 aircraft of the Gruppe keeping station on him.

As the aircraft straightened out on a course for home, the observer leaned back in his seat with a satisfied smile. Removing his flying helmet, mask and goggles, he donned his official gold-braided hat. He had eschewed flying overalls in favour of his fancy sky-blue uniform, and the sun, lowering in the west, glinted on the blue and gold Maltese cross which hung around his neck on a black and silver ribbon. It was the Pour Le Mérite, commonly known as The Blue Max, Germany's highest decoration for valour in the Great War. With it hung the Grand Cross of the Ritterkreuz, a decoration unique to the wearer. The scene was recorded for posterity by the on-board photographer, who mentally captioned it: 'Reichsmarschall Göring leads crushing attack on London. English surrender certain within days!'

Hermann Wilhelm Göring was often portrayed abroad as a buffoon and a poltroon. The truth was that he was not only multi-talented and energetic but also extremely popular in the Third Reich. Despite his vanity, which made some of his detractors assert that he even wore his Blue Max in bed, he was not averse to a joke against himself — provided, of course, that he had made it! In his famous 'guns before butter' speech in Munich in 1938, he had asked his audience: 'After all, what does butter do?' Slapping his ample girth, and grinning broadly, he answered his own question: 'It makes you fat!' The crowd roared with laughter. Here was the decorated Great War hero, the second most powerful man in the Third Reich, saying in effect, 'Look, I am human too!' The laughter was warm and affectionate. Göring had the common touch to a rare degree!

He wore many hats — Prime Minister of Prussia, Reich Minister of Aviation, Reich Minister of Economics, plus several other posts, and finally, Commander-in-Chief of the Luftwaffe, the world's mightiest air force. Outranked only by Adolf Hitler, he was the second most powerful man in Nazi Germany. So what on earth was he doing, flying a combat mission against the capital city of the greatest empire that the world had ever seen?

The truth is that he was paying off old scores. A lover of pomp, ceremony and his own importance, he had expected to be an honoured guest at the Coronation of King George VI in London in 1937. Alas, the less salubrious parts of his past had caught up with him. Founder of the infamous Geheime Staats Polizei (Gestapo), and deeply involved in the equally infamous 'Night of the Long Knives', he was not welcome in

England. Unbelieving, he had flown into Croydon, from where he was driven secretly to the German Embassy. Ambassador Joachim Ribbentrop had finally convinced him that his presence in London would result in an international incident, to the detriment of the Fatherland. He returned to Berlin on the following day.

The slight had rankled, but personally dropping bombs on the capital of the British Empire soothed his ruffled feathers. Moreover, if the English knew it, so much the better. And they would know: that little *Schwanz* Goebbels would tell the world. Not that he would want to, but he would have no choice.

There was no love lost between Göring and Propaganda Minister Josef Goebbels, that lecherous antithesis of Aryan manhood. When the Führer's prohibition on bombing London had been lifted, the Reichsmarschall had announced that he would take personal command of the air assault on England. But Goebbels had twisted his words so as to make it sound as though the Reichsmarschall would lead the attack in person.

Göring, well aware that commanders-in-chief had no business getting into the firing line, originally had no intention of doing any such thing, but, hopping mad, he refused to lose face. There was no great risk in flying over London; moreover, not only would it silence his critics, he would gain popular acclaim in the country at large. Hitler would act annoyed but, presented with a *fait accompli*, could do little other than forbid a repetition. In any case, his friend Adolf admired bravery. Finally, Göring positively chortled at the thought of the weedy little Propaganda Minister being forced to sing his praises *ad nauseam* over the next few days.

A third, albeit minor, score remained to be settled. Just days ago, the Reichsmarschall had upbraided his fighter leaders for failing to give close protection to the bombers. Having said his piece, he then asked them what they most needed. Adolf Galland, Kommodore of JG 26 and 32-victory ace, had had the incredible crust to ask for Spitfires for his unit. He had not meant it, but it could not be allowed to pass. For the Luftwaffe Commander-in-Chief, it had been a very simple matter to have Galland's outfit assigned to protect the leading bomber Gruppe, without, of course, Galland knowing of his presence. If he could criticise the 109s from personal observation at close quarters, then that would be absolutely perfect. Thus far, however, there had been too little action.

Göring's thoughts drifted into more pleasant channels. The crew that he was flying with were a great bunch, and he would see that they were suitably rewarded — Iron Crosses all round, and a signed photograph of himself at the centre of the entire crew, taken in front of the bomber, should do it. And now here he was, increasing his already heroic stature with an operational sortie over London that might just, if he were lucky, herald the capitulation of the island nation. At this point, *Der Dicke* ('The Fat One'), as he was pleased to be known, was jolted out of his reverie.

'*Achtung, Spitfeuer!*' came the cry, closely followed by an appalling tinny rattle as bullets ripped through the cockpit, showering shards of metal and glass everywhere. Ice-cold air howled through the broken window panels, almost drowning the bomber's guns as they returned fire.

Looking down, Göring saw blood spattered across his sky-blue uniform. Stunned by the suddenness of the attack, his first reaction was that this would make a superb picture — a guaranteed cover for *Signal*. Then he saw that the photographer was bleeding heavily, lying across the hatch leading to the nose compartment. Wims was slumped in his seat, his left arm almost severed and his face almost unrecognisable behind the remains of his oxygen mask. Prone on the floor behind him was wireless operator Jonni Dahl, who had manned the beam guns.

In shock, the Commander-in-Chief's thoughts wandered to the banter they had exchanged on boarding the aircraft. To Wims, he had said, 'If you shower don't get me back safely, I'll transfer the lot of you to the infantry!'

'If we do, I shall expect promotion to Major at the very least!' Wims had quipped back.

Dahl, an irreverent Bavarian, unabashed by the presence of his Commander-in-Chief, had rudely chipped in, calling Wims an *Arschlecker*. Before the pilot could reply, Göring riposted: 'Yes, it tastes great. But is it best with pickles or sauerkraut?'

The tail gunner had been a thin, sad-faced man called Armin Stumke. Göring had told him that he was sure to survive the coming mission.

Slapping his ample girth, he had commented that he, the Reichsmarschall, was a much bigger target than a scrawny Obergefreiter. The laughter only subsided when the crew got down to preparing for take-off. Now neither Wims nor Dahl would return home, while the chances of the photographer looked poor.

When the attack occurred, they had been flying over a solid cloud layer. Hit by the enemy fire, Wims had fallen forward on the stick, sending the big bomber into a steep, diving spiral amongst the cloud. As they emerged, Göring snapped out of his reverie. The co-pilot's controls were in front of him. Seizing the unfamiliar yoke, he checked the spiral, then eased the aircraft out of the dive. The port inboard engine was dead and trailing smoke, and the inboard fuel tank on that side was streaming petrol. Aloud, he snarled, 'Where the hell is Galland? I'll court martial the *Scheisskerl!*'

But this was nothing that a Great War fighter ace couldn't handle. Or was it? Flying a Fokker D.VII biplane fighter in 1918 was a poor preparation for flying a stricken four-engine bomber in 1940. The big Dornier kept trying to crab into the dead engine and the rudder seemed to have little effect. The compass was smashed, but the sun was over to starboard, so they were going in roughly the right direction.

As the bomber regained level flight, Egbert Karvola, usually the observer/co-pilot in this crew but relegated to bomb-aimer for this sortie, struggled up from his position in the nose, forcing the body of the unconscious photographer aside. Taking in the situation at a glance, he completed the messy job of getting Wims out of his seat and taking control. Juggling the throttles, he managed to get the Dornier on a straight course, then dropped the nose slightly to trade altitude for speed.

The rest of the formation was nowhere in sight, nor were there any escort fighters around. With one of its engine stopped, and trailing black smoke and fuel, the damaged German bomber, by now somewhere over Surrey and vibrating with the three remaining engines on full power and almost 330kph (178kt) on the clock, made a run for the Channel and safety. The men inside almost made it. On 7 September 1940 the British had other things to worry about than a single damaged German bomber.

With less than 500m (1,600ft) on the aircraft's altimeter the coast appeared dimly through the haze, safety seemingly assured. But not quite. The Dornier was spotted by three Hurricanes returning to Tangmere from the Canterbury area. That they had never before encountered a Do 19 was plain from the radio exchange:

'What the hell is that?'

'Dunno, but it's huge!'

'Who cares? The bastard's got black crosses all over it! Line astern . . . line astern . . . attacking. Go!'

Diving, the leader made a quartering attack, but the sheer size of the big bomber caused him to misjudge the range and break away early. His Number Two, in close line astern, was slow to react and almost collided with it, but his shots went home from very close range. The inexperienced and over-excited Number Three, lagging badly in the dive, opened fire at far too great a distance. As he pulled away, the Dornier, trailing flame from a second engine, crossed the coast at low level and vanished into the sea haze. Low on fuel, the Hurricanes broke off the action and headed for Tangmere. Unfamiliar with the silhouette of the Do 19, they claimed an FW 200 Condor probably destroyed.

They had been more effective than they knew. The leader had liberally sprayed the fuselage, wounding both remaining gunners, but the real damage had been done by his Number Two. His long burst of fire, delivered from close range, riddled the cockpit and the starboard inner engine. Flames from the punctured fuel system invaded the cockpit. As the Hurricane roared close overhead, avoiding a collision by barely three metres, Karvola was already dead and Göring badly wounded.

With three bullets in his left thigh and two in his chest, the Reichsmarschall fought his last battle, but in vain. As the all-consuming flames enveloped his body, his vision faded and his grip on the yoke relaxed. The stricken bomber dived steeply into the water some ten kilometres offshore from, by a supreme irony, Goring-on-Sea, Sussex. There were no witnesses and no survivors.

✦ ✦ ✦

First World War fighter ace, winner of his country's highest decoration for valour, and spiritual heir to the great 'Red Baron', Hermann Göring had risen to command the mightiest air force the world had ever seen. Having personally led it into battle over the capital city of the world's greatest and most enduring empire, he vanished, never to be seen again. This was the very stuff of myth and legend: he was Siegfried, Lohengrin, Parsifal, the last of the Teutonic Knights.

Göring's aircraft was photographed in the act of bombing, but seconds later the formation was attacked by two squadrons of RAF fighters. This got everyone's attention. When the mêlée was over, the Reichsmarschall's Dornier was nowhere to be seen: it had simply vanished. The Nazi hierarchy was baffled. All they knew was that Göring had set out — and then disappeared.

They sat tight. If the British had taken him prisoner, or had identified his body, they would certainly have announced it. The silence indicated that they had not. Nor was there any mention of a Do 19 being shot down. Days passed, and it became obvious that the British knew no more than the Germans.

For the Nazi hierarchy, the problem was what to do now. The Reichsmarschall could not simply vanish, as this would invite malicious rumours of insanity, assassination, suicide and so forth. Spurious car or aeroplane accidents would be almost as bad. Nor could the truth be suppressed for ever: too many people knew it. Hitler finally grasped the nettle on 16 September 1940, some nine days after the event, stating that the mighty Hermann had fallen in battle against superior (obligatory in this context) odds but giving no details and no date. The British, who could possibly have filled in some of the gaps, had other things to think about. The neutral press had a field day. Speculation ran riot, even to having the Reichsmarschall meet his end while flying the mythical Heinkel He 113 fighter!

1 Countdown to War

T HE Luftwaffe was officially revealed on 1 March 1935. Consisting of some 1,888 aircraft and 20,000 officers and men, to the outside world it had apparently sprung into existence full-grown. This was, of course, not the case. The Treaty of Versailles of 1919 permitted Germany a small standing army for internal security, but was worded in such a way as to prevent the establishment of military aviation. A small, dedicated group in the Weimar Republic had worked covertly to circumvent this restriction, using civil aviation as a shield.

A military aviation nucleus was formed in the early 1920s, and over the years was gradually expanded to the position where further concealment became extremely difficult. At this point, the German Chancellor, Adolf Hitler, correctly judged that the political climate was favourable for a *fait accompli*, and the Luftwaffe (the Great War air arm had been the Luftstreitkräfte) was unwrapped, to the accompaniment of much propaganda.

The Luftwaffe was only part of a bigger picture. Germany's expansion and rearmament plans for the Army and Navy were also in contravention of the Treaty of Versailles. Had they been discovered at an early stage, it was thought possible that Britain and France would have intervened to prevent them from reaching maturity. What action could be taken to prevent this?

The solution adopted was to build up a deterrent in the shape of a strong bomber force, even though this was largely bluff. Back in 1921, the Italian Generale Guilio Douhet had published a book called *The Command of the Air*; an expanded second edition followed in 1927. Douhet's theory was that nations could be defeated by having their war potential systematically destroyed by means of carefully planned bombing raids on selected targets. Given the state-of-the-art of the time, Douhet's teachings were nonsense: the degree of bombing accuracy, and the degree of destruction necessary, were simply unattainable. Even the degree of navigation needed to keep the schedule of destruction on time was very questionable. The fact was that Douhet had got almost everything wrong — and this included his proposals for countering the enemy's defending fighters — and took no account of the possibility of effective anti-aircraft gun defences, or even an enemy bomber force that could hit back equally hard.

As is so often the case, common sense did not prevail. 'The bomber will always get through!' wailed the doom-and gloom-merchants; writers such as H. G. Wells produced horrifying novels such as *The Shape of Things to Come*, forecasting the end of civilisation. On the other hand, national treasury departments liked the theory: it appeared to offer a cheap method of settling international conflicts. Muddled thinking prevailed. At the end of the day, however, Douhet had made strategic bombing fashionable, and Germany wanted a strategic bombing force. From 1933 until 1937/38, the Third Reich assigned bombers top priority.

✦ ✦ ✦

A bombing force was of course in the pipeline, in the shape of the Dornier Do 17, the Heinkel He 111, and the Junkers Ju 86. Developed in the guise of civilian airliners or mailplanes, these were all twin-engined, and none had the development potential for a true strategic bomber.

A brief skim through Adolf Hitler's manifesto *Mein Kampf* (it seems hardly fair to call it a book), makes it quite obvious that war against the Soviet Union was inevitable. This being the case, a long-range strategic bomber would be needed to attack targets deep in the Russian heartland. Oberst Wilhelm Wimmer, Head of the Technical Office of the Reichsluftfahrtministerium (RLM; German Air Ministry), sold the idea of a long-range strategic bomber to his chief, Generalmajor (later Generalleutnant) Walther Wever, whose task it then became to convince his commander-in-chief. Wever, who had become the Chief of Staff of the nascent air force in May 1933, two years before the Luftwaffe had been formally created, was a fully trained staff officer, as essential to a new service as a sergeant-major is to a battalion. Lacking aviation experience, he nevertheless learned to fly in his late forties, becoming an enthusiastic pilot who flew himself around his command in a fast, modern Heinkel He 70 Blitz. Wever had other qualities. Allied to an instinctive grasp of technical and administrative problems, he had an exceptional flair for getting the best out of people, from his energetic if amateurish Commander-in-Chief, through the prickliest aircraft designers and the most lethargic suppliers, to the youngest pilot.

Wever's talents and ability were critical. Neither the Commander-in-Chief nor his deputy were career military men. The Luftwaffe C-in-C was Hermann Göring, a Great War fighter ace with a distinguished record. As the final commander of the Richthofen Geschwader, he had to a degree inherited the mantle of the Red Baron. Despite this, however, he was a political appointee — a crony of Hitler. He had ended the war as a Haupt-mann (captain), and his political leap to general officer rank had omitted those valuable years between captain and colonel in which he would have received a thorough grounding in command and staff work. On the political side, as Reichsminister of Aviation he had been instrumental in building up the covert Luftwaffe. Despite his later reputation as a dilet-tante, this was well conceived and executed, and his hard work was exceptional. As Albert Kesselring later said admiringly of him, 'He was always at his best under pressure; when the rest of us were completely exhausted, he was still able to go on.'[1]

Although, when he came to power, the basis for a new air service already existed, Hermann Göring can rightly be regarded as the creator of the Luftwaffe. He was the 'mover and shaker' who got things done, frequently at the expense of the other services. However, there was a price to be paid. His vanity led him into a too-proprietorial attitude towards the new service. It became 'his' Luftwaffe; but at the same time his wide range of duties and interests increasingly curtailed the time he could devote to it.

Göring's deputy was Erhard Milch. An undistinguished Great War pilot, he was a superb organiser. He was made Managing Director of the state airline Deutsche Lufthansa in 1926, and he built this into the best airline in the world. He was named State Secretary of Aviation in February 1933. Although a civilian, he was then given general officer rank. Further promotions followed rapidly, culminating in Generalfeldmarschall in July 1940. Hard working and competent, he was also ambitious — a suspect quality in the backstabbing atmosphere of the Third Reich at that time, not helped by rumours of his Semitic ancestry.

Wever's ideas having prevailed, studies for a strategic bomber commenced in 1934. Called the Langstrecken-Grossbomber, it was intended to carry a payload of about two tonnes to targets in the Ural mountains, a distance of some 2,800km (1,500nm) from the nearest German bases. At the time this was completely impractical, but the potential was there. Widely, if unofficially, known as the Uralbomber, this aircraft could, if a future war took an unexpected turn, easily reach the primary British naval anchorage at Scapa Flow. This might prove vital: for the German Fleet to break out into the Atlantic, it had to run the gauntlet of the British Home Fleet at Scapa Flow, and if the latter could be threatened from the air the task would be that much easier.

Studies quickly established that the payload/range needed for strategic bombing could not be attained by any of the twin-engine aircraft then in the development stage. A four-engine machine was essential, although even this would be pushing current technology very hard. Submissions were made by three aircraft companies, and in the summer of 1935 Dornier and Junkers received orders for three prototypes each.

The Dornier Do 19V-1 first flew on 28 October 1936, and it was followed into the air by the Junkers Ju 89V-2 in December of that year. Both aircraft were large, and while neither initially remotely approached the Uralbomber's payload/range requirement, both had a great deal of potential for development. The mid-1930s was a time when aviation technology was moving fast.

By the standards of the day, the Do 19 was huge: how huge is best judged by comparison with the closely contemporary Boeing B-17 prototype, which first flew fifteen months earlier, in July 1935. In round figures, the span of the Dornier was one-tenth greater, its wing area a fifth larger and its length a fifth more than that of the American aircraft. The German bomber was rather heavier, but carried a smaller projected bomb load. Performance was roughly comparable except for range, which was inferior. The proposed defensive armament was rather heavier, but this was understandable as, unlike the American aircraft, the Uralbomber mission involved a lengthy penetration of hostile territory.

The Do 19 was angular, with a slab-sided fuselage reminiscent of the obsolescent twin-engine Do 23 bomber, a low/mid-set wing and twin fin/rudder assemblies set inboard on the tailplane and braced to the fuselage. A nine-man crew was proposed — pilot and co-pilot/observer, a radio operator, a bomb-aimer and five gunners. Four of these last were needed to operate two-man dorsal and ventral gun turrets; the other permanent gunner was located in the tail. A nose gun was manned by the bomb-aimer.

The Junkers Ju 89 was dimensionally slightly larger than the Dornier 19, and had some 15 per cent more wing area. The greatest difference concerned empty weight, the Ju 89 being 43 per cent heavier. The Junkers' performance was superior to that of its rival, its maximum speed at sea level of 350kph (189kt) being 10 per cent greater. More importantly, its cruising speed at operational altitude — 314kph (169kt) — was 25 per cent higher, as was its service ceiling of 7,000m (22,965ft), while its maximum range of 2,000km (1,079nm) was 19 per cent greater.

Based on the bare figures, there was 'no contest', and the Ju 89 should have been selected for production, but, at this stage, the statistics told only half the story. The Daimler-Benz DB 600A liquid-cooled, V-12 engines of the prototype Ju 89 produced some 34 per cent more power than the Bramo 322 nine-cylinder, air-cooled radials of the Do 19V-1, and this shortfall on the part of the latter aircraft largely accounted for the differences in performance. The Do 19V-2 was given the more powerful BMW 132F radials, which all but closed the gap, while the production Do 19A was powered by BMW 139 radials, each rated at 1,550hp. These gave the Dornier a maximum speed of 400kph (216kt) at 4,000m (13,124ft), an economical cruising speed of 350kph (189kt) at the same altitude, a range increase of 30 per cent to 2,185km (1,179nm)' a service ceiling of 8,500m (27,889ft) and a much improved rate of climb. Whilst these figures could have been matched by an up-engined Ju 89, one final factor gave the Do 19A the advantage in the *Uralbomber* contest. Empty, the Ju 89 was 43 per cent heavier than the Do 19, although its overall dimensions were only slightly larger. Why was this? Only part of the difference could be accounted for by the fact that liquid-cooled engines, with their associated plumbing, were inherently heavier than radials. The main difference lay in the fuselages: that of the Dornier was sleek, whilst that of the Junkers was fat. Whereas the Dornier was designed as an uncompromised bomber, it was probable, although never confirmed by designer Ernst Zindel, that the Ju 89 was expected to double as a transport.[2]

At the prototype stage, the relative wing loadings showed a tremendous difference. The maximum take-off weight of the Do 19 had been held down to 19,000kg (41,890lb), giving a loading of 118.60kg/m² (24.29lb/sq ft), which was closely comparable to that of the Boeing B-17. By contrast, the Ju 89, at its maximum weight of 27,800kg (61,290lb), gave a loading of 151kg/m² (30.95lb/sq ft), which for 1936 was on the high side. Power loadings, which had at the early prototype stage been fairly similar, had now moved decisively in favour of the Dornier, with 4.75kg (10.47lb) per hp as opposed to 7.24kg (15.96lb) per hp for the Junkers.

Aircraft costs are closely related to weight, and the disparity between the Do 19 and the Ju 89 made the former more affordable, tipping the scales decisively in its favour. Just one final decision remained to be made. Germany was a country with limited resources of both labour and *matériel*. The question then became: more aircraft or bigger ones? Calculations based on cost and weight showed that, for each Do 19A built, almost three Do 17s, or slightly fewer than two He 111s, or as many as six Ju 87s, would have to be sacrificed. Of these, the Do 17, with its low payload/ range capability, was the most easily spared. The He 111, which fulfilled the need for a capable and versatile twin-engine medium bomber, was less so at the time, but would become more easily spared in the near future. As for the Ju 87, a battle was then raging about its acquisition, which will

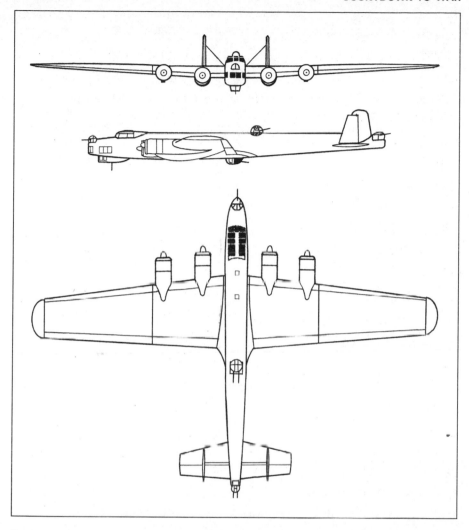

Rather larger than the closely contemporary Boeing B-17, the Dornier Do 19A was the Luftwaffe's first strategic bomber. Its payload/range capability posed difficult problems for its opponents on all fronts.

be examined in detail later in this chapter. One machine not considered for the trade-off was the new and fast Ju 88 Schnellbomber.

There were of course other factors, including the relative levels of aircrew and ground support needed, and that Junkers were heavily committed to producing the Ju 88, which had already been given top priority. In the event, Wever was never to be dissuaded of the importance

DORNIER Do 19 AND JUNKERS Ju 89: OUTLINE SPECIFICATIONS		
Type	Dornier Do 19V-1	Junkers Ju 89V-2
Span (ft/m)	114.83/35.00	115.71/35.27
Length (ft/m)	83.50/25.45	86.95/26.50
Height (ft/m)	18.95/ 5.76	24.94/ 7.60
Wing area (sq ft/m^2)	1,724.38/160.20	1,980.56/184.00
Empty weight (lb/kg)	26,158/11,865	37,480/17,000
Max weight (lb/kg)	40,785/18,500	61,290/27,800
Power	4 × Bramo 322 radials	4 × DB600A V-12s
Rating	715hp each	960hp each
V_{cruise} (kt/kph)	135/ 249	169/314
Ceiling (ft/m)	18,370/5,600	22,965/7,000
Max range (nm/km)	907/1,681	1,079/2,000
Wing loading (lb per kg/sq ft per m^2)	23.65/115.48	30.95/151.01
Power loading lb/kg per hp	14.26/6.47	15.96/7.24

of the strategic requirement, although at one point he was reduced to asking Göring to consider the propaganda effect of the visual impact of a whole Geschwader of these giant bombers in flight, on the rest of the world. This indirect appeal to the vanity of the Luftwaffe Commander-in-Chief worked, and towards the end of 1936 the Do 19A was ordered into production.

In general, the aircraft handled well, the main faults being its tendency to 'float' before touchdown, caused by the large wing area and low loading, and a degree of sensitivity to crosswinds on take-off and landing. However, these were judged acceptable for service use. Just one restriction was imposed: the big Dornier could only be operated from fixed bases with permanent hard runways.

The initial projected bomb load, carried internally in two bays, was 16 SC100s or 32 SC50s, for a load of 1,600kg(3,527kb), but this was quickly upgraded to eight SC250s, increasing the maximum internal ordnance load to 2,000kg(4,410lb). This later became standard for Luftwaffe bombers such as the He 111 and Ju 88, although the Do 19A could of course haul it much further. Larger bombs were in the pipeline, and the bulkhead between the two bomb bays was made removable to accommodate them.

Range was the next subject to be addressed. In the prototypes, fuel was carried in wing tanks between the engines and the fuselage; for the production article, extra tanks were added, both between the engines and outboard of them. Given the wing's huge area, and its depth, capacity was almost tripled. This increased the operational radius for the Do 19A to approximately 2,200km (1,187nm) with a full internal ordnance load. This was not quite Uralbomber range, but it was not far off: supplementary fuselage tanks, or even external underwing tanks, allied to a reduction in payload, could easily make up the difference. As a result of experience in the Spanish Civil War from 1936 onwards, all fuel tanks were made self-sealing.

The other main area of development was in defensive armament. Originally, this had been planned as a single, rifle-calibre machine gun in a nose turret, operated by the bomb-aimer; another in an open tail position operated by a specialist gunner; and hydraulic dorsal and ventral turrets each mounting a 20mm Oerlikon MG FF cannon, both of which were to have been operated by two men. Turrets for 20mm Oerlikon cannon were, however, heavy, and the complexity of two-man operation proved impractical. The 20mm MG FF was a drum-fed cannon, and changing a 60 round drum in flight was neither quick nor easy; moreover, the MG FF was probably the poorest performing cannon of its time. It fired a fairly heavy projectile at a cyclic rate of 350 rounds a minute and a muzzle velocity of 595m/sec (1,952fs) – half and about two-thirds, respectively, of the figures for the contemporary Hispano-Suiza – and it was, therefore, not really suitable for high-angle deflection shooting against fast-crossing targets, which would be necessary in the event of fighter interception. However, this last consideration did not prevent its installation in the German fighters of the era.

The MG FF cannon having been found wanting, it was replaced by the 7.9mm Rheinmetall-Borsig MG 15 machine gun in the dorsal and ventral turrets. Fitted also in the nose and the tail, this weapon could pump out nearly 17 rounds a second, but, as it was fed by a saddle magazine holding only 75 rounds, only about 4½ seconds of firing was possible before the magazine had to be changed, a procedure which took about five seconds. The concept of remote gun barbettes was explored, but the sighting technology was too immature at this time. From the early summer of 1940,

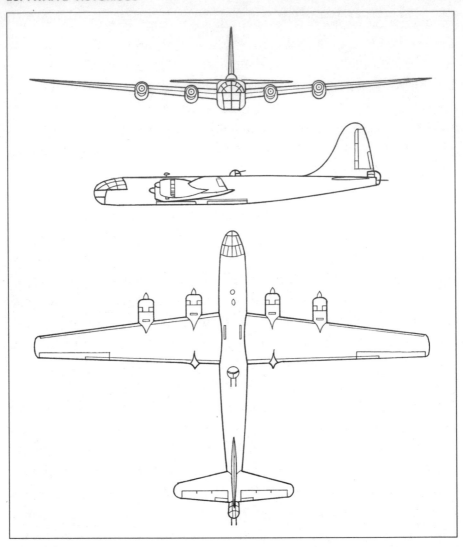

Engines of greater power, and a more efficient wing design, gave the Dornier Do 219A a higher economical cruising speed and greater range than its predecessor. Its tail surfaces were also radically modified.

however, a single MG 15 beam gun was installed on each side of the fuselage.

As with all aircraft programmes, creeping weight growth was a feature of the Do 19's development. The Do 19A's empty weight became 15,000kg (33,069lb) and its normal take-off weight 22,500kg (49,604lb), the latter giving a wing loading of 140kg/m² (29lb/sq ft) and a power loading of

3.63kg (8.lb) per hp—although both figures were rather better than those for the slightly later Short Stirling. The first production Do 19A, with a crew of seven instead of nine, was delivered to the Luftwaffe in July 1939 for evaluation.

By the late 1930s, aviation technology was moving fast, and the original Langstrecken-Grossbomber specification now began to look slightly old-fashioned. Early in 1938, the Reichsluftfahrtministerium issued the new 'Bomber A' specification. This called for an aircraft capable of carrying a 2,000kg bomb load out to an operational radius of 1,600km (863nm) at 500kph (270kt). The speed requirement was to make it difficult for 'Bomber A', which was to fly unescorted, to be intercepted. This apart, the 'Bomber A' requirement could be met by the Do 19.

Two proposals were submitted—by Dornier with the Do 219 and by Heinkel with the He 177. The Do 219 differed from its predecessor in having a narrower wing which was lavishly equipped with high-lift devices, and a bulged internal bomb bay to carry the largest Luftwaffe bombs.[3] The He 177 could be distinguished by its four paired engines, each pair driving a single huge propeller. This gave the aircraft the appearance of a twin-engined bomber, reduced profile drag and increased performance.

Whilst the Do 219 failed to match the performance of the He 177, it was for all practical purposes a proven design. It was selected for production in 1941, and entered service late in the following year. Whereas the Dornier proved extremely reliable, its Heinkel rival suffered from an alarming number of fires in the coupled engine bays.[4] Despite the best efforts of the aircraft's designers, this problem proved intractable, and the He 177 was redesigned as an orthodox four-engine bomber, the He 277. However, the delays incurred meant that it was the end of 1943 before it started to reach the first Kampfgruppe.

LEVEL VERSUS DIVE-BOMBING

Level bombing in the 1930s was notoriously inaccurate, as a result of several factors—altitude, visibility, speed over the ground, crosswinds, the shortcomings of the standard Goerz-Visier 219 bomb sight and, in war, being under fire. Before the war, flying at moderate speeds and altitudes in good visibility and still air, a practised crew could expect to land 50 per cent of their bombs within about 75m (246ft) of the centre of the target. Accuracy diminished as altitude and speed increased, and in the presence of strong ground and air defences the margin of error tripled.

What could be done to improve bombing accuracy? In poor visibility, a low-level bombing run might help. Drift sights might reveal the speed and angle of crosswinds, in which case an aim-off adjustment might be possible; in rare instances, an attack straight into the wind might reduce the margin of error. The bombs could also be released in a stick: it was possible to pre-set the spacing between them, typically from 10m (33ft) to 100m (328ft), greatly increasing the chances of scoring one or more hits.

The alternative was dive-bombing. Bomb-release height was relatively low, while the pilot could constantly adjust his aim during the dive. Moreover, in the dive, speed over the ground was greatly reduced: the steeper the dive angle, the slower the relative speed over the ground became, to the point where, if the bomber managed a 90-degree dive angle, it became nil. Therefore, dive-bombing was inherently more accurate than level bombing, and seemed to offer a reliable method of carrying out pinpoint attacks on small targets.

The idea initially stemmed from the United States. Ernst Udet, the ranking surviving German fighter ace of the Great War, became a dive-bombing enthusiast during a trip to America in 1933. On his return, he was co-opted into the Luftwaffe with the rank of Oberst in February 1936, at first as Inspector of Fighter and Dive-Bomber Forces. Then, just four months later, he succeeded Wilhelm Wimmer as head of the Technical Department. Here he gave free rein to his enthusiasm for dive-bombing. Wever tried to curb it, but this was difficult, as the impetuous Udet had the sympathetic ear of Göring, his wartime comrade-in-arms.

There was, however, an influential body of opinion that was strongly opposed to dive-bombing, led by Wolfram Freiherr von Richthofen,[5] a cousin of the famous 'Red Baron' and, at that time, Head of the Development Branch of the Technical Office. He categorically stated: 'Diving below 2,000m [6,562ft] is complete nonsense. Owing to the state of development of anti-aircraft artillery, every aircraft that descended to such a low altitude would be shot down by anti-aircraft fire.'[6] As at this time Germany led the world in anti-aircraft guns, he had a point. To keep the Ju 87 controllable in an 80-degree dive, and allow the lowest possible bomb release height, dive brakes were deployed to limit the aircraft's speed. The result was that the anti-aircraft gunners were given a sedate, close-range and non-manoeuvring target, at virtually zero deflection. In theory at least, a steep diving attack on a heavily defended target was potentially suicidal.

The Ju 87 was vulnerable for other reasons. It was not a fast aircraft at the best of times, and the externally carried bomb load reduced cruising speed to a snail-paced 260kph (140kt), typically at an altitude of about 3,500m (11,484ft) — much higher than this, and it would be difficult to identify the target. The combination of slow approach speed and medium altitude made the Stuka easy for fighters to intercept. Then, after the attack, formation cohesion was lost as the dive-bombers headed for home in a gaggle. Here again they were vulnerable to fighters.

Other weaknesses were that the Ju 87 could carry only limited loads over short distances. This being the case, it was only suitable for short-range tactical missions, and lacked versatility. Then again, it could only be used in its primary (i.e. dive-bombing) mission in conditions of good visibility, with a cloud base above 800m (2,625ft). Finally, although it was a cheap aircraft to build, if the losses were even remotely as predicted, it would be very expensive in terms of dead pilots. Nevertheless, even the anti-dive-bomber lobby agreed that the Ju 87 was the only aircraft to have a chance of consistently hitting a small target. All that was in dispute was the cost of doing so.

The debate grew heated, until only the Commander-in-Chief could settle it. Although 90 per cent convinced by the sound reasoning of Chief-of-Staff Wever, Göring, unwilling to upset the Head of the Technical Office so early in his tenure, compromised. He agreed to an initial low-rate production of Udet's choice, the Ju 87, but then succumbed to the blandishments of a Luftwaffe pressure group. This group, consisting mainly of young engineers on the General Staff, were dazzled by the potential accuracy offered by dive-bombing. They asked the obvious question:

should not all bombers be able to achieve this degree of accuracy? In a blinding flash of idiocy, they concluded that all bombers should be able to carry out steep diving attacks!

The most celebrated recipient of this dubious benefit was the Junkers Ju 88. Designed as a high speed bomber with a range sufficient to take in the entire British Isles, the decision to give the Ju 88 the capability of making steep-dive attacks increased the empty weight of the original design from about six tonnes to nearly ten. Not only were dive brakes added, but the airframe had to be completely re-stressed and strengthened. The extra weight made it tricky to handle, especially at low speeds. As former test pilot Peter Stahl commented, 'It is capable of suddenly doing quite surprising things without the slightest warning.'[7] Nor was the aircraft particularly effective in a steep dive: 60 degrees was the maximum angle that could reasonably be attained and held by an average pilot. One thing that Wever was able to do was to block an attempt to write a dive-bombing capability into the specification for Bomber A — a move in which he had the full support of Göring.[8]

The Ju 87 was Udet's pet project, and there is little doubt that the restriction of its production programme was a blow to him, the conversion of the Ju 88 Schnellbomber to a dive-bomber being only partial compensation.

The German-equipped and -manned Condor Legion took part in the Spanish Civil War, which served as a tactical and technical proving ground. While close air support rendered valuable aid to the ground forces in that conflict, the lack of effective opposition made conclusions misleading.

The Third Reich was never intended to take part in a major war before 1942, by which time it would have been a fairly well-balanced force, with an effective strategic bomber capability and a significant close air support element. In September 1939, however, the Luftwaffe was not really ready.

NOTES

1. Harold Faber (ed.), *Luftwaffe*.
2. The Ju 89 was in fact developed as the Ju 90 transport, although only a handful were built.

3. The largest German bomb originally intended to be carried by the Do 19 was the SC 250, of 368mm diameter and 1,640mm long. Much larger types were under development. The SC 1000 Hermann was the most widely used: it was 554mm in diameter and 2,580mm long. In addition there were the SC 1800 Satan (650mm and 3,500mm) and, largest of all, the SC 2500 Max (829mm and 3,895mm). Unlike the British, the Germans failed to develop really large bombs.

4. The British had similar problems with the twin-engined Avro Manchester, but, redesigned with four engines, this aircraft became the superb Lancaster.

5. This was ironic, as Richthofen became the greatest commander of Luftwaffe dive-bombing and close air support forces.

6. General der Flieger Paul Deichman, *Spearhead for Blitzkreig*.

7. Peter Stahl, *The Diving Eagle*.

8. In 1942 Göring condemned the fact that the He 177 had been designed for diving attacks.

2 Luftwaffe Rampant

SO STANDS the Luftwaffe today, ready to carry out every command of the Führer with lightning speed and undreamed-of might' — thus spoke Luftwaffe Commander-in-Chief Hermann Göring in August 1939. While the world at large did not exactly tremble at his words, it was distinctly uneasy. It was known that the German air arm was equipped with modern bombers and fighters, although numbers and strengths, and to a degree capabilities, had been grossly inflated by propaganda. The Luftwaffe had given an impressive demonstration of strength during the Anschluss with Austria in 1938, and repeated it during the occupation of the Czech Sudetenland early in 1939. However, these were bloodless victories: the air threat alone had been enough to cow the opposition.

THE SPANISH CIVIL WAR

The Luftwaffe had however been blooded, albeit unofficially, in the Spanish Civil War. This three-year conflict, fought between Nationalists and Republicans (thinly disguised Fascists and Communists, respectively), was used as a proving ground by three major European nations: Germany and Italy flew for the Nationalists; the Soviet Union for the Republicans. The German contribution was the Condor Legion. For all practical purposes, this was a branch of the Luftwaffe, although to maintain a fiction of legality it flew under Spanish Nationalist colours. At first it was manned by Luftwaffe 'volunteers', but when the value of such realistic training was recognised, the requirement for volunteers was dropped. Most personnel arrived in Spain via state-subsidised 'Strength Through Joy' cruises from Hamburg, and returned the same way. The Condor Legion allowed the Luftwaffe to use the Spanish Civil War as an extended live-fire exercise and proving ground for tactics and equipment. Personnel were rotated through at frequent intervals, and when the war ended in 1939 the Luftwaffe had a large pool of combat-experienced aircrew.

The Spanish experience taught many lessons. For the Jagdflieger, the most valuable was the abandonment of the three-aircraft Kette in favour of the widely spaced pair (Rotte) and four (Schwarm). This gave un-precedented flexibility in air-combat manoeuvring, putting German fighter tactics a step ahead of the rest of the world. What did, however, tend to be overlooked was the fact that the Spanish Civil War was atypical. The intensity of the air conflict was low, as was the quality of the Republican opposition, nor was there any serious attempt by either side at controlling air-defence interception from the ground. As a result, Condor Legion bombers and attack aircraft had a relatively easy ride. Against top-quality opposition, things would be entirely different—as would be proved in the summer of 1940.

One of the great myths of the era was that of Teutonic efficiency, which was supposedly much greater than that of any other nation. That this was not the case was demonstrated by the air raid on Guernica on 26 April 1937. Reconnaissance had reported that Republican troops were massing in the town. To delay them, the Rentaria Bridge over the Oca river was targeted, together with major roads to the south and east. As there were no anti-aircraft gun defences, bombing took place from the low altitude of 1,200m (4,000ft). In all, 26 bombers—Heinkel He 111s and Junkers Ju 52s—unloaded 40 tonnes of bombs on the hapless town. Guernica was badly damaged, and about 1,500 casualties, nearly all civilians, resulted.

The world's press labelled the attack a 'terror raid', and held it up as an example of sheer German ruthlessness, but in fact it was a classic example of sheer German incompetence. Reconnaissance misidentified civilian refugees in the town as Republican troops. Faulty intelligence had failed to detect the existence of a small arms factory in the town, which was thus not targeted. To crown a disastrous episode, pathetically inaccurate

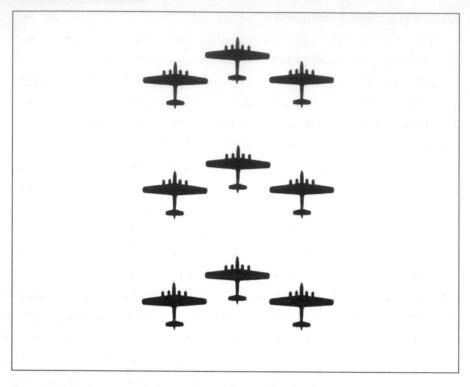

The Staffelkolonne was the preferred formation for the Do 19As of IV./LG 1, giving concentration of bombs on target. For Gruppe operations, the three Staffelkolonne flew in a Keil, or arrow, which gave the greatest flexibility when more than one industrial complex in the same area was targeted.

bombing left both the Rentaria Bridge and the rail terminus, another legitimate military target, unscathed. Just weeks earlier, inaccurate bombing of an arms factory at Durango had also caused heavy loss of life, but it was Guernica that caught the headlines, and for years the name became synonymous with Nazi 'frightfulness'.

One thing that the Condor Legion did establish was the effectiveness of close air support, albeit in the face of poor-quality opposition. This was mainly flown by Heinkel He 51 and, to a lesser degree, Henschel Hs 123 biplanes. In the final month of 1937, three Ju 87A dive-bombers arrived in Spain. Known as the Jolanthe-Kette (Jolanthe was a cartoon flying pig), this trio, flown by many different crews, successfully demonstrated accurate dive-bombing, although, as this was always done under conditions of complete air superiority, it was hardly a fair test.

SUBSTANCE OR SHADOW?

In 1939, the Luftwaffe cast a long shadow as an efficient, modern force both ruthless and numerous. The truth was, however, more prosaic, and only the crucible of battle would expose the flaws. On Hitler's orders, and with Göring as a willing accomplice, the Luftwaffe had undergone a too-rapid expansion. Despite Wever's best efforts at attaining a balanced force, it had breadth without depth.

The Luftwaffe had an impressive number of first-line fighter and bomber units, but, while it could fight a short war, aircraft production, which had remained at peacetime levels, was inadequate to replace attrition in an extended conflict. Moreover, despite the propaganda, its equipment was not all that it should have been.

The single-engine fighter in service was the Messerschmitt Bf 109, the E-model of which was reaching the Staffeln in 1939. To maximise performance, Willi Messerschmitt had wrapped the smallest possible airframe around the largest available engine. This had largely been successful, but it had imposed several penalties. First, poor low-speed handling caused a spate of take-off and landing accidents. For an inexperienced pilot, the Bf 109 was all too often lethal, and matters were not helped by the rather flimsy, narrow-track main undercarriage gear. Wing loading was on the high side for the time, and, to improve turning performance, automatic slats were fitted to the wing leading edges. During high-g turns, however, these tended to open asymmetrically, which could be embarrassing in combat. Finally, the aircraft lacked potential for development: the airframe was too small to take full advantage of more powerful engines and a heavier armament, and when, later in the war, these were fitted, wing loading increased and handling progressively deteriorated from poor to downright dangerous.

From 1937, the development of a fighter to supplement the Bf 109 was commenced, with the backing of Ernst Udet. This was the Focke -Wulf FW 190. Faster and more agile than the Messerschmitt, it was also sturdier, with a wide-track main undercarriage well suited to operations from semi-prepared strips. If the Bf 109 was a rather delicate thoroughbred racehorse, the FW 190 was a rough-and-tough cavalry horse. The prototype first flew in June 1939, although developmental problems delayed its service entry until late 1941.

Tactically, in 1939 the Jagdflieger were ahead of the rest of the world. The Spanish Civil War innovation of flying in widely spaced pairs and fours had been adopted. In air combat, this gave a tremendous advantage. Whereas air-combat training in other countries generally consisted of one-versus-one encounters, the Jagdflieger trained for multi-bogey, four-versus-four — or even Staffel-versus-Staffel — combats, accepting the potential hazard of mid-air collisions. This gave valuable experience not only of mutual support, but also of coincidental support in a confused fight.

The other Luftwaffe fighter in service was the two-seat, twin-engined Messerschmitt Bf 110 Zerstörer. This was an aircraft in search of a role. Initially it had been intended to pursue enemy formations raiding the Third Reich, and to hound them back over their own territory, for which its relatively long range and heavy armament made it well suited. The truth is that no one really knew how to employ it. During its development it had revealed many shortcomings, and attempts to correct these had seriously delayed production. However, nobody could deny that a long-range fighter was a useful addition to the inventory, and Göring settled the controversy by declaring that the Zerstörer was a strategic fighter to be flown by elite units — his 'Ironsides'. Even at this early stage, however, the 110 was scheduled to be replaced by the Bf 210 in a year or so. When Germany invaded Poland in September 1939, no fewer than ten Zerstörergruppen had been formed, but owing to production delays only three were equipped with Bf 110s. The remainder flew single-engined Bf 109s, mainly B, C and D models.

The bomber force was in no better shape. Strategic capability was lacking: service entry for the Uralbomber was still several months in the future, while the Dornier Do 17 and Heinkel He 111 level bombers were too limited in terms of payload/range to be effective in this role. The Junkers Ju 87 dive-bomber showed promise, but how it would fare against determined fighter and gun opposition was still an unknown quantity. Worse still, delivery of the potentially superb Junkers Ju 88 was well behind schedule tanks to an inordinate number of modifications and revisions, mainly arising from the need to make it capable of carrying out steep, diving attacks.

The final Luftwaffe weakness was training. Basic flying schools were adequate, but at the advanced level, in early 1939 all that existed were a mere three bomber and one fighter schools, plus one for naval aviation. The training of bomber pilots typically took two years, and of fighter pilots one year. The inadequate solution adopted was to give aircrew a final polish at their operational units. This totally precluded the building up of an operational reserve.

General Wever strongly objected to this, but was overruled by Göring on the grounds that the Führer's wishes for a rapid increase in the number of operational units were paramount. This was despite the fact that, on 23 May 1939, Hitler himself declared that preparations for a long war must be made — 'in case'. He then stated that there would be no war until 1942![1] When war broke out in September 1939, the Luftwaffe was forced to wage it with all their forces 'in the shop window' Reserves were almost non-existent, but Wever tried hard to minimise the worst effects. Production of the Dornier Do 19 was scheduled to reach 120 per month by mid-1940,[2] with three Geschwader of Uralbombers operational by September. Alas, these targets could not be met. Production of other types, notably the Bf 109, was increased, and two more fighter schools were formed.

POLAND

Luftwaffe operational doctrine clearly stated that its first task was to gain air superiority, preferably by destroying the enemy air force on the ground, but when the Polish campaign began at dawn on 1 September 1939 things went badly awry. Fog delayed the majority of the planned airfield strikes, and when they were finally launched the cupboard was bare of all but a few obsolete combat aircraft and trainers: alerted by the pre-war tensions, the Poles had dispersed their first-line units to secondary bases.

However, this merely delayed the inevitable. The Polish Air Force fought back hard but, outnumbered and outclassed, and handicapped by an inadequate early-warning and control system, it was shot from the skies. The two Gruppen of Bf 110s were used as bomber escorts, for which their long range suited them, but on this, their combat debut, they sustained losses owing to their lack of manoeuvrability— despite their superior performance. The four Gruppen of 'short-legged' Bf 109s were mainly employed for maintaining local air superiority over the battle-front, and for air defence. The Luftwaffe's top scorer of the campaign was Bf 109D pilot Hannes Gentzen with seven victories, five of which were scored over bombers. This indicated that his unit was primarily engaged on defensive duties.

Meanwhile the Ju 87 Stukas were learning their craft. As distinguishing between friendly and enemy troops from a high perch was impracticable, close support for the ground forces was not a viable option. For the most part, they were used for battlefield air interdiction, attacking targets behind the lines — supplies, troop concentrations, etc. — and they were aided by level bombers, which attacked communications targets such as marshalling yards, junctions, and other choke points. With a fair degree of air superiority assured, single bombers carried out armed reconnaissance missions, penetrating deep into Polish territory. Following railway lines at low level, they attacked by crossing the line at a shallow angle and dropping sticks of bombs at regular intervals to make as many cuts as possible.

This strategy was very effective. In all, the Polish Army had mobilised 45 infantry and sixteen cavalry divisions, and ten brigades of border guards, and, thanks to the damage inflicted on the railway system, eight infantry and five cavalry divisions, and three border guards brigades — almost 25 per cent of the effective troops, were prevented from getting into action.[3] By 8 September so much damage had been inflicted on the railways that the hapless Poles were forced to take to the roads. However, even here, continuous air attack precluded an orderly retreat to the line of the River Vistula.

A massive raid on Warsaw had been planned for the first day of the conflict, but this was cancelled because of adverse weather. Instead, a few raids were made on selected military targets in the capital, including the PZL aircraft works. Sporadic attacks followed, aimed at marshalling yards and the Vistula bridges, but without great success. Then, on 13 September, the Wehrmacht having arrived outside the city, the first so-called 'terror raid' on Warsaw took place. Planned at very short notice, it was a shambles. As General Wolfram von Richthofen later observed, 'The chaos over the target was indescribable. Not a single unit attacked at its appointed time, and aircraft nearly collided in the act of bombing. Below there was just a sea of flame and smoke, so that an accurate assessment of the results was impossible.'[4]

Was it a terror raid, or was it a Guernica-type débâcle? Opinions vary. The French Air Attaché in Warsaw stated that only military targets were attacked, but as his main concern was that France and England should not escalate the war with reprisal raids, his report is possibly biased. On the other hand, the Kommodore of KG 77 was relieved of his command for disobeying orders to attack Warsaw, and leading his men against alternative, strictly military, targets.[5] On the balance of probability, Warsaw was a terror raid, but we cannot be certain. What is certain is that after a series of leaflet raids calling on the Poles to surrender, an all-out attack was launched on 25 September. Besides orthodox bombers and dive-bombers, about 30 elderly Ju 52 transports flew over the city. They were loaded with incendiaries, which were literally shovelled out of the side doors with no attempt at accuracy. Burning, Warsaw surrendered on 27 September. While most air action in the Polish campaign took place in daylight, four raids were made at night by the specialist unit LnAbt 100, using a radio blind-bombing system. Given the technology of the times, it was remarkably effective.

The Polish campaign confirmed the validity of the concept of Blitzkrieg, or 'lightning war'. Air superiority had been assured from the outset, and by the end of the second week the outcome was hardly in doubt. The Stukas, acting as flying artillery to support the Army, had gained a fearsome reputation, while the level bombers had left a swathe of destruction across the land. The Zerstörer had not done as well against the antiquated P.11s as they should have, given their performance advantages, but, as the Bf 110 was scheduled for replacement, this was not considered important.

WAR IN THE WEST

Britain and France had declared war on Germany following the invasion of Poland in September 1939. The Franco-German border was protected on either side by heavily fortified defensive lines — the Maginot and Siegfried Lines, respectively — which for all practical purposes ruled out major ground offensives. Only in the air was there any real activity, and even that was limited in scope.

The Polish campaign had caught the Luftwaffe in the middle of its expansion. Time was needed both to continue this and to replace losses, which had been considerable. In any case, the Führer confidently expected a negotiated peace in the West, and civilian casualties would have adversely affected the chances of this. Consequently, land targets were placed off-limits. Nor were the Allies willing to escalate the conflict at this stage. Thus the only valid targets for either side were warships, at sea or anchored offshore.

Before the war, Göring's vainglorious edict 'all that flies belongs to me' had been endorsed by Hitler, with the result that only a handful of units had been assigned to the Kriegsmarine, mainly obsolescent types such as the Dornier Do 18 flying boat and the Heinkel He 59 floatplane. At the outbreak of war, the Heinkel He 115 floatplane was just entering service as a minelayer, while a below-strength Kampfgruppe 806 flew Heinkel He 111s. The only specialised anti-shipping units in the Luftwaffe were I and II./KG 26, with He 111s. Most of its pilots and observers had been drawn from the Kriegsmarine, and were supposedly experts in ship recognition. KG 26 flew against Poland, but in mid-September 1939 it was redeployed to the Heligoland Bight for operations over the North Sea. It was joined shortly afterwards by a mere Staffel of the new Junkers Ju 88-equipped I./KG 30.

Over the featureless and cloud-laden North Sea, the main difficulty was finding the enemy. Even if the Luftwaffe knew where the British warships were, it availed them little if they were uncertain of their own position. A Gruppenkommandeur described navigation at this time as being 'by guess and by God'. The results were less than impressive. On 26 September, three Do 18s spotted the British Fleet, losing two of their number to carrier fighters in the process. The Luftwaffe response was feeble; a single Staffel of Heinkels from KG 26, and a mere four Ju 88s from KG 30. Only the latter made contact, and the aircraft carrier HMS Ark Royal was mistakenly reported sunk. Then, on 9 October, a force of 148 bombers failed to find the British Fleet. One week later, a Staffel from I./KG 30 attacked warships in the Firth of Forth, damaging three but losing two Ju 88s to defending fighters. In all, the anti-shipping specialists had achieved little: during that month, KG 26 lost thirteen Heinkels while failing to sink a single ship. The misery was compounded on 22 February 1940, when 4 and 6/KG 26 scored a spectacular own goal by sinking a German destroyer with a single hit from a 50kg bomb.

Meanwhile the Jagdflieger were doing rather better. Several RAF bombing raids on Kriegsmarine targets had sustained heavy losses to the defending fighters. On 18 December, 22 Wellingtons were detected off the coast by radar, and the Messerschmitts were scrambled to intercept. In all, twelve Wellingtons were shot down, and another three were written off on their return. Losses on this scale were too high to be borne, and the RAF was forced to abandon daylight raiding by unescorted bombers.

A British attempt to interdict supplies of Swedish iron ore sparked off the simultaneous invasion of Denmark and Norway in April 1940. Denmark was swiftly overrun, with the aid of a single airdrop of paratroops, but Norway proved much more difficult. The small Norwegian air force was quickly overwhelmed, and paratroops, followed by air landed troops, captured two important airfields, despite heavy fog. Aided by level and dive-bombers, resistance on the ground was largely overcome, and soon the Wehrmacht had a firm foothold.

The British and French responded in force, and for a time the issue hung in the balance. The British Home Fleet appeared off the Norwegian coast, and was subjected to intensive air attack, despite cover from carrier aircraft. The most difficult task was the support of German troops at Narvik, in the far north and out of range of most German bomber forces. Nevertheless, help was at hand. A long-range reconnaissance Staffel, 1(F)/ 120, had been established on 1 October 1939, equipped with the Focke-Wulf FW 200 Condor, a converted airliner. This unit had become operational on 8 April 1940, and three days later three Condors bombed Allied shipping off Narvik in a mission lasting seventeen hours. Later, Condors flew resupply missions to the area. The Norwegian campaign was successfully concluded at the end of May.

Meanwhile, the stand-off in Western Europe had continued. Air activity had been restricted by exceptionally bad winter weather, although probing flights along the Franco-German border had led to occasional small-scale clashes. The impasse was broken on 10 May 1940. With a total disregard for international law, Germany bypassed the virtually impregnable Maginot Line, violating the neutrality of Luxembourg, Belgium and Holland, before sweeping into France. The Belgian fortress of Eben-Emael and two of the three bridges over the steep-banked Albert Canal were carried by an audacious glider-borne assault. Elsewhere, in a Poland-style bid for instant air superiority, Luftwaffe bombers attacked 47 French, 15 Belgian, and ten Dutch airfields. Raids on airfields at Amsterdam Schiphol, Ypenburg (near Den Haag) and Rotterdam Waalhaven were closely followed by paratroop drops, and then, when the bases had been secured, by air-portable troops, albeit at an enormous cost in Ju 52s. Infantry were also flown into Rotterdam by twelve He 59 floatplanes which landed on the River Maas in the city centre, losing four of their number in the process.

The Dutch and Belgian air forces were quickly reduced to impotence. Not so the French and British. In all, 91 airfields in Northern France housed first-line units, but a major Teutonic intelligence failure saw only 31 attacked on 10 May. Of these, five housed bomber units, only two of which sustained significant damage, while a dozen were home to fighters. The remainder were occupied by reconnaissance and liaison units.

On 14 May came the notorious bombing of Rotterdam. The air-landed German troops were desperately trying to hold the bridges in the city centre. A knock-out blow was ordered, to be carried out by two Gruppen of He 111s of KG 54. With the Dutch expected to surrender momentarily, cancellation signals were arranged but were not received by the Heinkels. The bombs from one Gruppe went down, starting huge fires. At the last moment, the leader of the second Gruppe spotted red Very lights and also an agreed signal to cancel, and led his force away to an alternative target. The majority of buildings in the heart of Rotterdam were timber-framed, and the fire service was inadequate to deal with the ensuing conflagration. This was also dubbed a terror raid, although the Luftwaffe had made every effort to prevent it.

Meanwhile the Panzers, spearheaded by the Stukas and backed by the level bombers, stormed into France, having crossed the Meuse at Sedan. The French, lacking an effective early-warning and fighter-control system, were unable to put up an organised resistance, and the RAF in France was in little better shape. Interceptions were a matter of chance, and as Allied air units were forced to retreat across country, often to emergency landing grounds with few facilities and non-existent communications, all semblance of an effective air defence was lost.

As in Poland, the Luftwaffe level bombers, having first attacked airfields, concentrated on road and rail communications targets, ports, troop concentrations, and stores depots. The short-legged Stukas, tasked with supporting the Panzers, were hard-pressed to keep up with the advance. With the aircraft moving forward on an almost daily basis, and flying six or more missions a day, the supply demands were enormous, and the wear and tear hardly less so. On 21 May, the Panzers reached the sea near Abbeville, cutting the Allied armies in half. The assault then switched to the Channel ports.

First Boulogne fell, and then Calais. In the north, therefore, only Dunkirk was left. At this point, Göring, in a vainglorious gesture, suggested that the encircled Allied forces around Dunkirk could be overcome by air power alone. Wever was appalled by this, as was the commander of Luftflotte 2, 'Smiling Albert' Kesselring, but their vigorous objections were overruled. The Führer, aware that, in the south, the bulk of the French armies remained unsubdued, and anxious to conserve his Panzer strength, halted them, leaving the reduction of Dunkirk to the Luftwaffe.

Had the weather been kinder, the German flyers might just have achieved a victory of sorts, but low cloud, heavy rain and fog hampered operations for almost 75 per cent of the time, while RAF fighters based in southern England put up a spirited resistance for the remainder. In all, 338,000 British and French troops were successfully evacuated, albeit minus their heavy equipment. Had the weather favoured the Third Reich, the probable figure would have been fewer than 50,000, making Dunkirk at least a partial Luftwaffe victory.

With Dunkirk neutralised, the focus switched. Operation 'Paula', a massive attack on aircraft factories and airfields in the Paris area on 3 June, and carried out by no fewer that 640 bombers with strong fighter escort, was at first hailed as a great victory. This is not borne out by the statistics: fifteen factories sustained slight damage, while heavy damage was inflicted on only six of the sixteen airfields that came under attack. Just four German bombers were lost, and a mere twenty French aircraft were destroyed on the ground. Following this, the Luftwaffe turned southwards, attacking troop concentrations and communications links. Her armies badly battered and thoroughly demoralised, on 25 June France capitulated.

◆ ◆ ◆

By any standards, this was a stunning victory. The atmosphere throughout Germany was euphoric. The fledgeling Luftwaffe had, with few exceptions, acquitted itself magnificently, and had played a major role in proving the Blitzkrieg concept. In just ten months, German arms had overrun Poland, Denmark, Norway, Belgium, Holland and France in short order, while Britain, the sole remaining enemy, had been driven from the continent and now stood alone, her only option apparently a negotiated peace.

Most euphoric of all was Generaloberst Ernst Udet, Chief of Supply and Procurement and the Technical Office. At the Armistice he exulted that the war was over, and that development of new aircraft types could take a low priority. In fact, this was in line with a decree issued by Göring on 7 February 1940, to the effect that work on all new aircraft that could not be ready to enter front-line service within a year should be halted[6]. Udet, always fascinated by 'higher and faster', had, with Wever's connivance, turned a blind eye to various projects under development, including jet propulsion. So in fact had several manufacturers, who had hoarded stocks of raw materials such as aluminium unbeknown to Udet, thereby creating artificial shortages.[7]

Hitler, almost equally euphoric, handed out Generalfeldmarschall batons on 19 July. Among the Luftwaffe recipients were Walther Wever, Albert Kesselring, Erhard Milch and Hugo Sperrle, while Commander-in-Chief Hermann Göring was given the unique rank of Reichsmarschall. However, Wever's promotion was accompanied by compulsory retirement. He was 56 years old, and had been Chief of Staff for the last five years. A straight talker, he had little time for Göring's crony Udet, whom he regarded as a dilettante. Neither was he on the best of terms with the empire-building Milch. Furthermore, at a time when the Luftwaffe was floating on a sea of glory, he irked his Commander-in-Chief by pointing out flaws in the new service. It was time he went.

His replacement was his own nominee — Hans Jeschonnek. General der Flieger Jeschonnek[8] was a career officer, just 41 years old. He had been credited with two victories while flying Fokker DVIIs with Jasta 40 in 1918, completed his General Staff training in 1928 and become a protégé of General Wever[9] in the 1930s — surprisingly, as he had a rather abrasive, very Prussian personality. Having said that, Kesselring, one of the most able Luftwaffe commanders, stated after the war that 'the most impressive personality among the Chiefs of the General Staff was Generaloberst Jeschonnek — an unusually intelligent and energetic person.'[10] Jeschonnek met favour with Göring on two counts: he was young; and he was devoted to Hitler. There were, however, hidden flaws.

THE ORPHANS

As the saying goes, 'Success has a thousand fathers; failure is an orphan.' And so it proved: the few Luftwaffe failures were masked by the overwhelming successes. However, Wever had identified the following weaknesses.

1. Attrition replacements of aircraft and crews were inadequate.
2. Better navigation training was needed (the German city of Freiberg was bombed in error, while six Heinkels were lost to Swiss fighters following an accidental border violation).
3. Bombing results were not commensurate with the effort expended, mainly due to inaccuracy.

4. Better liaison with the ground forces was needed (on at least two occasions, Stukas attacked Panzers).

5. The advantage of radar early warning had been amply proven but was not being followed up.

6. The Bf 110 was inadequate as a fighter, and should be used as a fighter-bomber.

7. The Bf 109 should be replaced by something that handled more benignly and had more potential for development potential. Meanwhile, its range should be increased by means of external tanks.

8. More dedicated transport units were needed. Ju 52s had been 'borrowed' from training units to meet the needs of paratroop and air mobile forces. Losses had been very high, and this virtually halted multi-engine training. Wever suggested that the Ju 86 could be fitted with petrol engines to make up the shortfall.[11]

NOTES

1. General der Flieger Paul Deichmann, *Spearhead for Blitzkrieg*.
2. This was actually the projected figure for the He 177.
3. Deichmann, op. cit.
4. Cajus Becker, *The Luftwaffe War Diaries*.
5. Ibid.
6. Harold Faber (ed.), *Luftwaffe*.
7. Ibid.
8. Jeschonnek actually became Chief of Staff at the age of 39.
9. Faber, op. cit.
10. Ibid.
11. This suggestion was actually made by Deichmann. See Faber, op. cit.

3   Assault on England

FOLLOWING the French capitulation on 25 June, many observers expected that the Luftwaffe would immediately turn its full might against England. That it did not was due to two main factors. The first was that Hitler confidently expected the island nation to sue for peace. The British Expeditionary Force had been comprehensively defeated in the field. Only by a miracle had it managed to escape complete destruction at Dunkirk, where almost all its heavy equipment had been lost. The Royal Air Force's bomber squadrons in France had taken a terrible beating, while its fighter squadrons had also lost heavily. In addition, the Royal Navy had sustained significant losses both off Dunkirk and off Norway. In the face of these calamities, could the British realistically hope to continue the war? The Führer thought not. Only in late July, apparently reluctantly, did he issue orders for the reduction of Britain.

The second factor was that the Luftwaffe was in no fit state to carry out anything other than the most minor of operations. Aircraft losses had been horrific: 459 fighters, 635 twin-engine bombers and 147 Stukas had been written off, with hundreds more damaged in varying degrees. Even more seriously, some 3,000 aircrew were dead or missing, and almost 1,400 had been wounded. These were not nearly offset by the return of about 400 Luftwaffe aircrew from French prison camps, even though they included top-scoring fighter ace Werner 'Vati'[1] Mölders and bomber Kommodore Josef Kammhuber, the future architect of Germany's night air defence.

Exhaustion was also a factor. The short-legged 109s and Stukas had flown intensively. Several sorties a day while continually moving forward had tested the flyers to their limits, while the 'black men' of the ground crews were worn out by the daily struggle to refuel, rearm, and keep often damaged aircraft serviceable. All needed rest.

The result was that many of the units were withdrawn to Germany in order to re-equip with machines and personnel. The training of many of the latter was incomplete. For example, a bomber pilot normally spent three months at an Ergänzungskampfgruppe for advanced tactical training. Otto von Ballasko was there for just two days[2] before being posted to a front line unit. Nor was he exceptional: many others suffered the same treatment. This imposed a heavy burden on the front-line units, which became responsible for giving the new men a final, operational polish.

Redeployment was another problem. Most permanent airfields in north-western France, Belgium and Holland had suffered during the campaign, and had to be repaired. Nor were there enough of them. The short-ranged, single-engine units, equipped with Bf 109s and Ju 87s, had to be based close to the Channel if they were to reach southern England. For these, primitive airstrips were established by the simple expedient of rolling a more or less level field. Basic servicing and repairs were carried out in the open, although sometimes rough buildings were cobbled together from old crates. Accommodation consisted of requisitioned farmhouses and tents. Communications, water supplies and sanitation all had to be organised, while 'goulash cannons' (field kitchens) fed the troops. Adequate stocks of fuel and munitions for sustained operations had to be established and camouflaged against air attack. Finally, anti-aircraft gun defences were put in place. It all took time.

Multi-engine training had been hard hit. With little dedicated transport capacity, the Luftwaffe had 'borrowed' more than 350 Ju 52s and their instructor pilots from the training units, firstly for the Scandinavian campaign and then for the paratroop and air-landing operations in the Low Countries. Losses had exceeded 50 per cent, and, even with the French campaign over, the aircraft were still needed to supply the new bases facing the Channel, pending the restoration of damaged road and rail links. Few found their way back to the training schools.

Wever's last act before retirement was to force through the re-equipment of the multi-engine training schools with Ju 86s.[3] Enough parts existed for 1,000 of these obsolescent bombers, and, with their unreliable diesels replaced by petrol engines, some 400 were built. In this Wever was backed by Milch. Göring was initially opposed to the idea, but, newly promoted to Reichsmarschall and flushed with victory, he finally acquiesced. This decision had two far-reaching consequences. The Luftwaffe could now set up a dedicated Ju 52 transport force, whilst multi-engine aircrew training could proceed uninterrupted.

THE FIRST NIBBLES

The Luftwaffe opened the ball in mid-June with sporadic small-scale night raids on England — mainly minelaying, with occasional incursions inland against aircraft factories and airfields. This could not last. A successful invasion demanded air superiority over the English Channel, and this became Phase 1 of what became known as the Battle of Britain. Daylight operations commenced in early July with attacks on English ports and convoys, mainly by escorted Do 17s and Ju 87s. From 4 July this was supplemented by Freijagd (fighter sweeps) over south-eastern England. These were counter-productive. If the RAF could identify them in time, they were left strictly alone to wear out their engines in peace (if that is the right word).

At first, the only single-engine fighter unit on the Channel coast was JG 51, led by First World War ace 'Onkel Theo' Osterkamp, who always referred to his English opponents as 'The Lords'. This term of respect did not, however, prevent him from claiming six victories to add to his Great War score of 32.

By mid-July Geschwader serviceability had dropped below 40 per cent. This was only partly due to the hard-fighting Spitfires and Hurricanes; attrition caused by operating from semi-prepared airstrips had also taken a significant toll. JG 51 was supported by the Bf 110s of ZG 26, led by the one-legged Great War veteran Joachim-Friedrich Huth. Outmanoeuvred and outperformed by the British fighters, the Bf 110s generally entered a defensive circle when attacked. A furious Göring demanded that it be renamed the offensive circle, but, as one pilot sadly remarked, 'It's still the same old circle!' Be that as it may, against single-engine fighters the Bf 110 was a 'turkey'.

Over the next few weeks, the Luftwaffe built up its strength for the assault on England, as the Jagdgruppen deployed to the Channel coast and revitalised Kampfgeschwader occupied bases inland.

PREPARATION

Phase 2 of the Battle was to consist of attacks on the RAF infrastructure — airfields and production centres — supplemented by raids on ports. This was scheduled to start on 10 August. Fighter Command was to be reduced to near-impotence within four to six weeks, making a seaborne invasion a practical proposition.

Three Luftflotten faced Britain: Luftflotte 2, commanded by Albert Kesselring, was based north of the Seine and faced south-eastern England; Luftflotte 3, commanded by Hugo Sperrle, was based south of the Seine facing southern England and the West Midlands; and the relatively small Luftflotte 5, commanded by Hans-Jürgen Stumpff, was based in Norway and Denmark and faced the enemy across the North Sea.

Before such attacks could be launched, however, accurate reconnaissance was needed. This began on 1 July but it was less than successful. In the space of five weeks, 50 reconnaissance aircraft were lost, half of them from the dedicated Aufklärungsgruppen. Radar detected them as they approached the coast, and once inland they were tracked by the Observer Corps. Flying singly at medium altitude, they provided excellent practice for the English fighter control system. When circumstances permitted, and they often did, RAF fighter squadrons vectored sections of three, or even flights of six aircraft, against each intruder.

To survive against such odds, the reconnaissance aircraft were forced to ever greater altitudes, to the point where their cameras lost definition. The Luftwaffe photographic interpreters could tell which airfields were active, but not the aircraft types on them. This was a failure of the first order. When the assault was launched, too many attacks were wasted on Coastal Command or training airfields.

THE BACKROOM BOYS

Meanwhile, Generalmajor Wolfgang Martini, head of the Luftwaffe signals organisation, was busy. In both the Channel battles and the reconnaissance missions of July, his organisation had noted that the RAF fighters were being accurately controlled from the ground. It was clear that the emissions coming from the 100m-high towers around the coastline provided some form of radar detection and early warning. The Germans themselves had radar, and so knew very well how it worked. Some mobile British radar sets had been captured at Dunkirk, and detailed examination had pronounced them to be primitive. Martini was less than impressed.

His staff continually monitored RAF radio communications. It was obvious that the British knew where the German formations were, and roughly the direction in which they were heading, even when they were past the radar cover and penetrating inland — to within certain rather imprecise limits. That was no great surprise. It was also obvious that RAF fighter-control was not centralised, but emanated from several major airfields. Direction-finding and triangulation quickly identified those in south-eastern England as Middle Wallop, Tangmere, Kenley, Biggin Hill, Hornchurch, North Weald, Debden and Northolt, the locations of which were known through pre-war reconnaissance and intelligence. Each of these airfields typically seemed to control three or four fighter squadrons, even though some of the latter were based elsewhere.

The Luftwaffe signals monitoring service quickly discovered that the British ground controllers issued remarkably precise interception instructions. The fact was that, in the early days, single aircraft or small formations, and not many of them, were relatively easy to track. Later in the battle, large multiple raids created confusion, and a smaller proportion of units ordered to intercept made contact. Early experience created a misleading impression, however, and one that was never entirely dispelled.

This raised the question: how did the RAF controllers know so precisely where their own fighters were? British fighter leaders rarely gave a clue as to their positions, neither were their voice transmissions long enough to allow cross-bearings to be taken. So it must be something more. But what? A dedicated transmitter perhaps? Martini's men continued their listening brief.

Not until the third week in August did they come up with the answer, and then it proved ridiculously simple. One radio in each RAF fighter formation automatically transmitted a steady signal of dashes for fourteen seconds in each minute. This was just long enough to allow British direction-finding stations to triangulate for a position. Martini had discovered 'Pip-Squeak'.[4]

THE STORM BREAKS

For the Luftwaffe, the assault on England truly began in the second week in August. Called 'Adlerangriff', its purpose was to destroy Fighter Command, in the air or on the ground (it mattered little). Once this was done, the way would be open for the invasion which would settle the hash of the turbulent islanders once and for all. Mass daylight bomber raids protected by a heavy fighter escort, aimed primarily at the fighter airfields and backed up by attacks on the aircraft industry should do the job. They had all the necessary intelligence, or so they thought.

Oberst Josef 'Beppo' Schmid, Head of Intelligence, was not the brightest star in the Luftwaffe galaxy. His faulty analysis and appreciation resulted in the initial assault on airfields becoming a fiasco. Of the targets attacked, Sheerness was a naval establishment. Airfields at Eastchurch, Odiham, Farnborough, Andover, Rochester and Detling were not fighter bases. A raid on Southampton damaged the docks but ignored the Spitfire factory at Woolston; Beppo's lot had it down as A. V. Roe, manufacturing bombers! In fact, faulty intelligence bedevilled the entire campaign against Fighter Command. This was not all. Navigational errors meant that the Luftwaffe completely failed to find two fighter airfields, Middle Wallop and Warmwell. The cost was high: eleven twin-engine bombers, six Stukas, eight Bf 110s and five Bf 109s failed to return. The RAF's losses were thirteen fighters, including one on the ground at Eastchurch. Teutonic efficiency had not improved much since Guernica!

The value of the British early-warning system had previously been recognised. If this could be taken out, 'The Lords' would be seriously

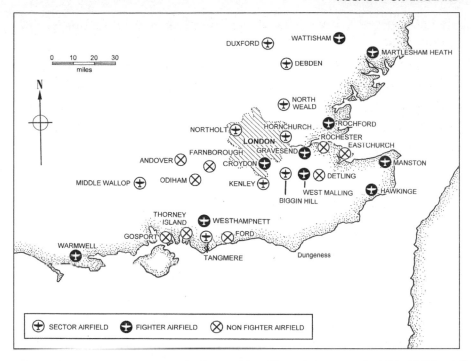

Major reconnaissance and intelligence failures led the Luftwaffe to attack nine non-fighter airfields, plus the non-operational West Malling, in the first few days of 'Adlerangriffe'. Nor did they identify the vital sector stations.

disadvantaged. On the previous day, the task had been given to Erpro-bungsgruppe 210. This was an operational evaluation unit scheduled to be the first to be equipped with the new Bf 210, the Stuka replacement. It consisted of two Staffeln of Bf 110s and one of Bf 109s, all fighter-bombers, or Jabos.

On 12 August EprGr 210 made shallow, diving attacks on radar stations at Dover, Rye, Pevensey and Dunkirk (Kent, not France). They were only marginally effective: while all except Dover were off the air for a few hours, rapid repairs saw them back on line that afternoon. On that same day, Ventnor was heavily attacked by Ju 88s of KG 51, and put off the air for nearly two weeks. The RAF rushed a mobile radar station to the Isle of Wight to plug the gap. Martini's listeners failed to notice the reduced signal strength from the mobile station; to them it appeared that Ventnor was still fully functional. In a major intelligence failure, the Luftwaffe concluded that the radar stations were impossible to knock out for any length of time.

The Reichsmarschall, whose technical knowledge was on a par with that of the average pot plant, concurred. He agreed with many of his fighter pilots that anything that drew the English up and into combat, where they could be shot down, was to the advantage of the Luftwaffe. This was of course to ignore totally the fact that fighters are at their most vulnerable when on the ground, where they spend the majority of their time. The upshot was that, henceforth, only sporadic attacks were carried out against the radar stations, apparently more in hope than expectation. Generalmajor Martini gave orders for electronic countermeasures to be developed to jam the British early-warning radars. This took time: the work did not begin until mid-September — too late to be really effective.

August 15 saw another major Luftwaffe intelligence failure. 'Beppo' Schmid had been seduced by Jagdwaffe victory claims. Had he divided them by three, his figures would have been far more accurate. His assessment now was that virtually all RAF fighters had been moved south, leaving the Midlands and North undefended.

This faulty assessment caused Luftflotte 5 to enter the battle for the first time. In accordance with American General Patton's dictum 'Hold 'em by the nose and kick 'em in the pants', a series of heavy raids was launched against targets in southern England. While these occupied the defenders, two major raids were launched against targets in the north, one escorted by Bf 110s and the other unescorted. Met by supposedly non-existent fighters, both were badly mauled, and, after just one day, Luftflotte 5 was out of the daylight battle. Things did not go well in the south either. Twelve airfields were raided, of which only seven housed fighters. Just three were sector stations; these suffered light damage, although three of the others were hit hard. One of the remainder, Odiham, was attacked in error. A mere two Spitfires were destroyed on the ground. Of the industrial targets bombed, not one was involved in fighter production. The Luftwaffe's losses on this day totalled 77, including aircraft that were written off on their return. Of these, no fewer than 28 were Bf 110s and 17 were Ju 88s. Many were the legacy of Luftflotte 5's fatal incursion. The RAF lost 32 fighters.[5] This was enough to convince Ober-kommando der Luftwaffe (OKL) that the Bf 110 was a failure, although, needing the numbers, they could not afford to dispense with it entirely.

Three days later the vaunted Ju 87 Stuka was blasted into oblivion. In a multiple raid on south-coast targets, eleven out of 28 Stukas of I./StG 77 were shot down or written off. This loss rate was unsustainable: from 18 August the Stukas were out of the battle, although they were retained in place to support the planned invasion.

Not counting 17 August, when adverse weather precluded much action, the Luftwaffe's losses were running at an unsustainable 49 aircraft a day. At this point the Reichsmarschall intervened. First, he insisted that the bombers be given closer protection. Secondly, he started to replace Jagdgeschwader Kommodoren with younger men, with success in combat as the criterion. Adolf Galland took over JG 26, Günther Lützow JG 3, Hannes Trautloft JG 54, and Hans Trübenbach JG 52. Mölders, who re-garded himself as the spiritual successor to the Great War fighter leader Oswald Boelcke, already commanded JG 51.

Close escort was unpopular with the Jagdflieger. Young Hans Schmoller-Haldy of JG 54 recorded that 'It gave the bomber crews the feeling that they were being protected, and it might have deterred some of the enemy pilots. But for us fighter pilots it was very bad. We needed the advantages of altitude and speed so that we could engage the enemy on favourable terms.'[6] Surprisingly, Göring's insistence on close escort, oft decried as a major error of judgement, seems justified by the record.

Adverse weather severely curtailed operations between August 19 and 23, and there was little activity on August 27. The remainder of the month saw daylight losses amount to 195 aircraft—excluding unescorted recon-naissance aircraft—of which no fewer than 107 were Bf 109s. Losses of twin-engine aircraft amounted to 88, an average of almost thirteen a day.[7] Even taking into account the withdrawal of the Stukas, this was a remark-able drop from the previous daily average of 38, but as average Bf 109 losses increased from eleven a day to more than fifteen, perhaps the Jagdflieger had a point. However, as the bombers were the offensive weapon, the broad picture seems to indicate that the Reichsmarschall was right. At least in part, the improvement could be directly attributed to the new close-escort tactics.

Naturally, the Jagdflieger were more vulnerable when, tied closely to the bombers, they were deprived of freedom of action, but there were of course other reasons for the grumbles coming from the 109 pilots. First, flying up to five sorties a day, they were becoming exhausted. Secondly, no one ever got a Ritterkreuz for protecting bombers!

Despite the dissipation of effort against non-essential targets, raids on the fighter airfields in south-eastern England were having a cumulative effect. Gradually the efficiency of the defenders was being eroded, although this was not immediately apparent. Another factor was that the sector station operations rooms were not only actually on the airfields, but virtually unprotected. Just one lucky bomb . . . !

German intelligence can hardly be blamed for failing to anticipate this. Instead, they made the sensible assumption that the vital operations rooms would be of reinforced concrete, deep underground, and impossible to knock out from the air. However, had the Luftwaffe concentrated its entire effort against the sector stations, they would have been wrecked from end to end, greatly reducing Fighter Command's effectiveness.

TARGET LONDON

The early battles had shown the Luftwaffe that at least two fighters were needed to escort each bomber, yet even this had not proved to be enough. The hard-pressed Jagdflieger were only able to provide escorts for about a quarter of the bomber force. This was a waste of resources.

Towards the end of August, Luftflotte 2 was reinforced by several Jagd- and Zerstörergruppen from Luftflotte 3. The main burden of daylight operations now fell on Kesselring's command, leaving Sperrle in a secondary role. At the end of August Schmid claimed that only 100 RAF fighters were serviceable, but upgraded this to 350 on 3 September. Kesselring was also optimistic, but many, including Sperrle, viewed these figures with extreme reservation.

To the Luftwaffe, the sustained airfield assault seemed to be having little effect on the ability of the British to strike back hard, and little over a fortnight remained to produce the air superiority needed for a successful cross-Channel invasion. Sperrle wanted to continue the airfield attacks, but Kesselring took the view (correctly) that, even if these were rendered inoperable, the British would withdraw their fighters to bases beyond the reach of the escorting Bf 109s.[8] A full-scale assault on London was the only feasible alternative. If it did not cow the recalcitrant islanders into submission, it would at least bring up the British fighters for a final Homeric battle against heavy odds.

Thus far the Führer had forbidden attacks on the English capital, but now a succession of mischances had given him a ready excuse to reverse his decision.[9] The order was given on 30 August, and the initial raid was scheduled for 7 September. Always the showman, Hitler made public his intentions before an audience at the Berlin Sportpalast. As a reprisal for the raids on Berlin, he shrieked, the weight of British bombs dropped would be repaid tenfold . . . fiftyfold . . . one hundredfold!

The largest German bomb that could be carried internally in 1940 was the SC 250, a light-case weapon containing about 138kg (303lb) of high explosive. A Heinkel He 111 carried up to eight of these. Bigger bombs, such as the SC 1000 Hermann, named after the rotund Reichsmarschall, had been developed, but these had to be carried externally, However, external carriage was — except for Stukas, which had no alternative — initially considered unacceptable for daylight operations. All that was about to change. For the first time, the new SC 1800 Satan heavy bomb was available.[10] Its light case was packed with 990kg (2,183lb) of high explosive, and trials had shown it to be extremely destructive. What was more, two Satans could be carried internally by the Do 19A Uralbomber.

The Dornier Do 19A had entered service a few months earlier with IV./Lehrgeschwader (LG) 1. Lehrgeschwader were operational evaluation units charged with developing tactics and methods, but in the Luftwaffe of 1940 the individual Lehrgruppen were also employed as front-line units. The working-up period complete, IV./LG 1 deployed to Antwerp/Deurne, a prewar Belgian airfield with hard runways and taxiways. To accommodate it, the Do 17-equipped II./KG 3 was withdrawn to re-equip with the new bomber.

It took little discussion before it was decided to lead the raid with IV./LG 1. To plant their Satans accurately, Uralbomber observers needed a view of the target uncompromised by smoke and fires from earlier raiders, which meant that they had to go in first. The propaganda effect of a whole Gruppe of these huge four-engine bombers leading the attack was not overlooked.

The raid was centred on the West India Docks, but took in the whole of London's dockland, Woolwich Arsenal and the oil storage tanks at Thameshaven. Bombers drawn from fifteen Kampfgruppen would take part — more than 350 in all. IV./LG 1 would be backed up by eight Gruppen of Heinkel He 111s, two of Junkers Ju 88s and four of Dornier Do 17s.

The bombers would fly in three columns on a 30km (19-mile) frontage, escorted by 22 Jagdgruppen of Bf 109Es and two Zerstörergruppen of Bf 110Cs, some 630 fighters in total. The plan was to launch the raid in the early evening, then keep the fires stoked up during the night with several hundred bomber sorties, mainly from Luftflotte 3, many of whose crews would fly twice. With a large percentage of the Heinkels carrying SC 1000 Hermanns externally, and others loaded with incendiaries, tremendous destruction was anticipated.

On the day after Hitler's hysterical outburst at the Sportspalast, Göring was interviewed on national radio. Upbeat, he stated that future operations would be decisive, and that he was taking personal command. The series of events related in the prologue led the Reichsmarschall to conclude that his best course of action was to fly in the leading Uralbomber. Whatever his faults, Göring was no coward, and this would leave his critics with egg on their faces — not that, statistically speaking, there was any great risk! His arrival at Antwerp/Deurne, complete with his entourage, caused a sensation, only exceeded by his announcement that he would fly in the leading bomber on the raid. Oberleutnant Hans Kamansky, then an observer with IV/LG 1, recalled:

> His presence filled the room. [He was] of medium height, [and] his chiselled features were only slightly blurred by excess weight. His startlingly blue gaze swept over us. He smiled, showing small but perfect teeth. His voice was a pleasant, light tenor, full of authority, as he gave us the expected pep-talk. Then he dropped his bombshell!

'I shall fly in the leading bomber. In a battle which will change the destiny of the world, where else should a commander-in-chief be, but at the head of his troops!'

His tone was almost indulgent. With an imperious wave of a plump, be-ringed hand, he defied us to protest. We stood there, stunned. Then someone cheered and, caught up in the moment, we all joined in.[11]

As was only right and proper, the Reichsmarschall flew with the Kommandeur, observer Major Egbert Karvola; his pilot the very experienced Hauptmann Erwin Wims. Fitting him out with a helmet and oxygen mask was no problem, but flying overalls of adequate girth could not be found. Göring brushed aside the difficulty: after all, his fancy sky blue greatcoat with white satin lapels would look best in the official photographs.

He spent the afternoon talking to the air and ground crews and watching the two huge blue-painted Satan bombs being hoisted aboard. Time to go. Wims taxied out, lined up on the runway and opened the throttles. The huge bomber gathered speed and lifted into the air. At altitude it circled, waiting for the other bombers to join up, then set course for London. Out over the North Sea, other Kampfgruppen slipped into their allocated places as though on a parade ground, while the protecting fighters took up station around them. Rounding the North Foreland, the huge formation headed up the Thames Estuary.

The absence of British fighters puzzled the Germans. They were not to know that the RAF had deployed to defend their airfields. Consequently, the German formation had a fairly clear run; few English fighter squadrons, hastily redirected, made contact. *Luftwaffe* losses were light — a mere seven twin-engine bombers, fourteen Bf 109s, eight Bf 110s and, of course, one Do 19.

◆ ◆ ◆

Antwerp/Deurne experienced something approaching panic when the Reichsmarschall's aircraft failed to return. As is typical of air combat, events had happened very fast, and, distracted by RAF fighters, no one in the formation had seen its going. One moment it had been there, the next — gone! Frantic calls to other airfields revealed nothing. There were no reports of crashes in France or Belgium. Was he down in England? Over the next two days, continental listening figures for BBC announcer Alvar

Liddell rose sharply. But still nothing! If the British knew anything, surely they would not keep quiet.

Someone had to tell the Führer that the Reichsmarschall was missing. 'Smiling Albert' Kesselring, Commander-in-Chief of Luftflotte 2, who had had no knowledge of Göring's escapade until after the event, baulked at the job, as did Göring's deputy Erhard Milch. The task fell to recently appointed chief of staff Hans Jeschonnek, whose career never really recovered from being the bearer of such bad news.

On 11 September Hitler finally accepted that Göring must be dead. For the time being, the assault on England was allowed to continue under its own momentum. However, the event allowed a badly needed reshuffle to take place, and the first question was: who should be the new Commander-in-Chief? Göring's deputy, Generalfeldmarschall Milch, was quickly eliminated on the grounds that, having no operational experience, he would be unlikely to command the respect of the seasoned air fleet leaders. His suspect ancestry was also a factor. Of the other three Luftwaffe Generalfeldmarschälle, Wever, now retired, was never seriously considered. This left Kesselring and Sperrle. Kesselring's distinguished record tipped the balance, and he was appointed. Command of Luftflotte 2 went to the hard-charging and ambitious Wolfram von Richthofen, who had led the Stuka-equipped Fliegerkorps VIII with distinction.

It was already apparent that Ernst Udet was totally unsuited to head the Technical Office; yet to sack such a distinguished and famous flyer would cause an outcry. The solution was to make him Inspector of the Fighters, a post he had briefly held in 1936 but one that in wartime was of increased importance. Udet, well aware of his own shortcomings, accepted his new position with relief. Milch, a superb organiser, added the Technical Office to his already large portfolio.[12]

PIP-SQUEAK COUNTERED

Meanwhile attacks on Britain continued without a break. The raid on 7 September had been extremely destructive, and fires were still burning three days later. London's ordeal had begun. At this point, the Luftwaffe introduced two new factors.

Martini's signals organisation had at last discovered how to jam 'Pip-Squeak'. Having rejected the use of ground stations, their solution was blindingly simple: by tuning the bomber radio transmitters to the 'Pip-Squeak' frequency, then clamping the Morse key down, they could corrupt the signals from the British fighters. The bomber crews were unhappy, however, fearing that the emissions would be homed on, but they were given no choice. The RAF control system was thrown into a state of confusion, which was only overcome by the expedient of having the fighter leaders radio back their positions at frequent intervals. This lowered efficiency, and to a degree reduced the number of successful interceptions.

The second factor was the introduction of drop tanks. The first Bf 109 subtype to carry the necessary plumbing was the E-7, which started to reach II./LG 2, based at Calais-Marck, in late August. The moulded plywood tank contained 300 litres (66gal), which would extend operational range and endurance by more than half as much again.[13]

With tanks, 109s based in the Pas de Calais could stay over London for more than half an hour rather than barely ten minutes, without having to worry unduly about the fuel warning light. Bombers could be escorted over the length and breadth of southern England and East Anglia and, if they took the most direct route, as far as the industrial areas of Birmingham and Coventry.

There were, however, problems concerning reliability. Not only did the tanks often leak, but airlocks in the feed system were common. The standard procedure was to take off using fuel from the main tank, then switch to the drop tank at altitude. If an airlock existed, the engine promptly cut out. When this happened, the procedure was to revert to the main tank and return to base. The ensuing landing, at high gross weight, often proved too much for the flimsy, narrow main gear legs. On 4 and 5 September, four Bf 109E-7s of II./LG 2 were damaged in landing accidents during non-combat missions.[14] Attempts to release the tank were not always successful. A hung tank made a landing perilous; it was always likely to come off at an embarrassing moment, as on touch-down, bursting and spraying highly volatile fuel in all directions. Even when the release mechanism worked properly, the pilot could still be in trouble. Released in anything other than straight and level flight and at modest speeds, tanks tended to pitch up and hit the tailplane, often with lethal results. The alternative was to retain the tank, accepting the reduction in performance and manoeuvrability caused by the extra weight and drag, but, against the agile Spitfires and Hurricanes, this was far from ideal.[15]

DAYLIGHT CRESCENDO

The next foray by the Do 19A took place on 15 September. Over the preceding week, the response of the defences to German incursions had been less than that in August, causing Beppo Schmid to conclude that Fighter Command had been fatally weakened. The phrase 'the last fifty Spitfires' was much in vogue.

To exploit this, two raids on London were planned. The first was at noon, and consisted of a mere 25 Do 17s drawn from I. and III./KG 76, covered by about 120 Bf 109s. The Dorniers were bait, calculated to bring the English fighters to a decisive battle with the 109s. The fighting was fast and furious, and the passage high above of 21 Bf 109E-7s from II./ LG 2 with long-range tanks passed almost unnoticed.[16] Meanwhile the Uralbombers of IV./LG 1 were out over the North Sea, escorted by 28 Bf 110s of V./LG 1, which had been deployed to Belgium for the occasion. This raid was detected well offshore by Bawdsey radar but was adjudged to be a feint. In any case, fighter squadrons from Martlesham Heath and Debden, plus the Duxford 'Big Wing', led by the indomitable Douglas Bader, were already airborne and heading south. Only when the bombers and their escorts crossed the coast near Felixstowe and headed inland was it taken seriously.

Near Cambridge, the Bf 110 escort turned back but was immediately beset by Spitfires from Coltishall, losing eight of its number. Shortly afterwards, with remarkably precise timing and navigation, the Dorniers rendezvoused with the long-range 109s of II./LG 2. It was barely in time: within minutes the formation was intercepted by Hurricanes and Spitfires from Wittering.

Outnumbered, the 109s fought hard and managed to keep the British fighters away from the bombers. The cost was high. Two Bf 109E-7s were lost when their drop tanks failed to disengage cleanly and another five fell to English guns, although they took three Hurricanes with them. Low on fuel, the escorts broke off and, widely scattered, headed for home.

IV./LG 1 rumbled on towards Coventry. Opposed only by anti-aircraft gunfire, the three Staffeln of bombers split to attack individual targets — Standard Motors, Alvis and Daimler. With eighteen Satans aimed at each, the damage was heavy, and production was badly hit. After bombing they reformed in a gentle turn to starboard, and set course for home. Lacking fighter escort, they headed for The Wash and the relative safety of the North Sea. Just past Spalding, with The Wash well in sight, however, they were intercepted by Hurricanes from Digby. In a running battle which lasted well out to sea, no Dorniers were lost, while the German gunners claimed two of their opponents.

Back at Antwerp/Deurne, the bomber crewmen were jubilant. They had successfully attacked industrial targets in the Midlands in daylight without a single aircraft loss, although five had received minor damage. Two gunners had sustained slight wounds. In the south, matters had gone less well. The noon raid on London had brought on the intended Homeric fighter battle, but without the anticipated losses to the defending fighters. Even worse, the arrival of the Duxford 'Big Wing' over the capital — five squadrons in parade-ground order — came as a terrible blow to German morale. The myth of the 'last fifty Spitfires' was finally demolished.

The second raid on London followed hard on the heels of the first. It consisted of 114 Do 17s and He 111s, covered by 361 Bf 109s. It was no more successful: the German losses were 21 bombers and a dozen fighters. However, the extent of the failure was masked by overclaiming — nearly triple the true British losses.

STRATEGIC OFFENSIVE

Photo-reconnaissance confirmed the high degree of destruction wrought by IV./LG 1 at Coventry. The Gruppe, under a cloud since the loss of the Reichsmarschall, had now redeemed itself. Over the next few days, although night raids continued, there was a hiatus in daylight operations. Unsuitable weather was a primary cause, plus high-level command changes, allied to the fact that the Führer had by now postponed the cross-Channel invasion indefinitely.

Generalfeldmarschall Kesselring, now the Luftwaffe's Commander-in-Chief, was keen to explore the strategic potential of the big Dornier. In this he was enthusiastically backed by his successor at Luftflotte 2, Generaloberst Wolfram von Richthofen. But how best to use it? The accuracy of daylight bombing gave the greatest return for the ordnance expended, but, as the Coventry raid demonstrated, it was prodigal of escort fighters. The question was: could even deeper penetrations be made without incurring prohibitive losses amongst the bombers?

The fact that IV./LG 1 had beaten off an attack by an entire squadron of Hurricanes without sustaining even serious damage, let alone loss, was viewed as significant. The Hurricanes had not pressed their attacks home to close range. As Hans Kamansky recalled, 'They seemed unwilling to close with us. Time and again they would begin an attack, open fire at very long range, then break away. It was as though they were intimidated by our sheer size and massed fire-power.'[17] Keeping up the pressure in the south while testing the industrial midlands and north with a series of damaging daylight raids might just be the straw that broke the camel's back. Richthofen, a tough-minded commander, decided that he would test the water.

The target chosen was Sheffield. Tracked by Stenigot radar, IV./LG 1 crossed the coast at Skegness at an altitude of 7,000m (23,000ft) to reduce the probability of interception. Meanwhile I. and II./LG 2 trailed their coats over East Anglia to draw off defending fighters. In this they were very successful. Engaged by three squadrons from Duxford and one from Coltishall, they were quickly embroiled in a major fighter action. However, with the advantages of height and numbers, and unencumbered by the need to protect bombers, they had slightly the better of things.

Near Lincoln, the Dorniers traded height for speed in order to get below the intermittent cloud and then make a fast run over the target. Fortuitously, this left the Digby Hurricanes floundering in their wake. Also in hot pursuit were eight Spitfires from Kirton-in-Lindsey, who only caught up as the raiders exited the target area at high speed. South of

Doncaster, the Spitfires were joined by ten Hurricanes from Church Fenton. Harried all the way by fighters, IV./LG 1 crossed the coast of England near Grimsby. Once again the fighters were unable to make their shooting tell. Eight Dorniers were damaged; three of them seriously, but all returned to base. The German gunners claimed five fighters shot down, although in fact only one was lost. The next target was the Bristol Aeroplane Works at Filton, deliberately chosen to keep the defenders guessing. This time the German bombers were escorted all the way out and back by the Bf 109E-7s. For the first time they lost a Dornier, to anti-aircraft gunfire.

Luftwaffe analysis indicated that, for sustained unescorted operations, a heavier defensive armament might be no bad thing. The replacement of the rifle-calibre MG 15s with 13mm MG 131 belt-fed machine guns was given top priority. The experienced IV./LG 1 was redeployed to Stavanger in Norway, from where it could attack the British Fleet anchorage at Scapa Flow and targets in Scotland. It was replaced at Antwerp/Deurne by the newly arrived II./KG 3.

The downed Do 19A had crash landed almost intact, and RAF investigators swarmed all over it. Two conclusions were drawn. Misled by the sheer size of the Dornier, and fearing a collision, the fighters had opened fire at too great a range.[18] Secondly, rifle-calibre guns were inadequate against such a large and well protected target: greater hitting power was needed.[19]

The Spitfire IB had been withdrawn owing to the chronic unreliability of its 20mm Hispano cannon. At this time, just two British cannon-armed fighter types had reached the squadrons. Both were twin-engine aircraft, both carried four 20mm cannon, and both were relatively long-ranged. The Bristol Beaufighter was being rushed into service as a radar-equipped two-seat night fighter, while the rather faster Westland Whirlwind was not yet operational. With a rehashed, cannon-armed Spitfire and the four-cannon Hurricane IIC still months away from service, for the British it was Hobson's Choice. The Beaufighter had already been accorded top priority to combat the night Blitz, and, despite engine problems, the Whirlwind was also rushed into service.[20]

The deterioration of the weather from October onwards resulted in the lessening, and final cessation, of the daylight offensive in favour of the night Blitz, as described in the next chapter.

NOTES

1. 'Daddy', so named because of his solicitous care for his men. Ahead of his time in recognising that killing often caused a profound psychological shock, he was concerned that his young pilots should gain their first victories without too much trauma.
2. Alfred Price, *Blitz on Britain*.
3. See Chapter 2, Note 11. Historically, Göring vetoed the idea.
4. 'Pip-Squeak' was the reason that the Fighter Command sector stations normally operated no more than four squadrons. It was a function of the standard radio, carefully timed to give no overlap. Four squadrons times fourteen seconds almost exactly filled one minute, leaving no further time.
5. Ramsey, (ed.), *The Battle of Britain Then and Now*, vol. 5.
6. Mike Spick *Luftwaffe Fighter Aces*.
7. Figures taken from Ramsey, op. cit.
8. Cajus Bekker, *Luftwaffe War Diaries*.
9. The accidental bombing of central London on the night of 24/25 August resulted in a series of retaliatory attacks on Berlin.
10. Bekker, op. cit.
11. Hans Kamansky, *Uralbomber Pilot*.
12. Milch actually took over the Technical Department in November 1941, following Udet's suicide.
13. The Bf 109E-7 seems to have been used entirely as a fighter-bomber in 1940.
14. They were, although this had probably nothing to do with drop tanks.
15. Adolf Galland, in *The First and the Last*, says that drop tanks would have been decisive in 1940. Given the problems involved, the reader can judge for himself.
16. In real life these carried bombs as *Jabos*.
17. Kamansky, op. cit.
18. In 1942 the Jagdflieger had the same difficulty against the Boeing B-17, which had a wingspan 10 per cent less.
19. The Do 19A in which Göring was lost had been the victim of happenstance — a first lucky attack which killed the pilot. Then, in the second engagement, an error of judgement by the second Hurricane pilot resulted in a lethal, ultra-close-range shot while narrowly avoiding a mid-air collision.
20. No 263 (Hurricane) Squadron received its first Whirlwinds at Drem in Scotland in the summer of 1940 and became operational on 7 December of that year. Given the scenario described, the type could have become operational some two months earlier.

4   The Blitz

AS SUMMER gave way to autumn, the daylight offensive drew slowly to a close. With the invasion postponed indefinitely, the campaign to gain air superiority over southern England had lost its urgency. In any case, worsening weather made the large-scale, close-formation daylight raids impractical. Losses had also been heavy. The hitherto all-conquering Luftwaffe had met its first reverse of the war.

It was not yet out of the fight. By switching the main weight of the attack to the hours of darkness, the German High Command still hoped that the will and capability of the British to continue the war would be seriously impaired. Night attacks had begun as early as June 1940. At first these were on a small scale, often no more than harassing attacks, but as the weeks passed they became progressively heavier. Whereas, in daylight, bombers were generally restricted by the operational radius of the fighter escort, night raiders had no such limitation and could reach targets anywhere in the British Isles. Although the defenders managed a few lucky interceptions on clear, moonlit nights, lacking radar and an efficient ground control system the fighters were impotent. At night, German bomber losses were acceptably low.

At night, bombing accuracy was far worse than by day, but this was offset by the ability to attack important facilities such as aircraft factories or docks, which would otherwise have been off-limits. The main problems to be overcome were finding the target in the first place, and then accurately finding the way home over a blacked-out, hostile landscape, or over the trackless sea. With commendable foresight, Erhard Milch had addressed both problems before the war. No fewer than three blind bombing systems had been developed, together with a network of navigational beacons.

The first bombing aid was Knickebein (a mythological magic crow), which transmitted two narrow beams with dots in one and dashes in the other. When the bomber was exactly on course, these overlapped to give a steady note. A cross-beam indicated that the target area had been reached. The maximum range of the system was about 400km (250 miles), but this could only be achieved at altitudes above 6,100m (20,000ft). With a beam just one-third of a degree wide, lateral accuracy was about 1.6km at a range of 290km (one mile at 180), which was only enough to allow area bombing. The beauty of the system was its simplicity: it needed no special equipment, and any operational crew could be trained to use it.

X-Gerät, which was used from 13 August, was more complex and, with an approach beam and three cross-beams, much more accurate, although shorter-ranged. Used only by specialist, well-trained Gruppen—of which KGr 100 was the first—it gave a theoretical accuracy of about 300m (328 yards) at a distance of 290km (180 miles). The technically more sophisticated Y-Gerät was an automated, single-beam system, tied into the auto-pilots of the bombers. It was, when it was first introduced, chronically unreliable, and the 'bugs' were not ironed out until January 1941, when it was used by III./KG 26.

To guide the bombers home, a network of navigational beacons had been set up across the occupied countries. By taking cross-bearings on two beacons, the bombers could establish their position fairly accurately. To avoid confusion, never more than twelve beacons were on line at any one time. It all looked very promising.

KGr 100 began operations with X-Gerät in mid-August, hitting the Spitfire factory at Castle Bromwich, the Dunlop Works and the Bristol Aeroplane factory at Filton in quick succession. The latter was bombed through solid cloud; night and weather were no longer sufficient protection. Large-scale night raids commenced on 28 August, when 160 bombers attacked Liverpool using Knickebein. On this and three subsequent nights, bombing, although heavy, was scattered, and little damage was caused.

The Luftwaffe bomber crews were supposed to fly along the steady-note beam of Knickebein, and they quickly became aware that the British were trying to jam it. As countermeasures went, the jamming was not very convincing, but the fact that it existed indicated that the British knew about it. The possibility that it could be patrolled by night fighters made the Kampfflieger twitchy, and they took the obvious step: they kept well to one side of the beam. Never too accurate, Knickebein was thus degraded before it had started.

Problems were also encountered with the beacons. Often the directional indications they gave were confusing, changing for no apparent reason, and many German bombers were led astray. Some force-landed in France out of fuel, while others simply vanished for no known reason. A few unfortunates even landed in England. An extreme example involved the Austrian Heinkel pilot Hans Thurner of KG 55. On the night of 14/15 February 1941, believing himself to be over France, he touched down at three English airfields in quick succession. On each occasion he discovered his mistake in time and took off again.[1] His comments to his observer on his eventual return to base are not recorded, perhaps fortunately. There was of course nothing wrong with the beacons, except that the perfidious Englander were managing to mask them with beacons of their own. Be that as it may, the Kampfflieger quickly grew to distrust the system.

X-Gerät was much more successful, and during the moonlit night of 14/15 November KGr 100 led a devastating raid on Coventry. Canisters of incendiaries started fires which lit the way for the bombers. These converged on the target from three directions, coming in over The Wash, the Isle of Wight and Brighton. In the space of eight hours, 449 bombers dropped 400 tonnes of high explosives, 57 tonnes of incendiaries and 127 parachute mines. The destruction was horrific. Production at Standard Motors, Alvis and Daimler, all hard hit by IV./LG 1 two months before, now ceased, as did other facilities. Parachute mines were thin-cased blast weapons, containing up to 70 per cent of high explosive. The parachute restricted the speed of impact to 65kph (40mph), giving a falling time of 47 seconds from the modest height of 3,000m (9,800ft). This was long enough for them to be blown well off course by crosswinds.

How best to use the two Dornier 19 Gruppen in this new phase of the war? The obvious answer was to use them at night, but Kesselring viewed this as a waste of scarce resources. Their long range would allow them to approach from unexpected directions — 'through the back door', as it were — thus keeping the defenders at full stretch. In the daylight role, the Do 19s were, potentially, far more effective. This view was reinforced by the knowledge that the US Army Air Corps, as it was then, anticipated using its new Boeing B-17 Flying Fortresses unescorted by day. Could the Luftwaffe be expected to do less?

At a mid-October conference involving Kesselring, Milch, Sperrle, Stumpf and von Richthofen, it was decided that the aircraft had to be used in the daylight strategic role. At the same time, an intervention by the Führer decreed that a full Geschwader should be formed with the honorific title 'Hermann Göring'. As a result, IV./LG 1 and II./KG 3 were formally redesignated I. and II./KG 5, respectively, with III./KG 5 forming back in the Reich.

The mission planning was precise. Having selected a target, an approach offering the greatest concealment was chosen — usually far out over the sea — to attack from the west. While this had the added advantage of giving the bombers the quickest route home, it was not to be done so often as to become predictable. Cloud cover was to be combined with extreme altitude to avoid interception. As they neared the target, the bombers were to trade height for speed at the discretion of the formation leader, and make fast bombing runs. This had two main advantages. The lower the altitude, the greater the bombing accuracy; and the faster they went, the greater the difficulty of interception for the defenders. After bombing, speed was to be converted back into altitude for the egress, the aircraft closing to very tight formation if fighters were in the vicinity. Confidence levels were high: the record appeared to show that the massed fire of the huge Dorniers could beat off fighter attacks.

The Bf 109E-7s of I. and II./LG 2, had taken heavy losses while providing long-range fighter escort to the big Dorniers. Not only were they handicapped in combat by their drop tanks; long overwater missions invariably made their single engines sound rough, even when they were not.[2] In future they would revert to their originally intended role as fighter-bombers, although if need be they could be used to provide a reception committee to cover the withdrawal of the bombers.

THE GRAND STRATEGY

By the autumn of 1940 supplies were pouring across the Atlantic into Britain. Food, fuel, raw materials, munitions, even aircraft, all arrived by sea in huge quantities. To a degree this was a repeat of the events in the Great War less than 25 years previously. Then, in the early months of 1917, the small U-boat force had almost succeeded in severing the transatlantic lifeline. It was only thwarted by the adoption of the convoy system. The margin had been narrow.

In the Second World War, Britain had adopted the convoy system at an early stage, although the escort vessels were at first too few, and their tactics largely untried. The U-boats were having considerable successes, although at present their numbers were small. This would be remedied over the coming year, and other measures were to hand (see below, Chapter 7). If only the surface units of the Kriegsmarine could be unleashed into the Atlantic, it would make a tremendous difference.

Commerce raiders had cut a deadly swathe through the British merchant marine in the South Atlantic and Indian Oceans, but this was not enough. A few short forays into the North Atlantic had been made by single German warships, with mixed results. What was needed was to get the heavy surface units out among the convoys.

The Kriegsmarine had started the war heavily outnumbered by the Royal Navy, and to date its losses had been disproportionate. Apart from an inadequate number of ocean-going U-boats, its effectives at the end of October 1940 consisted of two virtually useless pre-Great War battleships, two modern battlecruisers, two modern pocket battleships, two modern heavy cruisers, four light cruisers and about twenty destroyers. Against the overwhelming sea and air power of the British, a fleet action could only end in annihilation. Even break-outs by the heavy units risked being hunted down and the ships being destroyed by superior forces.[3] But if the Royal Navy could be weakened . . . ?

An accession of strength was on the horizon. Germany's most powerful battleship, *Bismarck*, was working up, having been commissioned on 24 August, while her sister-ship *Tirpitz* would be commissioned within three months. If that were not enough, the new aircraft carrier *Graf Zeppelin* was expected to become operational by the summer of 1941, followed in the spring of 1942 by a second carrier, *Peter Strasser*. Against a weakened Royal Navy, the revitalised Kriegsmarine might be able to achieve a good deal.

Luftwaffe Commander-in-Chief Albert Kesselring was not blinkered to the needs of his own service. A man of broad strategic vision (and an incorrigible optimist), he had established a good working relationship with the rather cautious but very professional Kriegsmarine Commander-in-Chief, Grossadmiral Erich Raeder. Having agreed that the North Atlantic was the key to the defeat of Britain, the two men planned how best to bring it about. Hitler, by now engrossed in plans for the invasion of the Soviet Union, and having resolutely shut his mind to the risks of conducting a war on two fronts, rather perfunctorily gave them a free hand.

Much now depended on what the Hermann Göring Geschwader could do. The summer had showed that warships manoeuvring in open water were nearly impossible targets for level bombers, even though, on 22 February 1940, the German destroyer *Leberecht Maas* had been sunk by a single direct hit from a small SC 50 bomb dropped by a Heinkel of II./KG 26. While this 'own goal' was rightly regarded as a fluke, it demonstrated the vulnerability of destroyers. On the other hand, warships were much better targets if they could be caught at their moorings. However, the OKL thought it unwise to tip their hand by concentrating exclusively on British fleet anchorages. Attacks on these should be interspersed with raids on major ports, thus hampering the unloading of critical supplies. Alternative targets would be shipbuilding facilities and, if necessary, the rail links to the dock areas. To avoid inter-Luftflotte friction, II./KG 5 was redeployed to Bergen in Norway, while III./KG 5 would be based at Aalborg in Denmark when it became operational in January 1941.

WIELDING THE SLEDGEHAMMER

The first raid took place on 6 November, against Scapa Flow, in the late afternoon. A weather reconnaissance aircraft had already signalled that the skies were almost clear. This was confirmed by a U-boat, which also provided a navigational beacon to act as a turning point. A nine-aircraft Staffel of Ju 88s of III./KG 30 was to provide a diversion by dive-bombing the fighter base at Wick, which housed a Hurricane squadron. Having bombed, it would depart, at full throttle and at sea level, into the gathering gloom in the east, drawing off the defending fighters as it went. Ten minutes later, 59 Dorniers of KG 5 were scheduled to approach the anchorage from the north-east, directly into the forecast wind, at 4,000m (13,124ft). Having bombed, they would turn for home.

As Robbie Burns nearly put it, the best-laid plans of mice, men, and Luftwaffe generals 'gang oft agley' — and so it proved. Arriving several minutes early, the Ju 88s were intercepted just short of Wick airfield by a flight of six Hurricanes. These managed to spoil the attack, but the homebound Ju 88s, at full throttle and trailing black smoke from their exhausts, got clean away. Meanwhile three Hudsons of Coastal Command, heading for the coast of Norway on an armed reconnaissance sortie, blundered across the surfaced U-boat. Pursued by a hail of anti-submarine bombs, it escaped into the depths. Aware of the importance of his mission, the U-boat commander twice tried to surface, but on each occasion was driven down again. Deprived of their improvised navigational beacon, the Dorniers wandered far to the west. A distant glimpse of the Faeroes finally showed their error, and they turned south-south-east, finally arriving over Scapa Flow nearly half an hour late.

A few wisps of cloud did little to obstruct the Germans' visibility, and a sizeable part of the British Fleet was laid out before them. As they descended to bombing height, they opened their formation into wide vics of three, allowing individual targets to be selected. As they did so, smoke pots were ignited to screen the warships. This was only partially effective, as was the fierce but woefully inaccurate anti-aircraft fire. Each aircraft released a stick of six SD 1000 armour-piercing bombs set for 30m (33yd) intervals.

Shortly after KG 5 had turned for home, it was assailed by the second flight of Hurricanes from Wick, which had been hurriedly scrambled in the face of the raid by KG 30. However, as Hans Kamansky recalled:

> They came in on our beam, and I had a brief glimpse of a Spitfire [*sic*] pulling high across us. We had quickly re-formed in tight formation, which I was so intent on holding that I saw little of the action other than the tail of the bomber directly in front of me but slightly lower, and another bomber close on my left. I heard the excited chatter of my gunners and the clamour of their machine guns, but otherwise could not describe the action in detail.[4]

The Hurricanes, too few in number to make much impression on the phalanx of Dorniers, scored few hits, while two of their number were seen to go down trailing smoke. A number of Fleet Air Arm Skuas were also scrambled, but, too slow to make contact, their presence passed unnoticed by the German flyers.

Luftflotte 5 hailed the raid as a great success. All the Dorniers had returned safely, three with bullet holes and two more with minor flak damage. Hits were claimed on two carriers, two battleships and five cruisers. Ten fighters were claimed shot down, which was hardly surprising considering that several dozen gunners were blazing away at each Hurricane.

Exactly what had been achieved? The carriers *Hermes* and *Furious* had both been hit, and would be out of action for several months pending repairs. The battleship *Nelson* had taken a glancing hit on the side of 'C' turret, but this had made little impression on its sixteen inches of armour. The bomb had bounced off and exploded close alongside, causing only superficial damage. One cruiser had been hit at the bows, causing moderate damage, while three destroyers, misidentified by the Germans as cruisers, had been sunk, two of them by near-misses. The greatest success of the day was the sinking of the battlecruiser *Hood*, which had taken three direct hits. In the air, one Hurricane had been lost, and another two damaged. Once again it appeared that the Dorniers could defend themselves against fighter attack.

For the next three days, bad weather prevented effective Luftwaffe reconnaissance. When it cleared, a Fernaufklärungsgruppe Ju 88 brought back pictures which showed Scapa Flow to be almost deserted. The superstructure of HMS *Hood* showed above the waves; also just visible were the wrecks of two destroyers. Beppo Schmid immediately jumped to the conclusion that the Luftwaffe had won a great naval victory. They had, although it was not quite so great a victory as they believed. Had Beppo stopped to think, he might have realised the obvious. That the British had moved their assets out of harm's way, and a more comprehensive reconnaissance would have revealed a truer picture. The propaganda department of Josef Goebbels also had a field day, although it hurt him to have to admit that these deeds were the doing of the Hermann Göring Geschwader. The one sour note was the disbelief of Grossadmiral Erich Raeder, who all too clearly remembered the 'sinking' of *Ark Royal* in September 1939.

The next major raid by KG 5 was aimed at British shipbuilding facilities and docks on the Clyde. It was timed for the morning of 15 November, there being some anticipation that the British defences would be reeling after the previous night's heavy attack on Coventry. And so it proved. Taking a circuitous route, the two Gruppen came in from the west and bombed virtually unhindered, causing massive damage. An unlooked-for bonus, which passed unnoticed at the time, was the destruction of HMS *Hermes*, in dry dock for repairs.

Having bombed, KG 5 then set course for the Firth of Forth — a deception move. As British fighters converged on Rosyth, the Geschwader turned south-east, the aircraft's radios tuned to the 'Pip-Squeak' frequencies and their Morse keys locked down to confuse the defenders. It worked. Narrowly evading interception, the bombers crossed the coast south of Berwick-upon-Tweed.

COUNTER-ATTACK

The Norwegian Resistance having confirmed the location of the Do 19A Gruppen, and fighter defence having failed lamentably, the RAF decided to bomb the airfields at Bergen and Stavanger. For this operation, Whitley bombers of Nos 10 and 51 Squadrons redeployed to Kinloss, while Wellingtons of Nos 9 and 37 Squadrons were sent to Lossiemouth. These were Operational Training Unit bases for the respective types; therefore all necessary facilities would be on hand.

During the night of 18/19 November, 21 Whitley bombers set out for Bergen, while nineteen Wellingtons aimed at Stavanger. The weather was foul. Heavy icing kept the Whitleys below 7,000ft (2,133m) and forced five of them to turn back. The confusion of islands off the Norwegian coast led many aircraft astray; nor did the proximity of mountains help matters. Only six aircraft claimed to have bombed, and fierce anti-aircraft fire accounted for two of them. No significant damage was caused.

The Wellingtons did slightly better, though they were also hampered by icing and low cloud. Stavanger was easier to find, and ten aircraft bombed, hitting a hangar and destroying two Do 19As and damaging various other buildings. German night fighters were about, but they were equally hampered by the weather. Two Wellingtons failed to return, the causes unknown.

Further raids were launched over the following nights, but, having no equivalent of the Luftwaffe blind-bombing systems, it was an achievement for the RAF aircraft even to find the target, let alone bomb accurately. Losses to weather exceeded those to enemy action.

The next objective for I. and II./KG 5 was the Vickers-Armstrong shipyard at Barrow-in-Furness, where an *Illustrious* class aircraft carrier was fitting out. For this raid, the biggest ever German bomb, the SC 2500 Max, was available.[5] As Barrow-in-Furness was on the Irish Sea coast, there was little point in planning a dusk raid: I. and II./KG 5 would have to fight their way in and out in close formation, and this demanded daylight. The unbroken string of successes had made the Luftwaffe planners overconfident, and for the first time little subterfuge was employed.

Single Staffeln of Ju 88s from III./KG 30 made hit-and-run raids on targets on the north-east coast — Jarrow, Sunderland, and Middlesbrough. Whilst these drew off the defending fighters, KG 5 crossed the coast south of Bamburgh and headed for the Solway Firth. Circumnavigating the Isle of Man, the aircraft passed close to the airfield at Castletown, which hurriedly scrambled a flight of Fleet Air Arm Fulmars,[6] but as the Dorniers turned east towards Barrow, losing height and accelerating, they left the slow and unhandy Fulmars trailing in their wake. Cloud cover was fairly heavy, but, despite this, over 100 huge SC 2500s caused massive

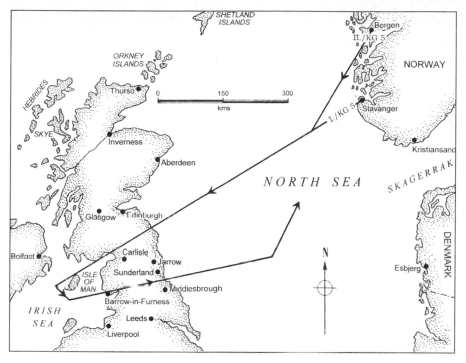

In late November 1940, I. and II./KG 5 raided the Vickers-Armstrong shipyard at Barrow-in-Furness in daylight. Ju 88s of III./KG 30, based in Denmark, drew off enemy fighters with hit-and-run raids on Jarrow, Sunderland and Middlesbrough while KG 5 crossed the coast further north. Emerging over the Irish Sea, the Dorniers rounded the Isle of Man and attacked Barrow from the west—the 'blind side'—before recrossing England for the safety of the North Sea.

destruction to the shipyards and the surrounding area. The aircraft carrier was completely wrecked.

Homeward-bound, the Geschwader headed out by the shortest route, towards Hartlepool, the Fulmars still in hot pursuit. Having crossed the Pennines, and by now back in immaculate formation, they were intercepted en route by a handful of Spitfires and Hurricanes, but once again the rifle-calibre machine guns of the British fighters proved unable to inflict mortal damage. However, there now came what was to prove a turning point. As KG 5 neared the coast, it was slowly overhauled by a twin-engine fighter which the German crewmen identified as a Ju 88C, a number of which were then engaged in flying night intruder missions over England.

Closing on the rearmost bombers, the stranger opened fire and nearly tore a wing off one of them. Burning furiously, it went down – the first Do 19A (insofar as the Luftwaffe knew) to fall to fighter attack. A storm of return fire was unleashed; hits were observed, and the twin-engine fighter broke off the action and vanished. The attacker was in fact a Bristol Beaufighter of No 219 Squadron based at Catterick. The RAF had concluded that only 20mm cannon-fire would suffice against the Do 19A; and this was the first time that a heavily armed fighter had been brought into action. While the Beaufighter had proved the point, it had been hard pressed to catch the bombers, and it was obvious that a single fighter could achieve little against such a massive formation. Nevertheless, RAF Fighter Command had not been idle.

Although it packed a lethal punch, the two-man Beaufighter, equipped with air interception radar, not only lacked performance by day but was far too valuable against the night raiders. There was, however, an alternative. The Westland Whirlwind twin-engine fighter was both fast and long-ranged, although it was plagued with engine problems. Like the Beaufighter, it carried four 20mm Hispano cannon – quite enough to cause lethal damage. Two squadrons of Whirlwinds had been hurriedly formed to counter the threat. No 263 Squadron was based at Drem, east of Edinburgh, while No 96 Squadron had hurriedly converted from the Hurricane and had been redeployed to Acklington on the north-east coast. While neither unit was fully worked up on type, both were hurried into action.

The loss of a single bomber to fighter attack was hardly a disaster to KG 5, but the misidentification of the Beaufighter as a Ju 88C caused a lot of static. It took a full week before it was finally established that none of NJG 2's Ju 88C intruders had been involved. Be this as it may, the next operation by I. and II./KG 5 took place at night. Early in December they took part in a raid on Liverpool, again carrying two Maxes each. The destruction was severe, and port facilities were reduced to barely 25 per cent capacity.

Having come close to neutralising Liverpool six nights earlier, the Hermann Göring Geschwader was assigned to a daylight raid on the second most important port receiving the Atlantic convoys—Greenock, on Clydeside. By now the huge SC 2500 Max bombs were in short supply, and the Dornier Do 19As carried six SC 1000 Hermanns apiece. They were painted sky blue, and it was a standing joke in the Luftwaffe that their girth and colour were reminiscent of the Reichsmarschall. For maximum area destruction, the Hermanns were set to release at 100m (109yd) intervals. The raid was once again planned for late afternoon, and would be followed up that night by Heinkels and Junkers, which would be guided by the fires started.

After several days' delay awaiting suitable weather, the Dorniers set out. Passing the Orkneys, they flew down the west coast of Scotland until they spotted the Dubh Artach lighthouse. From here they headed direct for Greenock and the Clyde. This time they had telegraphed their punch. They were spotted by several units of the British Fleet which were lurking in the sheltered waters of Loch Ewe on the west coast. With adequate warning, the British fighters reacted in force.

Eight Whirlwinds—all that were serviceable—were scrambled from Acklington and vectored in a north-westerly direction, while the Drem Whirlwind squadron was brought to cockpit readiness. Elsewhere, Spitfire and Hurricane squadrons at Turnhouse and Drem were placed at five minutes' readiness, while a recently formed Hurricane squadron based near Renfrew was hurriedly scrambled and ordered to orbit over Dunoun, thus interposing itself between the raiders and Glasgow.

Whilst the Glasgow area looked the most likely target, the defenders could not yet be certain. The problem was resolved when the Renfrew Hurricanes spotted a Balbo of 48 bombers inbound from the north-west. The squadron commander had previously been a flight commander with No 111 Squadron, which specialised in head-on attacks against split bomber formations. He had also studied the problems of judging range against such large aircraft. His pilots consisted of three Battle of Britain veterans; the rest were novices. He had instilled into them the importance of not opening fire until they thought that a collision was imminent, and told them to shut their eyes if they were frightened and keep shooting! Afterwards they were to break upwards, not down, and re-form, ready to attack once more. Putting his teaching into practice, he positioned his twelve Hurricanes in shallow echelon and led the charge.

For the first time, KG 5 encountered shock action. One of the leading bombers lurched out of formation, its pilot wounded. In another, the observer was dead. Three more sustained engine damage and began to lag, while one of the Hurricane pilots cut things a little too fine: his wingtip clipped the top of a Dornier's tail fin, making it difficult to control. Three leading Staffelkolonnen were left in disarray.

Now the Whirlwinds of No 96 Squadron arrived. Their initial quartering attack made little impression, but as they worked around to a no-deflection shooting position their 20mm shells started to strike home. However, with only 60 rounds per gun — approximately five seconds of firing time — they were quickly out of ammunition. Just two Dorniers had gone down, trailing fire and smoke, while two more were badly damaged. The Hurricanes had re-entered the fray with a series of unco-ordinated attacks from above and astern. Against the main formation this achieved little, but two of the experienced section leaders concentrated on one of the stragglers. A second engine out of action, this eventually crashed near Cumbernauld.

In the circumstances, with the Hurricanes still in attendance, it was understandable that the bombing was inaccurate and that relatively little damage was caused. The Dorniers headed for home, but they were not yet out of the wood. As they crossed the coast just north of Edinburgh, they were assailed from three sides in quick succession. Spitfires and Hurricanes from Turnhouse attacked from above. Then at the moment of greatest confusion, the Whirlwinds of No 263 Squadron arrived almost unnoticed from astern. Their 20mm cannon made short work of four bombers and damaged three more, while the single-engine fighters claimed several hits. In almost total disarray, the bombers fled out to sea. As they left the scene, they were pursued by the Hurricanes of No 111 Squadron from Drem, which dispatched two of the stragglers.

INQUEST

Before this raid, the Hermann Göring Geschwader had seemed invincible. Used sparingly, they had flown 252 sorties for the loss of just three bombers, one to an unknown cause, one to anti-aircraft fire and one to a fighter. The last aircraft might not have been lost had the attacker been recognised as hostile. Now, on a single raid, they had lost nine bombers (19 per cent), while a further eleven (23 per cent) had sustained serious damage. This loss rate was unaffordable. Kesselring and Stumpf were appalled. The question was: had KG 5 been lucky previously, or was it that this time the defenders had been lucky? Which was the true picture?

The reduction of the British Home Fleet remained the top priority, closely followed by the cutting of the Atlantic supply routes, but the OKL concluded that the Uralbomber was too precious an asset to be hazarded unnecessarily. From this point on, deep penetration raids in daylight were to be made only at the discretion of the Luftwaffe Commander-in-Chief, and then only in exceptional circumstances. Future daylight raids would only be made on targets within 30km of the east coast of England. With III./KG 5 operational from early January 1941, the full-strength Hermann Göring Geschwader would join the night Blitz, which its huge bomb-carrying capacity would greatly enhance.

This was a good decision. From early 1941 the RAF introduced reliable two-cannon Spitfires, and the four-cannon Hurricane IIC, which in daylight would have cut a deadly swathe through the four-engine bombers. Two more Whirlwind squadrons were formed to protect Scapa Flow, supplemented with four-cannon Hurricanes. At night the Beaufighter, with radar ground control, was slowly becoming more effective, but over the next few months only one Uralbomber fell to this combination. British west-coast ports suffered heavy damage during night raids, and shipyards were also hard hit. There was, however, another factor. Hitler was planning 'Barbarossa', the invasion of the Soviet Union, in which the Dornier Do 19As would play an important part. In early April KG 5 was redeployed to bases in the east, together with KG 3, then also re-equipping with the Do 19A. Would the Uralbomber would live up to its name?

NOTES

1. Later awarded the Ritterkreuz mit Eichenlaub, he failed to return from a sortie over England on 11 June 1944.

2. An illusion common to pilots of all single-engine aircraft over the sea, regardless of nationality.
3. This was, in fact, the fate of the *Bismarck* in May 1941.
4. Hans Kamansky, *Uralbomber Pilot*.
5. Max was first used on 20/21 November 1940. Carried externally by the He 111, it made take-offs so hazardous that at first only two crews of KG 26 were cleared to carry it. Stowed internally by the Do 19A, there would have been no such problem.
6. No 808 Squadron, under the operational control of No 13 Group.

5 Eyes of the U-Boats

A S NOTED in the previous chapter, a handful of U-boats had brought Britain perilously close to defeat in 1917. With the few ocean-going boats in commission in 1939, it did not seem possible that the feat could be repeated, but in the summer of 1940, when bases on the Biscay coast of France became available, circumstances changed. No longer did the U-boats have to skirt the British Isles to reach their hunting area: they now had direct access to the Atlantic, which increased the time available for patrolling by reducing the time spent in transit.

The greatest problem was finding the convoys. In good visibility a U-boat cruising on the surface could search an area of about 1,500km^2 every hour, reducing to barely one-tenth of this in poor weather or at night. In 1940 there were frequently fewer than six U-boats on station at any one time, which between them could visually search barely one ten-thousandth of the area of the North Atlantic each hour, in daylight only. By comparison, finding the proverbial needle in a haystack was child's play! There were, however, other methods. The Kriegsmarine radio listening service was active, and occasionally the German cryptographers succeeded in cracking the British naval codes, although, as these were changed at intervals, the advantages were generally short-lived.

The most important convoys were those eastbound, carrying supplies to the beleaguered British, usually sailing from New York or from Halifax in Nova Scotia. Westbound convoys were not ignored: a freighter sunk while sailing in ballast would be unable to make the return trip laden. Either way, convoys zig-zagged at irregular intervals, often making quite dramatic course changes. More often than not, a convoy would be quickly swallowed up in the vast wastes of the ocean, and all track of it lost. Commander-in-Chief U-Boats Konteradmiral Karl Dönitz summed up the problem succinctly: 'Imagine our situation as a land problem, with the enemy convoy at Hamburg and my nearest U-boats at Oslo, Paris, Vienna and Prague — each with a maximum circle of vision of 32km. How on earth can they expect to find a convoy unless directed to it by air reconnaissance?'[1] He had a point. A long-range aircraft, cruising at 335kph (181kt) 600m (1,970ft) above the ocean, could, in decent visibility, reconnoitre nearly 19,000km^2 per hour, more than twelve times more than a U-boat could manage.

The means were already to hand. To enable the 'weather frogs' to prepare their forecasts, data from far out in the Atlantic was needed. The first Fernaufklärungsstaffel (long-range reconnaissance Staffel). 1(F)./120, was formed at Bremen on 1 October 1939. It was equipped with a modified civil airliner, the Focke-Wulf FW 200 Condor, which was structurally strengthened, given a defensive armament and had provision for four SC or SD 250 bombs carried externally. 1(F)./120 became operational in April 1940, but later that month it was redesignated 1./KG 40. At first, reconnaissance was the main mission, and co-operation with the U-boat force was minimal. As the war escalated, Condors were briefly used for minelaying, but the weight and drag of a 1,000kg mine carried externally under each wing reduced the aircraft's performance and handling to unacceptable levels. After a month in which losses approached an unbearable 20 per cent, Condor minelaying sorties were discontinued. With the fall of France, 1./KG 40 redeployed to Bordeaux, where the addition of two more Staffeln brought it up to Gruppe strength as I./KGr 40. The first sorties were flown on 8 August 1940, on armed maritime reconnaissance, although a couple of night bombing raids were made on Liverpool later that month.

Despite the Allies' early adoption of the convoy system, there were still many singletons to be found in the Atlantic, which the Condors attacked at low level. By the end of the year they had sunk a total of fifteen ships with a gross tonnage of about 75,000, and this figure might have been higher had serviceability been better. The Condor's civilian ancestry made it unsuited to the rough and tumble of operations, and structural failures were far too frequent. Rarely were more than half a dozen aircraft serviceable on any one day, and sometimes only one.

Co-operation with the U-boats was less than effective. Even when a convoy was found and its position reported, unless a U-boat happened to be within about 100km (62 miles) it stood no chance of making contact before the Condor had to turn for home. The obvious answer was a relay of Condors, but there were never enough aircraft available.

For months Raeder and Dönitz had been pressing for a long-range reconnaissance force under naval command, arguing that as a consequence U-boat successes would soar. Previously their ideas had foundered on Göring's dictum 'All that flies belongs to me!', but with the Reichs-marschall now in Valhalla the way was clear for further representations to be made. Having secured the wholehearted backing of Luftwaffe Chief of Staff Jeschonnek (Kesselring was reluctant), Raeder and Dönitz app-roached the Führer. On 10 November 1940, he responded by giving Dönitz operational control of I./KG 40,[2] with II. and III./KG 40 to follow when they were formed. Shortly afterwards the Kriegsmarine was given operational control of KGr 606, KüflGr 106 and two Staffeln of AufklGr 123. Nor was this all. The serviceability rate of the Condor, typically between 20 and 30 per cent, was patently unacceptable. By Führer decree, its replacement by the Do 19 was given absolute priority, and a second Gruppe of KG 40 was to be formed on type. The Condors reverted to the more suitable transport role.

Kesselring, who wanted to build up his strategic bomber force for the forthcoming invasion of the Soviet Union, was less than pleased. However, overruled by Hitler, he consoled himself with the thought that, if the Atlantic campaign could be brought to a quick and glorious conclusion, not only would the nightmare of war on two fronts be avoided, he might even get his strategic bombers back in time.

The first unmodified Do 19As arrived at Bordeaux in mid-November, and two Staffeln had re-equipped by the end of the year. They were followed by the Do 19B, with a 20mm Oerlikon MG FF cannon in the nose and extra fuel tanks in the fuselage. This reduced the warload to eight SC 250 bombs, adequate against merchant ships and escorts, while increasing the operational radius by 400km (250 miles) — almost to mid-Atlantic. II./KG 40, formed in February/March 1941, was based at Trondheim in Norway, from where it could range out well past Reykjavik in Iceland or Spitzbergen to the north.

ATLANTIC ASSAULT

Initial Do 19 operations were hampered by appalling weather, and only when it eased could I./KG 40 begin hunting in earnest. With no shortage of aircraft, co-ordinated multiple missions could be flown, while to reduce fatigue on 12–14-hour missions the establishment was increased to the point where there were effectively two crews for each serviceable aircraft. This had been made possible by the equipment of the training units with the Ju 86 (as related in Chapter 2). After the starveling days of the Condor, this was sheer luxury.

Typically, the first Dornier took off in darkness and headed for its assigned patrol line. It was followed by others at about twenty-minute intervals, on tracks offset to give the greatest possible search area, but which also allowed mutual support to be quickly provided. Single ships could be attacked on sight, using the low-level 'down the centreline' method pioneered by the Condors. Whenever convoys were sighted, they were to be reported and shadowed, and constant position reports were to be made in order to guide in the U-boats. As a Dornier neared its prudent limit of endurance, it whistled up its nearest fellow, and when this arrived the first Dornier aimed its bombs from a safe altitude before departing for home, causing alarm and confusion below, if not actual damage. In this way a convoy could be shadowed from dawn to dusk, but at nightfall contact was inevitably lost, and the search had to be resumed next morning.

While convoy sightings increased dramatically, however, it was the same old story. Only rarely was a U-boat within steaming distance before nightfall, and while sinkings did increase they did not represent the dramatic improvement for which Dönitz had hoped. There were other problems. Navigation over the trackless ocean was far from easy, and often neither the Dorniers nor the U-boats knew their own positions with any precision, with the result that contacts were often missed.

To improve matters, a Fliegerführer Atlantik was appointed on 1 February — Martin Harlinghausen, widely known as 'Iron Gustav'.[4] An anti-shipping specialist since the Spanish Civil War, he had been mainly responsible for developing the 'Swedish Turnip' attack, an ultra-low-level approach from the beam. Trials soon showed that the 'Swedish Turnip' was unsuitable for use by the huge Dornier, but, optimising the number of aircraft available, he rewrote the book.

Once sighted, a convoy was reported as before, but now all the other Dorniers within hailing distance came to lend a hand. If the convoy escort was weak — and indeed it usually was — an attack could be launched. What happened next is best described by one of the participants:

Having received the report, we hastened to the convoy. Other Dorniers in the vicinity converged on the scene like hungry vultures. [This felicitous turn of phrase stuck: before long the big Dornier became universally known as 'The Vulture'.

Soon there were five of us circling above the convoy, which consisted of 23 ships in three columns. Only three escorts could be seen, one ahead and one far out on each flank. We kept well clear of them. Fritz Reinhardt, who had made the first sighting, pulled high and made a level bombing run from rear to front. He didn't hit anything, but his attack threw the convoy into confusion as the ships tried to evade his bombs.

While the escorts were distracted, I seized my chance. Having selected a large freighter at the rear of the nearest column as my target, I came in low and fast from the stern quarter. Having released a stick of four bombs, I reefed into a hard right turn, nearly sticking my wingtip into the sea in my excitement. As I pulled out, my rear gunner called out, 'A hit! A hit!'

I had not been alone. Looking back, I saw Fred Aumuhle streaking towards the starboard escort, his nose gunner trading fire with it. He only just missed colliding with it. Like us, he had scored hits on a freighter. Most successful of all was Ulrich Repke, who had flown straight down the line of the central column at 100m and hit two ships, one of which was already sinking. He then got shot up by the leading escort, losing an engine, although he got home safely on the other three.

I was not aware of being fired at, but three holes in my fuselage showed that I had been. After the attack, Fred and I pulled high and expended our remaining bombs in a level attack — unfortunately with no observable result.

The rule was, the last one to arrive, and thus hopefully the one with the most fuel, should not take part in the attack, but had to continue to shadow the convoy. We set course for home, leaving poor Joseph Karzten unhappily circling out of range of the guns of the escorts. It was not all bad: he confirmed that the ship that I hit had later sunk.[5]

This form of attack often paid dividends; and, of course, just sometimes the system worked as planned and several U-boats made contact with the convoy. Perversely it sometimes also worked in reverse. On 9 February 1941, a U-boat discovered a convoy and reported it. With no other U-boats within reach, it homed in bombers which sank five ships.[6]

Even before Dönitz had assumed control of I./KG 40, his U-boats had begun to make serious inroads into Allied merchant shipping as he massed them in 'wolf packs' in the Western Approaches, north and south of neutral Eire, through which the convoys had to pass. Losses quickly became so serious that the southern route had to be abandoned. West-coast ports became congested, and some convoys were routed around the north of Scotland, offloading at ports from Aberdeen to Humberside, where they were exposed to night attacks by medium bombers.

Aware of the dangers posed by the Vulture Gruppen, the RAF tried to strike back. A daylight raid on Trondheim by Blenheims and Beauforts ended in disaster when it was intercepted offshore by a Gruppe of Bf 109Es. Night bombing raids on Vulture bases at Bordeaux and Stavanger achieved little.

The first half of 1941 saw no fewer than 423 Allied ships sent to the bottom.[7] Prospects for the survival of the island race looked bleak as sinkings outstripped shipbuilding capacity. With their backs to the wall, the British fought on with all their might. A huge shipbuilding programme churned out escorts, sloops and corvettes. Many land-based bombers were diverted to Coastal Command to the detriment of the air offensive against the Third Reich, while Catalina and Sunderland flying boats gave long-range cover. At this stage aircraft sank few U-boats, but they often forced them to submerge and lose contact with the convoys.

From this point, Vultures increasingly encountered British aircraft, which they engaged on sight. Outgunned by the Do 19B, several were shot down and most of the rest were driven off. The Sunderland, known to the Luftwaffe as the 'Flying Porcupine', proved a more worthy opponent because, while the Vulture was rather faster, the British flying boat was slightly more agile. The battles between these giants were generally inconclusive.

LOST IMPETUS

Convoys became fewer but larger, and more heavily escorted, while merchant ships were given heavier defensive weaponry. By mid-1941, German losses to anti-aircraft fire had increased to the point at which low-level attacks by Vultures were discontinued. They now shadowed convoys from a safe distance, or 'laid their eggs' from medium altitude. Few direct hits were scored, but near-misses sometimes caused serious damage to merchantmen.

Other Vulture losses occurred nearer to home. The RAF had commenced long-range fighter patrols: two Whirlwind squadrons covered the UK–Iceland gap, while two Beaufighter squadrons prowled the Bay of Biscay. Only rarely did they make contact, but when they did the Vultures stood little chance of survival:

> Horst Blenz, our tail-gunner, gave the first warning as four black shapes swung in behind us. At first we thought they were Ju 88s, but we were quickly disillusioned when they attacked in pairs from both stern quarters at once. 20mm cannon shells tore into our right wing, setting both engines on fire.
>
> At once my Vulture became almost uncontrollable, slewing into the dead engines. My observer, Rolf Pabst, joined me on the controls, and somehow we kept our stricken bird on a more or less even keel. Losing height, and with flames pouring from our punctured wing tanks, I prepared to ditch. But one of our opponents had other ideas. Guns blazing, he attacked from head-on. Cannon shells tore through the cockpit, killing Pabst and radio operator Zuchmann. The sea was so very close— grey and unfriendly.
>
> The impact, when it came, was violent, and I lost consciousness. When I came round, I was being hauled into our dinghy by our two surviving gunners, puking litres of salt water.
>
> By sheer chance we were rescued shortly after dusk by U 184 when it surfaced to recharge its batteries.[8]

On 16 June 1941 a patrolling Vulture sent a sighting report of a large westbound convoy south of Iceland at 58°N 23°W; eight minutes later it reported that it was under attack by single-engine fighters. This far out? The report was regarded with suspicion, but the big bomber was never heard from again. Another Vulture hastened to the scene, only to vanish without trace. Two more were ordered to investigate. Both reported single-engine fighters before contact was lost. Four Vultures down in little more than 90 minutes? How could this be?

The mystery deepened the next day, when three U-boats, hastening on the surface to intercept the convoy, reported being attacked by single-engine biplanes. Obviously there was an aircraft carrier in the vicinity. But where? Two days later, an extremely circumspect sortie located it some 80km (50 miles) north-west of the convoy.

It was a large carrier, with four destroyers in attendance. But could it possibly be American? Certainly the destroyers, all elderly four-stackers, were of American origin, but this was inconclusive.[9] Although nominally neutral, units of the US Navy had already taken an active part in defending the convoys. The Führer, in an attempt to avoid open warfare with the United States, strictly forbade his U-boat commanders to retaliate. How much worse would it be if an American carrier was sunk?

A daring photographic sortie eventually allowed the carrier to be identified as British, and therefore it was fair game. Two Staffeln of II./KG 40 set out from Stavanger on a search and destroy mission but, in poor weather conditions, failed to find it. Low on fuel after an extended search, the weary Vultures took the most direct route home, using a nearly deserted Scapa Flow as a target of opportunity. Minutes later, they were pursued out to sea by a flight of avenging Whirlwinds. Four Dorniers were damaged, two of them beyond repair.

In fact the British, with merchant shipping losses running at unsustainable levels, had detached two fleet carriers to provide air cover over the convoys, each with a complement of cannon-armed Sea Hurricane fighters and Albacore bombers. While these could be ill-spared from other tasks, it was an indication of how grave the situation in the Atlantic had become.[10]

To reduce the risk, Vultures patrolling in areas where carriers were thought to lurk flew in Ketten of three aircraft, for mutual support against fighter attack. They suffered few losses during this period, but the total area reconnoitred unavoidably fell by two-thirds, making them that much less effective. Understandably nervous when a fighter was sighted, on at least two occasions they broke off patrols when confronted by a single 'Hurricat', a one-shot fighter rocket-launched from a specially adapted merchantman. Their problems were compounded from September when the first escort carrier, converted from the German prize *Hannover*, entered service on the Gibraltar–UK run. In quick succession it was followed by others.

External factors also affected the Battle of the Atlantic. Kesselring commandeered the entire production of the Do 19 to maximise his strategic bomber force for the attack on the Soviet Union, which commenced on 22 June 1941. Consequently the proposed III./KG 40 was never formed.

In the autumn of that year, Vulture pilots got a nasty shock. The Liberator Mk I, which was entering service with RAF Coastal Command squadrons, carried four 20mm cannon in a ventral tray. Intended for strafing U-boats, these proved equally lethal against the Dorniers, despite the lack of a dedicated air-to-air gun sight. Nor could the Dorniers easily refuse combat, as they were generally outperformed by the big American-built bomber.

The entry of the United States into the war in December 1941 had significantly altered the situation in the Atlantic. Dönitz was quick to take advantage, sending the majority of his U-boats to the US eastern seaboard, where they enjoyed rich pickings with minimal losses. This took much of the pressure off the Atlantic convoys. Not until June 1942 did the inexperienced Americans get their act together, forcing the U-boats back into mid-Atlantic.

With the reduction of U-boat operations in the eastern Atlantic, 2. and 3./KG 40 were deployed to Eleusis, near Athens, leaving a single Staffel to hold the fort from Bordeaux. Eleusis was a classic example of the strategy of the central position. Malta, the 'unsinkable aircraft carrier' from which the British could interdict Axis supplies to the Western Desert, was within easy reach. To the south-east, Alexandria was the home of the British fleet in the eastern Mediterranean, while further away, but still within reach, was the Suez Canal. The latter was the bottleneck through which all Allied supplies had to pass.

With hindsight, it is obvious that, had Malta been invaded and captured, the advantage in North Africa would have lain heavily with the Axis forces. For various reasons, few of which concerned the Luftwaffe, this subjugation was not attempted. In the face of Axis air power from Greece, Crete and North Africa, the British fleet at Alexandria was unable to do much at this stage. The Suez Canal became the priority target almost by default.

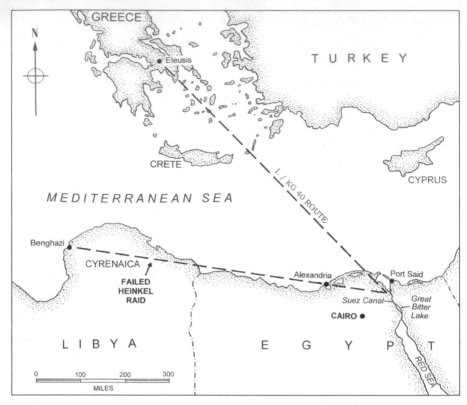

Mounted from Benghazi, the first raid on the Suez Canal saw seven out of eight Heinkels force-land in the desert, out of fuel. Operating from Eleusis, near Athens, I./KG 40 succeeded in delaying the enemy build-up in North Africa.

It had been tried before. On 17 January 1941 eight He 111s set off from Benghazi to attack a convoy reported entering the Canal. It was a fiasco. Operating at the very limit of their range, the Heinkels failed to find the convoy and seven of the eight ran out of fuel on the homeward leg and came down in the desert.[11]

Where the Heinkels had failed, a true strategic bomber might well have succeeded — and indeed it did. A Ju 86P high-altitude reconnaissance bomber brought back photographs of a convoy about to enter the Canal and a raid was planned. The convoy was in the Great Bitter Lake, and three ships were sent to the bottom by near-misses. I./KG 40 returned two nights later, sinking another two ships in the Canal itself, temporarily blocking it.

This immediate success saw 1./KG 40 transferred to Eleusis, while 5./KG 40 was redeployed from Stavanger to Bordeaux to fill the gap. More attacks on the Canal followed, which even the transfer of an Australian Spitfire squadron to the area failed to prevent. By July 1942 only four Vultures had been lost, one to mechanical failure, one to anti-aircraft fire and two to Beaufighter night fighters. Three Allied fighters were claimed as shot down.

Continual raids on the Suez Canal took their toll of Allied supplies. Thus deprived, the Allied commander General Montgomery was forced to defer his offensive at El Alamein by four months, until February 1943. By the same token, the long-planned Allied landings in French North Africa were also delayed.

Ships arriving at Suez had first to round the Cape of Good Hope, in a voyage lasting weeks. To speed the process, crated aircraft were landed at Takoradi in Ghana, where they were assembled, then flown across Africa. This could not be done in one hop; there was a series of staging posts. These were obvious targets for interdiction, but the range was extreme, even for the Vulture. However, if successful attacks could be made, scarce British resources would be tied up in defence. Navigation over the trackless wastes of the Sahara was a major problem, and a staging base on Lake Chad was selected as most suitable target, as the 150km (96 mile) long lake made an ideal landmark.

Four Vultures, one of them a reserve, arrived at Tripoli to refuel on 23 February 1942, and a Kette of three started out on the following day. They found and bombed the base with virtually no opposition, causing damage to buildings and destroying a fuel dump. All three returned safely.[12] There were, however, doubts about the effectiveness of this raid, given the disruption to normal operations that it caused and the fact that there appeared to be no aircraft on the ground.

It was, therefore, ten weeks before the raid was repeated. This time the intruders were met with anti-aircraft fire, and were pursued by three Hurricanes. One Vulture had an engine knocked out; it force landed in the desert near Sebha. The Germans were convinced by this that the game was not worth the candle, and no further attacks took place.

FROM MED TO ARCTIC

Meanwhile II./KG 40 was ranging the Arctic. Now allied with the Soviet Union, but appalled by her early reverses, Britain and America were trying to sustain her by supplying war materials. This was made possible by the notorious Murmansk convoys, which commenced in February 1942.[13] Taking a northerly route, the ships assembled at Reykjavik in Iceland, where they met up with their escorts, which almost invariably included an escort carrier. From Reykjavik, the convoys passed through the Denmark Strait between Iceland and Greenland, and then, staying just outside the limit of the drift ice, passed south of Jan Mayen Land, north almost to Spitzbergen, then east before turning south to the Russian ports of Murmansk and Archangelsk.

Fog, squalls and scarce hours of daylight hampered the Vultures. Often it was days before they managed to establish that the convoys had sailed. When they did, the shipping was hard to find, even with the new Hohentweil air-to-surface radar. The German crewmen also were aware that there was often a strong surface force in the vicinity — battleships, cruisers and destroyers — as a defence should any Kriegsmarine surface units sally forth. It did not pay to blunder across these.

The Germans generally knew when a convoy was gathering at Reykjavik, and full-strength raids might have caused maximum disruption. However, on the one occasion this was tried, the weather turned foul, and it was aborted. A few raids by Ketten of three aircraft were made, but these were generally ineffective.

The main function of II./KG 40 was to find the convoys and report their positions. They would then be attacked by a strike force assembled in northern Norway. This force consisted of about 100 aircraft — Ju 88s of III./KG 30 and III./KG 26, He 111s of I./KG 26 and He 115 floatplanes of 1./KüFlGr 406.[14]

Results were variable, even when the hours of daylight increased and the weather improved. When Vultures located a convoy — and poor visibility often prevented this — they were harassed by carrier fighters. Not until the convoys passed Jan Mayen did they come within range of the strike forces. In the main, these made torpedo attacks since conditions were rarely suitable for dive-bombing. They scored only two notable successes, against convoys in July and August of that year.[15] With the coming of the autumn bad weather, interdiction of the Murmansk convoys lapsed and II./KG 40 reverted to co-operation with the U-boats.

NOTES

1. Cajus Becker, *The Luftwaffe War Diaries*.
2. This actually occurred on 6 January 1941, while Göring was on extended leave. When the Reichsmarschall found out, he objected strongly, and the decision was reversed on 28 February.
3. This did not happen, but, given the circumstances, it would have made sense.
4. This appointment was actually made a month later, but tinkering has been necessary to fit the narrative.
5. Silbert Müller, *Vultures of the Atlantic*.
6. An 'action replay' of a real event on this day, when five Condors were homed on to a convoy by U 37.
7. About one-third more than the historical record indicates.
8. Müller, op. cit.
9. In 1940 the Unites States had supplied Britain with 50 mothballed destroyers in return for the use of bases in the West Indies.
10. This is an indication of how bad things could have become given this particular scenario.
11. This raid was led by Harlinghausen, who walked for four days after force-landing.
12. An attack on the Lake Chad staging post was actually made by a single Heinkel 111 with extra fuel tanks and a minuscule bomb load. It ran out of fuel on the homeward leg and force-landed in the desert. It was not discovered for a week.
13. These actually began in August 1941, but, given the loss levels postulated previously, February 1942 looks far more realistic.
14. Correct as at March 1942.
15. PQ.17 and PQ.18. Given the conditions, it is doubtful whether the Do 19 could have made more than a marginal difference.

6   Below Stairs

FROM beginning to end, progress in aircraft design never ceased, although once or twice it slackened when the war looked as good as won. However, these were false dawns. Fairly typical was the development of the Bf 109, the E sub-type of which was the mainstay of the Jagdflieger in 1940.

CONVENTIONAL FIGHTERS[1]

The quest for increased performance saw the installation in the Messerschmitt fighter of the 1,200hp Daimler-Benz DB 601 engine in a redesigned, sleeker cowling, with an enlarged spinner. A redesigned wing with rounded tips, new ailerons and plain rather than slotted flaps was supplemented with a retractable tailwheel, while the braced tailplane was replaced by a cantilever structure. This new aircraft was the Bf 109F, which entered service in January 1941. It was widely regarded as the peak of Bf 109 development.

The Bf 109G, initially powered by the 1,475hp DB 605 engine, started to reach operational units in late summer 1942. Over the next two years the engine was continually 'tweaked' for more power, and as the threat changed so the aircraft's armament was increased. This was not achieved without penalty. The extra weight increased wing loading, adversely affecting turning radius and low-speed handling — never one of the strong points of the type. In landing configuration, with wheels and flaps down, it could only be flown at full throttle, and its characteristics, both on take-off and landing, were often described as malicious. Both operational and training accidents increased sharply. It was often argued that the type should phased out, but it was retained because at high altitude it was superior to the Focke-Wulf FW 190.

Although the Messerschmitt had been selected as the primary Luftwaffe fighter in the 1930s, Ernst Udet ordered the FW 190A to be developed in the summer of 1938. Powered by the BMW 801 radial engine, it was designed as a rough and tough 'cavalry horse' to complement the Bf 109 'thoroughbred'. Heavily armed, it entered service in July 1941 and immediately established its superiority over the Spitfire V in speed and rate of roll, although it was unable to match the turning capability of the British fighter. It was immediately successful as an air combat fighter, and its rugged landing gear made it well suited to operations from semi-prepared strips. It was quickly pressed into service as a fighter-bomber and attack aircraft – in the latter role eventually replacing the Stuka – and flew short-range anti-shipping sorties.

The FW 190 was briefly used as a makeshift night fighter and – with a heavier armament and armour protection (the weight of which severely degraded performance and manoeuvrability) – as a daylight bomber-destroyer. Production simply could not keep up with demand. The final years of the war saw the advent of the FW 190D high-performance fighter powered by the Jumo 213A inline engine, and the Ta 152 high altitude fighter.

Even before the war, the Bf 110 Zerstörer was known to be deficient in many respects, and, as we have noted, it was scheduled to be replaced by the Bf 210 fighter-bomber. The latter was also detailed to replace the Ju 87 Stuka, but the failure to give it a credible dive-bombing capability was largely responsible for its demise. Continual redesign resulted in the Me 410 Hornisse, which entered service in May 1943. Variants of the Hornisse were used as fast bombers by night and bomber-destroyers in daylight, although in the latter role they proved too vulnerable to enemy escort fighters.

Meanwhile, still in search of a role, the Bf 110 soldiered on. As a Zerstörer, it peaked during 1940 but was thereafter rapidly run down, and by mid-1944 it had all but vanished from the scene. It was used on the Eastern Front as a Schnellbomber during 1941–42 but was phased out during the following year. A few were used for reconnaissance, where its limited endurance permitted.

There was, however, an area where the perceived shortcomings in performance and manoeuvrability of the Bf 110 were of less importance, and where its solid virtues of heavy firepower, reasonable endurance and vice-free handling could all be put to good use. This was the realm of night fighting. The high-performing but difficult-to-handle Ju 88 would have been a better choice, but in 1940 this was in great demand as a bomber and anti-shipping aircraft. Few could be spared for other roles, and because it was available when needed the Bf 110 became the principal Luftwaffe night fighter more or less by default. Production ceased in December 1944, and until this time, when it was supplanted by the Ju 88, it was numerically the most important German night fighter.

The one attempt by the Luftwaffe to produce a purpose-built night fighter was the Heinkel He 219 Uhu. It first flew in November 1942 and the brochure figures were impressive. Yet few Uhus entered service, for two reasons: first, the brochure figures could not be matched by production aircraft; and secondly, the incredibly high (for the time) wing loading made it a very 'hot ship', especially at altitude.

JETS[2]

Before the war, Germany led the world in jet propulsion. The He 178 experimental jet first flew in August 1939. Udet, always excited by technical progress, gave Messerschmitt a green light to design the twin-jet Me 262. There were, however, technical problems. Gas turbine engines operated at higher temperatures, and at greater rotational speeds, than anything previously encountered. New alloys were badly needed if jet propulsion were to become a practical proposition. It was a time for trial and error, and the development could not be rushed.

The first prototype Me 262 was flown (with a reciprocating engine substituting for the jets) on 25 March 1942. Whilst Milch was lukewarm, Kesselring, keenly aware of the industrial potential of the United states, which was now in the war, backed development to the hilt. Then, on 18 July 1942, the Me 262 flew on jet power alone. Far faster than any standard

Luftwaffe fighter, the aircraft demonstrated a remarkable performance, but the reliability of the Jumo engines was lacking.

Nickel and chromium were required to produce the high-quality alloys demanded by the engnes, and neither of these metals was available in Germany. The main source of nickel was Petsamo in Finland, while chromium was mined in Turkey. The Führer, preoccupied at this time by events in the Soviet Union, gave priority to obtaining them[3] and the German metallurgists set to work. By October 1943 the Jumo 004 turbojets had achieved a degree of reliability that allowed the design to be frozen, and mass production to begin. Me 262s started to reach the operational research unit EprKdo 262 in December 1943, which in late February 1944 was redesignated III./JG 7. Other units followed, and the jet fighter defence of the Third Reich quickly became a reality.

Hitler's vaunted intuition now came into play: he demanded that a significant number of Me 262s be converted to carry bombs. Protests by the Luftwaffe High Command that, while the Me 262 could carry bombs, it had no means of aiming them with even a modest amount of accuracy were overruled. This decision, often criticised by post-war armchair strategists, had a logical basis, as we shall see in a later chapter. By the summer of 1944, five Gruppen of Me 262 fighter-bombers had been formed.

Slightly in arrears of the Me 262 was the world's first jet bomber, the Arado Ar 234 Blitz. First flown on 15 June 1943, the Blitz was a twin-engine single-seater, able to carry a single PC 1400, or one SD 1000 and two SC 250s, or three SC or SD 500 bombs externally. Its maximum speed was 742kph (461mph) and its maximum range 1,555km (967 miles), reducing to 1,100km (684 miles) with a full bomb load. Its endurance at low level was 1 hour 15 minutes, rising to 3 hours 15 minutes at 10,000m (32,800ft). The Ar 234 entered service in April 1944, and it proved invaluable for reconnaissance duties, its combination of high speed and high altitude making it almost immune to interception.

TACTICAL BOMBERS

Largely discredited in the summer of 1940, the Ju 87 Stuka soldiered on through the next three years of the war in ever decreasing numbers.[4] Low-rate production continued into 1944, by which time Soviet anti-aircraft gunners had taken its measure. The final variant was the Ju 87G, a tank-buster with a 37mm cannon pod under each wing. The Dornier Do 17, with its low payload/range, had been almost entirely phased out by 1942 in favour of the Do 19 and Ju 88. The Do 19 also caused its projected replacement, the Do 217, to be abandoned. By the same token, production of the Heinkel He 111 was also reduced, although it remained in service until the end of the war, Heinkel concentrating on the He 177 and He 277.

The most successful tactical bomber in service in 1940 was the Junkers Ju 88. Designed as a fast level bomber, it was then, as noted earlier, handicapped by the added requirement to carry out steep, diving attacks. It was later modified for reconnaissance and night fighting, and during 1945 it became numerically the most important Luftwaffe night fighter. It was then developed into the Ju 188 and the ultra-high-altitude Ju 388.

STRATEGIC BOMBERS

The Dornier 19 was never intended to be more than an interim type, and its success surprised OKL considerably. The 'Bomber A' specification issued early in 1938 called for something much faster, and therefore more difficult to intercept, with even greater range. The radical Heinkel He 177 was the front-runner, with the Dornier Do 219 regarded as back-up, 'just in case'.

Designed in the interests of efficiency and low drag, the Heinkel had a slim, cigar-shaped fuselage, a span of 31.44m (103ft 1:in) and a wing area of 102m^2 (1,098 sq ft). Its most radical feature was the use of pairs of coupled engines, each driving an enormous four-bladed propeller. This concept, which gave the aircraft the appearance of a twin-engine type, reduced drag and improved performance. It was first flown on 19 November 1939.

By contrast, the Do 219 retained the boxy fuselage and bulged bomb bay of the Uralbomber, and its basic four-engine configuration. Its wings, however, were the subject of a total redesign. They became slimmer and narrower, and with a small reduction in span, coupled with a lavish use of slats and flaps. A single fin and rudder replaced the previous twin, braced assembly. The first flight took place on 16 February 1940. Provisionally named Fafnir (the serpent in the Volsung Saga), the Do 219 performed admirably from the outset, with few modifications needed. The same could not be said of the He 177, named Greif, which, although rather faster than its rival, gave nothing but trouble from the start. Not only did the Greif have serious aerodynamic problems: its coupled engines showed an alarming propensity to overheat and catch fire in flight.[5] Several experimental and pre-production aircraft were lost to various causes before, in mid-1941, the Fafnir was selected for production. It entered service late in 1942.

At this point, Ernst Heinkel did what he should have done much earlier. He abandoned the coupled engine layout in favour of a standard four-engine configuration.[6] This resulted in the He 277, the development of which was ordered in autumn 1941.[7] Not until December 1943 did it enter service, however, and by that time the Do 219 was regarded as the premier Luftwaffe strategic bomber.

The Third Reich, like the United States, was trying to develop nuclear weapons. Little enough was known about these, except that they would be very large and very heavy. In anticipation, two Do 219s and two He 277s were modified to carry atomic bombs.[8]

The largest German strategic bomber was the Messerschmitt Me 264. Conceived at a time when the United States seemed certain to join the war, it was designed to carry a bomb load of 1,800kg (3,968lb) to New York. It was enormous, with a wingspan of 43m (141ft 1in), a wing area of 127.7m² (1,370sq ft) and a maximum loaded weight of 45,540kg (100,416lb). The first flight took place in December 1942, but for various reasons, not the least of which was the inability of its warload to produce more than a psychological effect, only a handful were built.

NOTES

1. This section is historical and factual.
2. This section is what might have been. It is based on Price, Alfred, *The Hitler Options*, Chapter 8.
3. In practice, never enough nickel and chromium reached the Third Reich to permit this.

4. Production actually increased in 1942–43, thanks mainly to the non-arrival of suitable replacement types. I have postulated the decrease as being due to a lack of capacity directly attributable to the construction of strategic bombers.
5. The British Avro Manchester suffered similar problems with its Rolls-Royce Vulture engines, and was withdrawn from service.
6. This is exactly what the British did with the Manchester, to produce the classic Lancaster. Historically of course, the Luftwaffe persevered with the He 177 and finally got it into service years late.
7. Göring vetoed this, and only eight were eventually completed. None saw service.
8. Historically, two He 177s were so modified.

7 Carrier Task Force

PRIOR to 1914, Imperial Germany had had substantial overseas colonies — Samoa and New Guinea, Togoland, Cameroon, German West Africa and German East Africa. From 1915 these were progressively overrun by British or British Empire forces, aided in Cameroon by the French. This was rendered relatively easy by the almost total British control of the seven seas, despite the fact that the Imperial Navy had vastly increased its strength during the preceding years.

In the Great War, the High Seas Fleet mounted only one serious challenge to the supremacy of the Royal Navy. Although the Battle of Jutland in 1916 was indecisive, it was a strategic defeat for the Germans, which for the remainder of the war was bottled up in the North Sea and the Baltic. By default, the offensive passed to the small U-boat force which, as noted in Chapter 4, came close to severing the Atlantic sea routes.

The Imperial Navy, reduced to a rump after the Armistice, was renamed the Reichsmarine in 1921, and its strength remained small. It would remain so until after August 1934, when the ageing President Hindenburg died. This allowed Adolf Hitler, the Chancellor since January 1933, to assume full power. In March 1935 he repudiated the Treaty of Versailles; and two months later the Reichsmarine, commanded by Grossadmiral Erich Raeder since 1928, became the Kriegsmarine.

Hitler at first ruled out the possibility of war with the British, but quickly changed his mind. The result was the Z-Plan of 1938, which assumed that there would be no hostilities before 1948. It called for two large and powerfully armed battleships for North Atlantic operations, supported by two aircraft carriers. The battleships duly emerged as *Bismarck* and

Tirpitz. In addition, six even larger and more powerfully armed battleships were planned, carrying eight 405mm (16in) and twelve 150mm (5.9in) guns, plus a strong anti-aircraft armament and, unusually for modern battleships, six torpedo tubes. Possessed of extremely long range, these were earmarked for commerce raiding in distant waters. The underlying idea was that the Royal Navy would have to detach strong forces to protect merchant shipping, at the expense of weakening the Home Fleet.

The concept of long-distance commerce-raiding was far from new: the three pocket battleships, *Admiral Graf Spee*, *Admiral Scheer* and *Deutschland*, had all been built with this in mind, but they lacked the firepower necessary to survive if cornered. In addition, eleven merchant ships were fitted out as auxiliary cruisers for distant waters, to spread British naval strength even further. Support was given by a fleet of supply ships and tankers.

OVERTAKEN BY EVENTS

War with England began in September 1939, and not in 1948 as Hitler had predicted. At this time, both *Bismarck* and *Tirpitz* had been launched and were fitting out, as was the first aircraft carrier, *Graf Zeppelin*. Two of the new battleships had been laid down, one at Blohm & Voss at Hamburg and the other at Deschimag at Bremen. The second carrier, *Peter Strasser*,[1] was also under construction at Germaniawerft, Kiel.

The Führer gambled on a short war, and in any case had his long-term sights set on the Soviet Union. With Poland conquered, he confidently expected a negotiated settlement with Britain and France. Work on the two new commerce-raiders was terminated in April 1940, and later both were broken up. The capitulation of France in June 1940, and the projected invasion of England later that year, appeared to justify this decision.

The two German carriers almost suffered the same fate. *Graf Zeppelin*, able to carry up to 40 aircraft, had been launched on 8 December 1938, although fitting out had been delayed owing to problems with its arrester gear and catapults. Work on this and *Peter Strasser* (still on the slips) was suspended in April 1940. However, Grossadmiral Raeder, citing the use of carriers by the British, Americans and Japanese, persuaded the Führer that naval air power would be essential for the future, and work on the two carriers was resumed in July 1940.[2]

Two factors later that year injected a note of urgency into the German carrier programme. The failure to subdue England in the summer of 1940 meant that the war would continue at least well into the next year. Then, in November, the Italian Fleet, supposedly safe in the well-defended harbour at Taranto, was crippled in an audacious night attack by a mere 21 British carrier aircraft. Not only were the purpose-built carriers immediately assigned a high priority; the heavy cruiser *Seydlitz* was earmarked for conversion.[3] Plans were also drawn up for the conversion of the liners *Europa*, *Gneisenau* (not to be confused with the battlecruiser of the same name) and *Potsdam*, although these last three did not proceed.

THE CARRIERS

Graf Zeppelin was well protected, with belt armour of 100mm and a further 50mm on the deck, but, as with every other carrier in the world apart from the British *Illustrious* class, this was the hangar deck, not the flight deck — a crucial difference. She was also well defended. The main armament consisted of eight pairs of 150mm (5.9in) guns, while for anti-aircraft defence she mounted six twin high-angle 105mm (4.1in), eleven twin 37mm and seven quadruple 20mm guns. On trials she reached her design speed of 332 knots, and while cruising at 19 kots her range was about 13,000km (7,000nm). These figures also applied to *Peter Strasser*.

The rather smaller *Seydlitz* had similar hangar-deck armour and slightly thinner belt armour. She was less well defended against aircraft, with six twin high-angle 105mm, ten twin 37mm and five quadruple 20mm guns. Her designed speed was 31 knots and her range at cruising speed about 11,000km (5,900nm).[4]

Ideally, German carrier aircraft should have been purpose-designed for the task, as was the case with every other nation with shipborne striking power. However, for Germany this was not really a practical proposition. The aircraft industry of the Third Reich was heavily committed to rearming the Luftwaffe, and the relatively small numbers of carrier aircraft needed would have diverted scarce resources from this primary aim. A secondary consideration was that the performance of dedicated carrier aircraft was generally inferior to that of their land-based equivalents.

The obvious solution was to modify existing land-based types for carrier operations—a classic case of having one's cake and eating it too! After a brief flirtation with biplanes, rejected as having too inferior a performance, the Messerschmitt Bf 109 was selected as the fighter, and the Junkers Ju 87 became the dive- and torpedo-bomber.

The choice was flawed. Hermann Göring's dictum still held sway, and, lacking experience, neither the Luftwaffe nor the Kriegsmarine fully appreciated the need for extended endurance in carrier operations, and both the Bf 109 and the Ju 87 were short-legged. The difference is easily explained. Land-based fighters could warm up their engines quickly and perform a mass or a stream take-off. Returning damaged, or low on fuel, they could land at any airfield along the way, or even, *in extremis*, lob in on a suitable field to await recovery. Furthermore, their airfield was still exactly where they had left it! No such options were available to carrier aircraft. Having warmed up, they queued for their turn to take off. After launching singly, they had to climb out and form up, all of which took time. On their return, they had first to find the carrier, which could possibly be up to 80km (43nm) from its original position. This was no easy task: the sea has few if any waypoints, while poor visibility often makes matters much worse. Sometimes a time- and fuel-consuming square search was needed.

Having found 'mother', with any luck already heading into wind, the aircraft then had to circle and await their turn to land. Even when things went well, orbiting the carrier with the fuel warning light glowing could give rise to some nail-biting moments. All it needed was for one pilot (possibly wounded or with battle damage) to make a hash of his landing and block the deck, and the rest of the Staffel could run out of fuel and end up in the wate. To add to these woes, replacement aircraft and pilots were simply not available in mid-ocean. Losses were therefore permanent until the end of the sortie.

To take some specifics, the operational radius of the land-based Bf 109E, allowing ten minutes for combat at full throttle, was little more than one-third of its stated maximum range,[5] typically 200km (108nm) — and even that left little margin for contingencies For carrier work, the realistic operational radius expressed as a proportion of stated range would be barely one-fifth — say, 135km (73nm). The only answer was to fit auxiliary fuel tanks, increasing the radius of action by possibly half as much again, but by naval standards this was still inadequate. The Ju 87 would be similarly range-limited. A further factor was that while auxiliary fuel tanks could be carried, they were undesirable, as they reduced striking power by occupying hardpoints which would otherwise have been used for bombs.

Initially the air complement (Trägergruppe) of the *Graf Zeppelin* was to consist of 30 Messerschmitt Bf 109 fighters and twelve Junkers Ju 87 dive-bombers, but the authorities felt that a mere Staffel of dive-bombers was an inadequate return for the expenditure on an aircraft carrier. While fighter defence was obviously needed, the carrier would operate in conjunction with a powerful surface force which, theoretically, would provide an effective shield of anti-aircraft fire. The air complement was then changed to twelve fighters and 28 dive-bombers; that of *Seydlitz* consisted of twelve fighters and 20 dive-bombers.

THE CARRIER AIRCRAFT

The Bf 109T[6] was derived from the Bf 109E, from which it differed in having a wing span 1.21m (3ft 112in) greater with 1.33m^2 (14.31 sq ft) more area, modified flaps, an arrester hook with a strengthened fuselage and main gear, a catapult spool, and provision for manual wing folding. Retractable spoilers on the upper wing surfaces allowed a rather steeper landing approach, albeit at a flatter angle. The added weight of these modifications resulted in a slightly higher wing loading, despite the extra area, and a marginal reduction in performance compared with that of the basic Bf 109E-3, but low-speed handling was rather more benign. An auxiliary fuel tank was carried on the centreline as standard.

The shipboard variant of the Stuka was the Ju 87C,[7] which entered service in 1939. Like its Messerschmitt shipmate. it was navalised with catapult spools, arrester gear and fuselage strengthening. With hangar and deck parking space at a premium, it was fitted with electric wing folding. The sturdy fixed main gears were, however, a liability in the event of a forced landing in the sea: as the wheels dipped below the waves the Stuka would go straight over on its back. To improve the crew's chances of survival, the main gear legs could be jettisoned before ditching.

The standard Ju 87C was, like the Bf 109, short-legged, but help was at hand. This was the Ju 87R, a specialised long-range anti-shipping variant was fitted with integral, 150-litre wing tanks. In addition, it was plumbed for two 300-litre underwing drop tanks. It was a compromise solution, trading bomb load for fuel; and the normal warload consisted of a single SC or SD 250, or a light torpedo. As a carrier bomber, its maximum effective reach became a fairly acceptable 280km (150nm).

THE GRAND PLAN

The first two years of the war had seen the *Kriegsmarine*'s heavy units raiding out into the Atlantic, generally operating individually. However, with few exceptions they had been hunted down by superior forces before they could inflict damage upon the convoys. In 1941 this was to change.

For Grossadmiral Raeder, the die was already cast. He knew that the British Home Fleet had been weakened by the Uralbomber attacks, although he was, like most Navy men, sceptical about the optimistic Luftwaffe intelligence estimates. But this did not alter the fact that if the Kriegsmarine, with its recent great accession of strength, were ever to challenge the Royal Navy on the high seas, the time had come. The risks were great, but so were the rewards.

An innately cautious man, Raeder was caught on the horns of a dilemma. On the one hand, he could delay several months until all his heavy surface units were ready, then put a vast armada to sea. The real problem was: how would his opponents react? Such a large fleet could not be concealed, and the British, given sufficient time, could reinforce the Home Fleet by stripping the Mediterranean and Indian Ocean and concentrate on bottling his forces up. While the British would obviously be reluctant to take this step, the enormity of the threat to the motherland might make it inevitable.

If this were the case, the result would be a decisive make-or-break battle, historically as important as Trafalgar. In this scenario, Raeder was keenly aware that his small carrier air arm, around which everything centred, would be heavily overmatched. Moreover, if matters went awry—and in war there are no certainties—he would have no reserves.

Another option open to the enemy would be to play for time, refusing a major surface action while skirmishing with the German fleet to reduce its strength. Convoys which could not be turned back in time would be ordered to scatter, accepting the inevitable heavy losses but hoping that some ships might get through. This would leave the Kriegsmarine in control of the North Atlantic until fuel ran low. Having returned to port, it would be some considerable time before it could sail again.

Never a great admirer of the Führer's 'victory or death' attitude, Erich Raeder quickly rejected the all-or-nothing solution, choosing instead to divide his forces. Banking on the advantage of surprise, he could seize the initiative by sailing a powerful force at soon as possible, with a second, equally powerful force to follow later.

His reasoning was as follows. A sudden breakout into the Atlantic by a strong force with its own organic air cover would catch the British on the hop. Having created mayhem across the convoy routes, and, with luck, overwhelming a few British surface units on the way, it would relocate to a base in Brittany. His second force would be based at Trondheim in Norway. Even if his first sortie proved indecisive, the two would act as lethal pincers, poised to close around the British Isles. This would have the added benefit of weakening the Home Fleet by forcing it to divide against the twin threat.

SCHLACHTGRUPPEN

Raeder divided his forces into two Schlachtgruppen, each centred on a carrier and supported by a battleship, and named after the admirals commanding. Schlachtgruppe Lütjens consisted of *Graf Zeppelin*, supported by the *Bismarck*, the battlecruiser *Gneisenau* and the heavy cruisers *Prinz Eugen* and *Ziethen*,[8] attended by the light cruisers *Emden* and *Köln* with a screen of eight destroyers. Schlachtgruppe Ciliax consisted of the carrier *Seydlitz*, supported by *Tirpitz*, the battlecruiser *Scharnhorst* and the heavy cruiser *Hipper* and attended by the light cruisers *Leipzig* and *Nürnberg* with a screen of nine destroyers.

In addition to the carrier aircraft, the major warships carried Arado Ar 196 floatplanes of Bordfliegergruppe 196. The main functions of BFGr 196 were reconnaissance, anti-submarine patrols and, if surface action were joined, spotting for the big guns. Endurance apart, its performance was derisory, with a maximum speed of just 310kph (168 knots) and the rate of climb of a tired brick. On the other hand, Schlachtgruppe Lütjens carried seventeen Arados, while Schlachtgruppe Ciliax had just one fewer.

The Arado was launched by catapult but could only be recovered by landing on the sea alongside its parent ship, after which it was hoisted inboard by crane. Recovery in rough seas was therefore difficult, if not outright impossible. A technique had been developed before the war whereby the parent ship steamed in a tight circle, thus creating a calmer area for landing, but the formation integrity demanded by Schlachtgruppe operations virtually ruled this out. In dire need, a light cruiser could be detached to recover the aircraft, whether or not it was 'mother'. Flying (and recovery) conditions permitting, at least one Arado was to be aloft on anti-submarine patrol during the hours of daylight. An obvious secondary task then became to drive off enemy shadowing aircraft.

The Ar 196A-3[9] packed a respectable punch, with two 20mm MG FF wing cannon and two MG 17s in the rear cockpit, but its performance was so poor that it was hard-pressed to get near even a lumbering Whitley or Catalina, let alone drive one off. The obvious answer was for the carrier to launch a Bf 109T, but, with a complement of only twelve, every aircraft had if possible to be preserved for more important tasks. However, the large total complement of Arados provided a solution of sorts: three or four of them would provide a shadower with a very tricky problem.

COMMAND OF THE OCEAN

Although the admirals commanding were given considerable operational discretion, their overriding priority was to wrest control of the North Atlantic from the British, thereby cutting the sea lanes and starving the island nation into surrender. However, while each admiral could risk a great deal, as part of a greater plan he could not allow his force to be effectively neutralised. Whatever happened, the two forces had to stay in being, to pose a constant and deadly threat.

To Raeder, there seemed little risk if only surprise could be achieved. Against such forces as he could put into the field, the British could only respond with equal or greater strength. Surprise would ensure that they would not be given enough time to concentrate, and, it was hoped, they could be defeated in detail.

The priorities assigned to the German carrier air units were essentially as follows:

1. The timely location of enemy surface units. Reconnaissance would mainly be the task of the Bordflieger, but, when conditions prevented the Arados from operating, Ju 87s could be used at the discretion of the force commander.

2. Enemy carriers were the primary targets for air attack if and when they were encountered, and, if possible, the air units should be reserved for this purpose. The action was to commence with a full-strength first strike with bombs and torpedoes, or both. If enemy fighters were known to be active, a Schwarm (four fighters) of Bf 109s could be sent to escort the bombers, while the other two Schwärme rotated to provide constant air defence.

3. Enemy surface units lacking air support were to be engaged, at the discretion of the admiral, by gunnery. The carrier was not to be risked in a surface action but sent, suitably escorted, out of harm's way.

4. It was emphasised that secrecy and surprise were of the greatest importance. If for any reason shadowing enemy aircraft could not be driven off by the Bordflieger, carrier fighters were to be used. It was of equal importance that shadowing enemy surface units were to be driven off, or preferably sunk. If the warships could not achieve this, then in the last resort bombers were to be used.

The final plan was for Schlachtgruppe Lütjens to break out into the North Atlantic in June 1941, create havoc across the convoy routes, attack and sink all major British surface units encountered and then redeploy to

St-Nazaire[10] in Brittany to prepare for further sorties. Schlachtgruppe Ciliax was to sortie into the North Atlantic in October 1941 with a similar brief to that of Schlachtgruppe Lütjens, before returning to Trondheim in Norway. A few cautious heads wanted to hold Lütjens back until Ciliax was ready, but, as this would almost certainly have lost the element of surprise and allowed the enemy to concentrate to thwart the breakout, Raeder refused.[11]

This, then, was the grand strategy: in essence, to divide and rule. Of the other major units, *Peter Strasser* would, when commissioned, replace *Seydlitz*, which would then revert to carrier training in the Baltic until needed as a replacement. The pocket battleships *Scheer* and *Lützow* (the former *Deutschland*) were to break out into the Atlantic under cover of the confusion caused by the first Schlachtgruppe and head south to interdict supply routes from South America and the Cape of Good Hope. The two museum pieces, the pre-war vintage battleships *Schlesien* and *Schleswig-Holstein*, would remain in the Baltic, ostensibly to counter the Soviet Baltic Fleet but equally to act as red herrings for Western intelligence.[12]

THE BREAKOUT

Raeder took every possible measure to ensure that the assembly of Schlachtgruppe Lütjens was kept secret. He chose a time to coincide with the start of Operation 'Barbarossa', the German invasion of the Soviet Union, guessing that the attention of the West would be focused on events in the East.

On 21 June 1941 *Schlesien* and *Schleswig-Holstein* left Gdynia and steamed towards the Gulf of Finland. Fresh from working up in the Baltic, *Bismarck, Graf Zeppelin* and *Prinz Eugen* sailed from the same port on 21 June 1941, but, once out of sight of land, headed westward. On the night of 23 June they reached Kiel, then passed through the Nord Ostsee Kanal, where they were joined by six destroyers off the estuary of the Elbe. As they headed north, *Emden* and *Köln* arrived from Wilhelmshaven.

The rendezvous with the rest of the force, *Gneisenau, Ziethen* and two more destroyers, was in Hardangerfjord, south of Bergen. After a top-up of fuel from depot ships, Schlachtgruppe Lütjens sailed at dusk on 26

June, course north-west, heading for the Denmark Strait. Its departure was masked from the prying eyes of enemy reconnaissance aircraft by low cloud and poor visibility.

The sailing of such a large force could not, however, be concealed from the Norwegian Resistance, which informed London by clandestine radio. This news was electrifying. A large-scale air and sea search was initiated. Convoys were immediately re-routed far to the south at maximum speed, leaving many stragglers in their wakes, while desperate efforts were made to concentrate units of Home Fleet across the likely lines of approach. Having rounded Iceland undetected, Schlachtgruppe Lütjens sped south-west through the Denmark Strait. But things had already started to go wrong. Three supply ships, *Belchen*, *Gonzenheim* and *Lothringen*, scheduled to refuel and replenish the force, had already fallen foul of the British.[13] For the thirsty heavy cruisers this was serious: the duration of the sortie had to be significantly reduced if the fleet were to stay together.

At dusk on 29 June the leading German destroyers emerged from a low-lying bank of fog, only to see a British cruiser on the horizon. Mindful of standing orders, four of them, supported by the light cruiser *Emden*, set off in pursuit, while the Schlachtgruppe made a radical change of course to the south. In a confused night action lasting nearly four hours, two German destroyers were sunk by gunfire and a third damaged, but not before they had succeeded in scoring two torpedo hits on the enemy cruiser. These slowed it down, allowing *Emden*, which was not particularly fast, to catch up. After a lengthy gun duel at long range, the damaged British cruiser was reduced to a burning hulk, although it had scored four hits on *Emden* with its six inch guns.

There was in fact another participant, but this went unnoticed by the Germans. Another British cruiser in the area, drawn to the distant gun flashes, steamed to the rescue, only to run almost into the rear of the darkened Schlachtgruppe. As the German lookouts were more interested in the gun flashes on the southern horizon, its approach remained undetected. Unable to reach its chummy ship in time to assist, it dropped back, shadowing the German force by radar. At first light it launched its Walrus amphibian, universally known as the 'Shagbat'. Staying low to the horizon, this trailed the Schlachtgruppe at the limits of visibility, plotting the position, course, and speed of the German fleet. Meanwhile the cruiser searched for survivors.

Admiral Lütjens was determined not to bump into anything without due warning, and at first light he ordered four Arados to be launched, with instructions to reconnoitre ahead and wide on the flanks. No thought was given to danger lurking astern, and the low-flying 'Shagbat' escaped detection, her sighting reports drawing Allied reconnaissance aircraft like wasps to a jam pot. By mid-morning no fewer than five were circling the German battle group. More Arados were launched, but no sooner was one aircraft driven away than another closed in. Their efforts were not entirely in vain: one Catalina was shot down, and another turned for home streaming smoke. One of the Arados was badly hit by return fire and sank on landing before it could be recovered.

Desperate to drive off the shadowers, Admiral Lütjens ordered a Rotte (pair) of Bf 109s aloft from *Graf Zeppelin*. One Allied reconnaissance aircraft was shot down almost immediately, but the others took refuge in broken cloud, popping out only occasionally to maintain contact with the surface force. When the first Rotte became low on fuel, a second was sent off. This also claimed a Catalina shot down, but a heavy deck landing by one of them collapsed an undercarriage leg. The damage suffered made it unserviceable for the remainder of the cruise.

At this point the weakness of the Flugzeugträger started to become apparent. It carried too few fighters to be truly effective, and those it did carry were not really suited to the rough-and-tumble of carrier operations.[14] The Arados, though numerous, lacked the performance needed for air defence. But, as the saying went, one could only fight the war one had with what one had, no matter how unsuitable. Darkness brought eventual relief from constant air surveillance, and another radical change of course during the night succeeded in shaking off the shadowers.

On 1 July Lütjens was heading for the predicted position of an eastbound convoy, but when he arrived he found only empty sea. At least the sky was clear of enemy aircraft, as he had passed beyond the effective range of the Iceland-based Catalinas. Scouting ahead, the Arados gained only one contact — a small freighter which had lost touch with its convoy. Rather than betray his position, he altered course to give it a wide berth.

On the following day his luck changed. A patrolling U-boat reported a convoy barely 200km to the south of his position, on a south-easterly course. Guided by reports from the U-boat, he timed his run to arrive at the predicted position of the convoy at first light, approaching from just south of west so that his targets would be silhouetted against the lightening horizon.

Observing strict radio silence, Schlachtgruppe Lütjens drove on through the night. Towards dawn *Graf Zeppelin*, escorted by the damaged *Emden* and the remaining destroyers, pulled out of the line to the north. The five major warships bored on, deploying into an offset line ahead. This was to be a gun action.

The force was first sighted by a lone sloop, on anti-submarine patrol some 8,000m astern of the convoy. A garbled reply was made to its challenge, and the resulting delay and confusion allowed *Ziethen* to close the range before unleashing a salvo from her secondary armament. Hit several times, the sloop was torn apart.

It was a huge convoy — no fewer than 52 ships on a twelve-ship frontage, accompanied by eight escorts, only one of which was a destroyer. A few quick-witted merchant captains tried to scatter at top speed, but it was already too late. The five German warships stormed through the convoy, firing to port and starboard as they passed between the columns. Only the light cruiser *Köln* used her main guns, but at ranges of just a few hundred metres the secondary armament of the major warships was adequately lethal.

The escorts tried desperately to protect their charges, but, heavily outgunned, they were quickly overwhelmed. The destroyer gallantly attempted to torpedo *Prinz Eugen* but was blown out of the water. Less than two hours later, it was all over. All that remained to mark the spot was flotsam, a few lifeboats and rafts, several massive oil slicks, and a huge pall of smoke, gradually dispersing on the wind. There were but two survivors — freighters that had taken advantage of the smoke and confusion to make good their escape.

Admiral Lütjens had achieved one of his objectives — the total destruction of a convoy — but now he had a hard decision to make. *Prinz Eugen* and *Ziethen* were running low on fuel, and *Emden* and a destroyer were damaged. He had two choices. Either he could detach the three cruisers and the destroyer to make their own way home while he continued raiding in mid-Atlantic, or he could bring his entire force into St-Nazaire intact, hopefully picking up further victims en route.

Several factors influenced his decision. The German monitoring service had informed him that two eastbound convoys had fled south at his approach; sooner or later they would have to come northabout. Another convoy had just left Gibraltar for England. With a little luck, he might catch something. Just one thing was certain: his destruction of the convoy could not possibly have gone unreported, in which case he could soon expect visitors. The Home Fleet and elements from Force H at Gibraltar had sailed to cut him off. If they combined, they would pose a deadly threat, but only if they were able to find him. By the same token, if the British forces could be located in time, he would be able to accept or refuse battle depending on the strength of the enemy. Everything now waited on air reconnaissance.

His final decision was based on two overriding factors. First, it was essential to keep his Schlachtgruppe in being, to become the southern half of the Kriegsmarine's 'pincers'. Secondly, he was a firm believer in concentration of force. To send the two heavy cruisers and the damaged *Emden* on ahead while he remained in mid-Atlantic would be to risk defeat in detail. He was also aware that the air complement of *Graf Zeppelin* was numerically inferior to that of a British fleet carrier, at least two of which would be sent against him. Rallying his force, he headed south once more, hoping to fool the enemy reconnaissance aircraft before making his final run to St-Nazaire.

THE NET CLOSES

As the Schlachtgruppe was still outside the effective range of Icelandic and British-based Catalinas, Lütjens' expected visitors failed to arrive. Then, on reaching latitude 47° 30'N at noon on 4 July, he turned east and set course for France. Lütjens had not, however, gone undetected. His force had been spotted by a U-boat. This was doubly unfortunate. The U-boat arm was noted for its tendency to use radio for inessential matters. Then, not long before, the Royal Navy had boarded a sinking U-boat and recovered an Enigma encrypting machine and its code books. The U-boat commander had promptly signalled the sighting to his base at Lorient; equally promptly, the British intercepted his signal and within hours had decyphered it.

Shortly after dawn a single Catalina arrived, only to be pounced upon and shot down by patrolling Bf 109s, though not before it had reported being attacked. This was good enough: other shadowers arrived from all directions and, despite further losses, followed the Schlachtgruppe. Meanwhile the wind was freshening, and clouds were gathering. Yet another Bf 109 came to grief on the heaving deck, and flying was halted.

Meanwhile Vultures from KG 40 were scouring a huge area of the ocean in an attempt to locate the British surface units. They were not given a clear run. RAF Sunderlands patrolled across their projected tracks with orders to attack Vultures on sight. Several battles of the giants took place, although these were generally inconclusive. Force H was finally located at noon on 5 July, some 600km (324nm) east of Cape Finisterre, heading north-west and almost on a collision course with Lütjens. Although harried by Fleet Air Arm Fulmars, the Vultures managed to establish that it consisted of a carrier, provisionally identified as *Ark Royal*, accompanied by four cruisers and a screen of destroyers.

To Lütjens, it seemed that battle was unavoidable. While he was outmatched in air power, in a surface action he had the edge. But this would be the first ever carrier battle;[15] there were no precedents to guide him. He planned to delay, timing matters so that he could launch a maximum air strike to arrive at dusk, with his Stukas coming out of the setting sun, then drive on at full speed to bring on a night surface action.

Graf Zeppelin, escorted by two destroyers, pulled out of line and headed into the brisk south-westerly wind to launch her six remaining serviceable Bf 109s. These were to drive off the shadowers. When it looked as though they had succeeded, Lütjens turned south-east with his main force. An hour later the German carrier again turned back into the wind to launch her Stuka strike force, while the rest of Schlachtgruppe Lütjens cracked on all possible speed, heading directly for the predicted position of Force H.

When the German force had been spotted leaving the Denmark Strait a few days earlier, a large eastbound convoy south of Iceland had been ordered to scatter, while a westbound convoy north of Rockall was turned back. With merchant ships scattered over half the North Atlantic, the British Home Fleet had sailed to protect them. However, it soon became obvious that the immediate threat had passed. The Home Fleet, concentrated in two groups within mutual supporting distance, steamed south, ready to block any German attempt to escape back to Norway. The net was closing, if slowly.

Admiral Somerville, commanding Force H, was in a quandary. The Home Fleet was still too far off to render him immediate assistance, but if he simply refused battle there was every chance that the German force would slip past him and reach the French ports safely. The thought of Schlachtgruppe Lütjens based on the Brittany coast, able to sally forth at will, was the stuff of nightmares. Yet Force H would be heavily outgunned in a surface action. Something had to give.

The opposing carriers were now within striking distance of each other, and a decision could not be long delayed. Admiral Somerville did, however, have certain advantages. When the RAF shadowers had been driven off, he had replaced them with two Fulmar fighters which had evaded the Messerschmitts. An hour before sunset, a Fulmar reported that *Graf Zeppelin* had turned into wind and was launching aircraft, while the main force was steaming on.

Shortly after the report was received, *Ark Royal* also turned into wind and began launching all her remaining aircraft. The British admiral was under no illusions: he knew what the Stukas had done to the carriers *Illustrious* and *Formidable* earlier in the year.[16] If *Ark Royal* suffered similarly, there would be no carrier to return to.

First off were the long-range Fulmars, followed by the shorter-legged Sea Hurricanes. The fighters took station well to the west, to intercept the incoming raid. They were followed off the deck by the entire complement of Swordfish. These were Admiral Somerville's second major advantage: equipped with ASV radar, they could attack by night. This was just as well, because, being slow biplanes, they would not arrive until after nightfall. Having launched, Force H turned south, maintaining full speed.

THE AIR BATTLE

All 28 Ju 87s from *Graf Zeppelin* were serviceable. Ten of them carried bombs, the rest torpedoes. The bombers flew in from the west at 2,000m (6,562ft), the highest altitude the cloud base allowed. The torpedo carriers were in two waves of nine at low level, one coming out of the setting sun to the west and the other approaching from the darkening sky in the north. No fighter escort was available.

Heavy laden and outnumbered, the Stukas were intercepted some 30km(16nm) out and shot to pieces. Even the poorly performing Fulmars had a field day. Just ten got past the fighters and, of these, four fell to anti-aircraft fire. *Ark Royal* suffered light damage from two near-misses by bombs; three torpedo hits were scored, sinking a destroyer and damaging a cruiser. One Sea Hurricane was lost, and two Fulmars damaged.

Meanwhile the ancient Swordfish droned on through the night. Distracted by lights in the distance, they missed the main German force, to find *Graf Zeppelin* trying to land on the last of the surviving Stukas. It was too good a chance to miss. Three Swordfish dive-bombed unopposed, scoring two direct hits which went through the unarmoured flight deck to explode in the hangar. As huge fires roared out of control, three more sneaked in with torpedoes, scoring two more hits. At this point the German gunners woke up and blazed away at everything in sight, shooting down two Swordfish and the final Stuka still airborne.

Two following squadrons of Swordfish found the German main force. Here the opposition was fiercer and they paid heavily, losing ten out of eighteen aircraft, but not before they had put two torpedoes into *Bismarck*, one into *Köln* and three into *Ziethen*, sinking her. *Bismarck's* speed had been reduced, and the plan for a night surface action thrown into disarray.

However, Force H failed to slip past the Schlachtgruppe undetected, and a long-range gunnery duel took place at dawn. Now, however, the

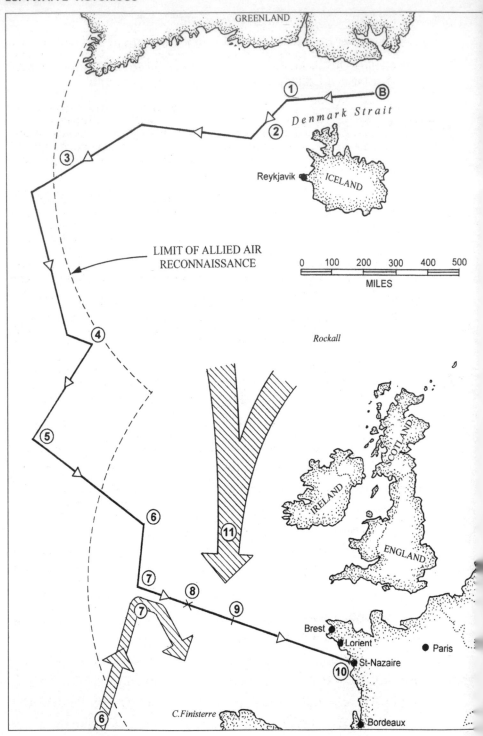

LIMIT OF ALLIED AIR
RECONNAISSANCE

Schlachtgruppe Lütjens, June/July 1941. Had it succeeded, Admiral Raeder's plan to have two naval carrier groups based at Trondheim in Norway and St-Nazaire in Brittany would have posed a deadly threat to Britain's Atlantic supply routes. Seen here is the sortie by Schlachtgruppe Lütjens, which failed by a narrow margin to achieve its objective.

A   The Schlachtgruppe concentrates in Hardangerfjord near Bergen. It sails at dusk on 26 June. Avoiding the heavily patrolled Iceland–Faeroes gap, it heads for the Denmark Strait.

B   The three ships scheduled to top up fuel off Greenland have all been caught and sunk. This will later leave Admiral Lütjens with a hard choice.

1   The Schlachtgruppe is detected quite by chance by a single British light cruiser in the Denmark Strait.

2   Attacked by four 'Z' class destroyers and the light cruiser *Emden*, the British cruiser is pursued and sunk. Unnoticed is a second British cruiser astern, which shadows the Schlachtgruppe, homing in land-based reconnaissance aircraft.

3   Schlachtgruppe Lütjens passes outside the limits of British land-based air surveillance.

4   The almost complete destruction of a convoy, 3 July.

5   Restricted by fuel shortages for his heavy cruisers, and with a damaged cruiser and a destroyer, Lütjens turns east to make a direct run for St-Nazaire.

6   Vultures of KG 40 detect the British Force H from Gibraltar approaching from the south. It is identified as one carrier, the *Ark Royal*, two heavy cruisers and two light cruisers, with a screen of destroyers. Lütjens, aware of his superiority in a surface action, steers to engage it.

7   The first ever carrier-versus-carrier battle. *Graf Zeppelin* and *Ziethen* are sunk; *Bismarck* and *Köln* are damaged. On the enemy side, one destroyer is sunk and a light cruiser and *Ark Royal* are damaged. By dawn, the two fleets are within gunnery range. *Bismarck*, *Gneisenau* and *Prinz Eugen* suffer damage, while, for the enemy, the battlecruiser *Repulse* and a light cruiser are sunk and *Ark Royal* suffers further damage. Knowing that the Home Fleet is now in position, Force H disengages.

8   By now the British Home Fleet has closed on the Schlachtgruppe and an air strike from the carrier *Victorious* sinks *Emden* and a destroyer and damages *Bismarck*'s steering.

9   Ordering the remnants of his once proud Schlachtgruppe to head for St-Nazaire at full speed, Lütjens sacrifices himself and his crippled flagship to facilitate their escape. *Bismarck* is pounded into a wreck by the battleships *King George V* and the *Prince of Wales*.

10   The remnants of Schlachtgruppe Lütjens—the damaged cruisers *Gneisenau*, *Prinz Eugen* and *Köln* and the remaining destroyers—all reach St-Nazaire but take little further part in the war.

11   The British Home Fleet, having initially positioned itself to prevent a return to the North Sea, comes storming south to intercept Schlachtgruppe Lütjens.

odds were shorter. Two of the four ships identified as cruisers were actually the 15in-gun battlecruisers *Repulse* and *Renown*. These scored hits on *Bismarck*, slowing her up still more, and caused damage to *Gneisenau* and *Prinz Eugen*. It was not without cost: *Repulse* sank after taking several damaging hits, as did a 6in-gun cruiser, while *Ark Royal* was hit twice as she escaped to the south. That afternoon, aircraft from the carrier *Victorious* attacked the remnants of the once proud German group, sinking *Emden* and a destroyer and damaging *Bismarck*'s steering. This allowed the Home Fleet to close, and Lütjens sacrificed his battered flagship to the guns of *King George V* and *Prince of Wales* to allow the others to escape.

Raeder's plan to sever the Atlantic lifelines had come badly unglued, and Hitler was not best pleased. He halted all further work on carriers, and the second Schlachtgruppe was never formed.

REALITY

The concept of Kriegsmarine carrier aviation was deeply flawed from the outset. The carriers were too small, the aircraft were not sufficiently specialised, and starting without peacetime experience was a bad idea. Having said that, the Schlachtgruppe concept could have posed very serious problems for the British had it been implemented. Historically, Bismarck was overwhelmed by sheer weight of numbers, and unless the Schlachtgruppe could have gained a rapid and resounding victory this would probably have also been its fate.

In 1942 the presence in Brest of *Scharnhorst*, *Gneisenau* and *Prinz Eugen* posed a broadly similar threat. It was a relief to the British when Hitler, acting on intuition, pulled them out. Another indication of how much of a threat was posed can be seen by British attempts to neutralise *Tirpitz*, even though the huge battleship rarely stirred from her safe anchorages.

NOTES

1. The name is speculative. Fregattenkapitän Peter Strasser had commanded the Imperial Naval Airship Division in the Great War and had been killed when Zeppelin *L 70* was shot down over the North Sea on 5 August 1918.
2. Work on the second carrier was never resumed. The ship was broken up at Kiel in 1940.

3. Historically, work on the *Graf Zeppelin* remained slow, and finally ceased in 1943, with the carrier still incomplete. Conversion of *Seydlitz* was seen as an emergency measure, but not until May 1942, as were the liners. None survived the planning stage.

4. Egbert Klessen-Wartmann, *Kriegsmarine Luft*.

5. The stated maximum range is a purely theoretical figure, of value only to dedicated 'number-crunchers'.

6. Two Staffeln of Bf 109T-1s (T = Träger = carrier) were formed for *Graf Zeppelin* — 5. and 6./Trägergruppe 186. They and the denavalised Bf 109T-2s served with the Luftwaffe as land-based fighters into 1943.

7. See Note 6. This was 4(Stuka)./Trägergruppe 186. Its Ju 87Cs were pressed into service with the Luftwaffe.

8. Originally called *Lützow*, and renamed *Ziethen* when the pocket battleship *Deutschland* was renamed *Lützow*. In fact, this heavy cruiser, still incomplete, was sold to the Soviet Union in 1940.

9. The shipboard variant was the Ar 196A-1, which carried a single, fixed, forward-firing machine gun and another in the rear cockpit. However, given the need to supplement the carrier air units, it seems only sensible to have replaced these with the more powerfully armed A-3.

10. St-Nazaire was chosen because it had dry-dock facilities large enough to take even *Bismarck* or *Tirpitz*.

11. This decision was hotly debated after the war.

12. They also acted as icebreakers in winter.

13. *Belchen* and *Gonzenheim* were sunk; *Lothringen* was captured. The actual dates are a bit early — 3, 4, and 15 June, respectively — but no matter!

14. The Fleet Air Arm had similar problems with the Seafire, more of which were lost in accidents than in combat.

15. Historically, the first ever carrier battles, Coral Sea and Midway, were still nearly a year in the future.

16. Both had been so badly damaged that they had to be withdrawn to the United States for repair.

8 Fliegen gegen Ivan

HAVING annexed Albania in 1939, Mussolini launched an invasion of Greece on 28 October 1940. The British responded by occupying Crete. For the Führer this was bad news, as it brought Romanian oilfields at Ploesti, so essential to future German operations, within range of British bombers.

The Italian invasion was quickly halted, and in March 1941 British land and air forces reinforced the Greeks. A month later, in a lightning campaign, German forces overran both Yugoslavia and Greece. Then, in May, German airborne forces captured Crete. This was a Pyrrhic victory, for German para- and glider-borne troops took such heavy casualties that they were never again used in a major air assault. Luftwaffe transport units also sustained heavy losses: 170 Ju 52s were destroyed or badly damaged — one-third of the total employed.[1] The need to rescue the Italians from their calamitous venture against Greece delayed Operation 'Barbarossa', the long-planned invasion of the Soviet Union. Originally scheduled for May 1941, it was finally launched on 22 June.

Even before hostilities began, the Wehrmacht knew that it was heavily outnumbered, not only on the ground but also in the air. In the months prior to the assault, many deep-penetration photo-reconnaissance sorties had been flown at extreme altitudes, but these had apparently failed to reveal the true picture. The reasons were probably twofold — a lack of photographic definition, which had bedevilled reconnaissance over England during the previous summer, coupled with the vast area to be covered.

Be that as it may, the Head of Luftwaffe Intelligence, 'Beppo' Schmid, concluded that Soviet strength in the European theatre was about 5,700 combat aircraft, of which 2,980 were fighters. This was an underestimate of about 50 per cent, although he judged correctly that the majority of them were obsolescent. Schmid also discounted a report from the German Air Attaché in Moscow to the effect that the capabilities of Soviet aircraft and aero-engine factories were impressive. However, he could hardly be blamed for this—the Führer counted on a quick victory, which would make Soviet industrial potential largely irrelevant.

For Operation 'Barbarossa', the Heer was divided into three army groups, each supported by a Luftflotte. Army Group North started from East Prussia. Its objectives were to sweep through the Russian-occupied Baltic states and head to and past Leningrad. It was supported by Luftflotte 1, with a single fighter Geschwader, JG 54 with 129 Bf 109s, of which 98 (76 per cent) were serviceable, and three bomber Geschwader, KG 1, KG 76 and KG 77, with 270 Ju 88s, of which 210 (78 per cent) were serviceable. Operations over the Baltic were the province of KGr 806, with 30 Ju 88s, of which 18 (60 per cent) were serviceable.

Army Group Centre swept over the frontier from east of Warsaw, aiming at Minsk, Smolensk and, eventually, Moscow. It was supported by Luftflotte 2, commanded by the dynamic Wolfram von Richthofen. More than double the strength of Luftflotte 1, it contained nine Gruppen of single-seat fighters from JG 27, JG 51, and JG 53 — a total of 316 Bf 109s, of which 272 (86 per cent) were serviceable. These were supplemented by two Gruppen of Zerstörer—78 Bf 110s, of which 51 (65 per cent) were serviceable; at least initially, these would mainly be used as fighter-bombers. Other fighter-bomber units were SKG 210[2] with 83 Bf 110s, of which 74 (89 per cent) were serviceable. II(Schlacht)./LG 2, with 38 Bf 109s and thirteen Hs 123s, one 109 being unserviceable, completed the inventory. Close air support was provided by StG 77 with 141 Ju 87s, of which 109 (77 per cent) were serviceable, while the level bomber complement consisted of II./KG 4 and KG 53 with 110 He 111s, of which 62 (56 per cent) were serviceable.[3]

Army Group South started from southern Poland, heading for Kiev, the Crimea and, eventually, the Caucasus oilfields. En route it was to combine with Army Group Centre in massive encirclements of the Soviet armies. It was supported by Luftflotte 4, numerically the strongest of all, with nine Gruppen of single-seat fighters from JG 3, JG 52, JG 77, and LG 2—a total of 337 Bf 109s, of which 259 (77 per cent) were serviceable. The medium bomber force consisted of KG 27 and 55, with 171 He 111s, 153 (68 per cent) being serviceable; and KG 51 and 54 with 163 Ju 88s of which 146 (80 per cent) were serviceable.

However, even before the invasion began, an almighty row was brewing at Oberkommando der Luftwaffe. The strategic bomber force was by now two full Geschwader strong. Moreover, back in the Reich, KG 2 Holzhammer was already trading in its elderly Do 17s for the Uralbomber: its first Gruppe was scheduled to be operational by late July 1941, with the other two following at six-week intervals. This was a very powerful force indeed.

Luftwaffe Chief of Staff Hans Jeschonnek argued strongly for the six strategic Kampfgruppen to be deployed among the three air fleets, but he was overruled by his commander-in-chief. Kesselring believed in concentration of force, and, for this, they had to be kept together. Kesselring was backed by von Richthofen, who wanted the strategic bomber force attached to his Luftflotte 2. Convinced that he was right, Jeschonnek thereupon appealed to Hitler, but his proposal was rejected. Nettled at being thus bypassed, 'Smiling Albert' severely reprimanded his Chief of Staff. Then, to eliminate friction between his three Luftflotte commanders, who all wanted a share of the pie, Kesselring moved the goalposts: he created Fernkampfdivision 1, directly under the command of OKL, a step not entirely unprecedented since OKL already directly controlled a large Aufklärungsgruppe. This solution not only kept the strategic bomber force together, it allowed a coherent targeting policy for the front as a whole, rather than a fragmented one organised to suit the ambitions of individual Luftflotten or army groups. The keynote was flexibility.

To command it, Kesselring appointed Generalmajor Günther Korten,[3] the former Chief of Staff of Luftflotte 4, with the new title of Angriffsführer Ostland. The diplomatic Korten could be relied upon to minimise friction with the Luftflotte commanders, although this was a difficult task as his bombers would have to operate from bases within their areas.

Although Jeschonnek was gifted in many ways, his character was deeply flawed.[4] He had barely avoided being court-martialled by Milch over a stupid training order which caused at least three fatal accidents, and relations between the two were never good thereafter.[5] Now he had annoyed both Hitler and Kesselring. His relative youth, his too-rapid rise and the fact that he had never held an operational command all diminished his influence with the 'fighting generals'. Chief among these was the ambitious von Richthofen, who, prior to Jeschonnek's intervention, had expected to have both Uralgeschwader as part of his Luftflotte 2. Jeschonnek's star was on the wane.

THE EASTERN FRONT, JUNE–DECEMBER 1941

When Operation 'Barbarossa' began, the Luftwaffe knew that it was heavily outnumbered. To redress the balance, it sought to cripple the Soviet Air Force from the outset with a destructive surprise attack. It was far from the first time that the Third Reich had contravened international law, but in total war it is results that count. The morality of the situation was best summed up some four decades later by American fighter pilot Colonel Lloyd C. ('Boots') Boothby: 'Pearl Harbor is called "The Day of Infamy". The Israeli pre-emptive strike of 1967 is called "a great tactical victory". It all depends whose side you're on!'

Be that as it may, the Luftwaffe attack on Soviet airfields was devastating. Before dawn, picked crews from II./KG 4 and KG 53 crossed the frontier at maximum altitude, routed over sparsely populated areas to evade detection. At 03.15 hours, throttled back, they swept down in Ketten of three aircraft, each Kette attacking an airfield with hundreds of SD 2 fragmentation bombs. Shortly after dawn the initial attack was followed up by Jabos — Bf 109s and 110s — many also carrying SD 2s. As the day progressed, level bombers joined in. The slaughter was tremendous, and more than a thousand Soviet aircraft were destroyed on the ground. Even so, the effect was, necessarily, limited: only 66 of nearly 200 airfields were attacked on the first day.

After the initial surprise had passed, the Soviet Air Force rose to defend the Rodina (Motherland), flying an estimated 6,000 sorties, albeit to little effect. Lacking combat experience and tactical know-how, their bombers were shot down in droves. Their fighters fared little better. On the first day, the Luftwaffe claimed a total of 1,811 aircraft destroyed, 1,489 on the ground, and 322 in the air, most of the latter falling to fighters. German losses were a mere 35 aircraft.

Although apparently a stunning victory, it was in fact less than decisive. The enormous destruction of mainly obsolescent aircraft on the ground simply created a large pool of Russian fighter pilots ready to convert on to newer and better fighter types as these became available. By 1941 industrial nations could produce combat aircraft far more quickly than they could train combat-ready pilots to fly them. Had Hitler achieved his planned quick victory over the Soviet Union, this would not have mattered, but in the long term it proved critical.

The months following the invasion were a happy time for the Jagdflieger. Even though the number of Soviet aircraft destroyed ran into thousands, hundreds more still rose to give battle. Undertrained, and flying inferior aircraft, they were little more than a target-rich environment for the German fighter pilots, many of whom started to amass huge scores. Leading the pack was Werner Mölders, who already had 68 victories (not counting his fourteen in the Spanish Civil War) when 'Barbarossa' commenced. In just eight days he passed Manfred von Richthofen's First World War total of 80 victories, and on 15 July his score reached 101. At this point he was withdrawn. (Hitler was solicitous of his more successful young warriors, and sought to preserve them.) Just days earlier, Ernst Udet, his health undermined by a combination of poor diet and an excessive use of stimulants, had entered a sanatorium. This presented Kesselring with the opportunity of retiring the old warhorse without

MAJOR ARMS FACTORIES IN MOSCOW, 22 JUNE 1941	
Factory	Product
GAZ (*Gosudarstvennyi aviatsionni zavod*) 1 fighters	MiG-1 and MiG-3
GAZ 24	Mikulin aircraft engines
GAZ 30	Il-2 attack aircraft
GAZ 49	Yakovlev fighters
GAZ 84	Li-2 transports
Zavod 37	Tanks
Zavod 40 (M'tischi)	Tanks

embarrassment. Mölders was recalled to replace Udet as Inspector of Fighters.

Fernkampfdivision 1 was also in action from the first day, although not against airfields. Moscow was a strategic target of the first order, on three counts. First, it was a major centre for rail and road communications. Secondly, it was a major centre of arms production. Not only did it contain almost all the Soviet weapons design bureaux, but it was also home to many aircraft and tank factories. Thirdly, and not by any means least, Moscow was the seat of government, and effective raids on the capital would not only disrupt military planning, but also have a powerful effect on morale.

In the early afternoon of 22 June, when it was judged that the Soviet defenders were fully occupied with the land battles, 180 Dornier Do 19As from KG 5 Hermann Göring and KG 3 Blitz set out from their bases near Warsaw. They crossed the front at 6,000m (19,686ft), heading north-east and still climbing. To confuse the defences, they flew a dog-leg course towards Moscow. All the aircraft carried two SC 1000 Hermann bombs and incendiaries.

As it was known that the gun defences of Moscow were heavy, their assigned bombing altitude was 7,000m (23,000ft), chosen because it was near the effective ceiling of Soviet 76mm M31 and 85mm M35 anti-aircraft guns. The day was cloudless, with only industrial haze to obstruct visibility:

> We turned in from the north-east and began our attack run, surprised that no fighters had yet intercepted us. Four Gruppen turned to search for specific targets; we bored straight ahead for central Moscow, taking drift sights to allow us to gauge wind strength and direction.
>
> Ahead, we could just make out the coloured domes of the Kremlin cathedrals. This was our aiming point. The defences woke up and treated us to desultory anti-aircraft fire. At first it burst well below us, but gradually the gunners got the range. It was only slightly heavier than what we encountered over England.
>
> With a cry of 'Los', our observer released the bombs, and we followed the formation around to a westerly heading. Not until we were homeward bound did Soviet fighters appear—Polikarpov I-16s and a few MiG-1s. Most seemed disinclined to close with us, but one I-16 pilot was more aggressive. Following a head-on attack, he collided with the outside man in our Staffel, shearing off his left vertical fin and rudder. We watched horrified as our comrade spiralled down out of control. Only three parachutes opened before we lost sight of him.[6]

From such a high altitude, the bombing was not very accurate. Nevertheless, it achieved its purpose. GAZ 1 and GAZ 30 were hard hit, as was Zavod 37. Bombs fell in and around the Kremlin area. The Cathedrals of the Annunciation and the Archangel were damaged, as was the fortress. Stalin's state apartments and the Praesidium offices were wrecked. Extensive damage was caused to the ministries area, and to two rail termini. A direct hit demolished the statue of 'Iron Feliks; in Dzerzhinsky Square, and blew out the windows of the NKVD building. Lenin's mausoleum in Red Square was rocked by a near-miss, and his left ear fell off.[7]

The cost to the Luftwaffe was light. Two Uralbombers had fallen to Flak, while a third had been rammed by the enthusiastic I-16 pilot. Five others had sustained varying degrees of damage. However, losses of less than two per cent were considered acceptable.

Having established that the Moscow gun defences were not as formidable as previously thought, the Germans launched further raids on Moscow at lower altitudes. Although ever-increasing numbers of Soviet fighters were encountered, losses remained light. Also attacked was Leningrad, home of three major tank factories and the Soviet Baltic Fleet anchorage at Kronstadt. Other strategic targets were Kiev, Kharkov, Rybinsk and Yaroslavl.

Meanwhile the Wehrmacht stormed through Soviet territory, taking over a million prisoners as it encircled and destroyed entire Russian armies. In the north, Leningrad was besieged, in the south the Ukrainian cornfields were overrun, and Army Group Centre came within sight of Moscow, but the delay in launching the invasion now made itself felt. Unseasonal rains turned dirt roads into quagmires, impassable to wheeled vehicles, while the destruction of the Soviet Armies had taken longer than expected. Then, in December 1941, with victory apparently in sight, the campaign was halted by 'General Winter'.

Even before 'Barbarossa', a few Soviet armament factories had begun to relocate eastwards, out of bombing range. The rapid German advance accelerated this process, and more than 1,500 factories and other installations were uprooted. This was a major undertaking; each day an average of more than 300 goods trains headed east, some with journey times of up to a fortnight.[8] Luftwaffe strategic reconnaissance failed to reveal either the extent or the import of these movements, and the chance to interdict them decisively was missed. Although thousands of railway interdiction sorties were flown, these were almost entirely in support of tactical operations.

THE EASTERN FRONT, 1942

By December 1941 the Heer, exhausted, and ill-equipped to deal with the extremes of the Russian winter, ground to a halt. Although it had inflicted incredible losses on the enemy, the Soviet Union had still been able to form whole new armies. In mid-December the Russians began a counter-offensive.

The Luftwaffe, hampered by problems with supply and maintenance as well as by the climate, had difficulty in achieving even a 30 per cent serviceability rate. However, it fought back as well as it could. The Fern-kampfdivision, by now three Geschwader strong, took no part in these operations; the logistics were too formidable. During October and November a dozen full-strength raids were flown by all three Geschwader. Including essential flight testing, nearly 20,000 tonnes of fuel had been expended – 41 trainloads, almost one-sixth of the total German fuel production! In the winter of 1941/42, this was unaffordable. Meanwhile the Army Group commanders, having been driven back by the Soviet winter offensive, were clamouring for more close air support. Seeking a short-term solution, Jeschonnek called for the production of strategic bombers to be halted in favour of more Stukas.

The Soviet winter offensive had seen the new Russian tank, the T-34, operating *en masse* for the first time. Although crude to the point where German experts dismissed it as unable to meet their own quality-control standards, it was in many ways superior to the latest German PzKpfw IV; and its sheer crudity lent itself to easy and rapid mass production.

In consultation with the Army Group commanders, Kesselring took the overview: hordes of 'cheap and cheerful' T-34s might easily overwhelm the badly outnumbered Panzers. While it was impossible to halt tank production completely by bombing the factories, output could be considerably reduced. Those that survived could be delayed, if not actually prevented, from reaching the front. The means were to hand. The strategic bombers of Fernkampfdivision 1 had the range and hitting power to accomplish this. Hitler, offensively minded as always, agreed. Jeschonnek[9] was quietly 'promoted sideways' and replaced as Luftwaffe Chief of Staff by the thrusting Wolfram von Richthofen.

The fuel restrictions imposed on the Fernkampfdivision during the winter had made Hitler more aware of the importance of seizing the Caucasian oilfields, and this became his priority. Army Groups North and Centre were limited to little more than holding actions, and divisions from them were sent south. Thus reinforced, Army Group South was then split into Army Groups A and B. The latter would advance eastwards, and, on reaching the Volga, would mask the important communications and production centre of Stalingrad. Army Group B would cross the Don east of Rostov and then make a two-pronged attack, to the Maikop oilfields and to the oilfields at Grozny, then on to Baku on the Caspian Sea.

Hitler saw the capture of Stalin's own city as a personal propaganda *coup*, but, persuaded by his ground and air commanders that it was only a matter of time, he agreed to hold off until the vital oilfields were secured. For the time being, it was to be invested on the west bank of the Volga. It could not, however, be totally isolated: not only were the Russians expert at building pontoon bridges, but many supplies were carried into the beleaguered city by river traffic.

'Smiling Albert' Kesselring also spotted another Luftwaffe failing during the summer of 1942. Attaching Luftflotten to army groups tended to give the latter proprietorial rights that they were reluctant to relinquish. In quiet sectors, and there were many of them, the *Kampfgruppen* tended to be used for inessential operations. Thus massaged, the figures indicated that the parent army group needed the units in question, whereas in practice they could be better employed elsewhere.[10] Having assessed individual needs, Kesselring reinforced the Mediterranean with spare units; the others were centralised under Generalmajor Kurt Pflugbeil as Fliegerkorps Ostland. This move was vigorously opposed by the Luftflotte commanders, but they were overruled by Kesselring.

URALBOMBERS GO FORTH

In April Fernkampfdivision 1 concentrated its efforts on reducing the flow of Russian tanks to the front. It was time for the Uralbomber to live up to its name. The first problem was strategy. Was it best to go for the nearest (and easiest) targets first and then gradually extend ever deeper? Or should the initial strike be distant, with later attacks working inwards? Korten argued that the effect of the first course would be to telegraph his punches, giving the Soviets time to strengthen their defences. For the same reason, it was preferable to attack several targets simultaneously. While follow-up raids would be necessary, they could be carried out at infrequent intervals. Both Kesselring and Richthofen strongly agreed. A long-range strike against multiple targets was best.

Accurate navigation was going to be difficult. In some areas, iron-ore deposits caused magnetic anomalies strong enough to affect aircraft compasses; neither, at such extreme distances were radio bearings sufficiently accurate. However, as the ultra-high-flying Ju 86P-2s of the OKL-controlled Aufklärungsgruppe had discovered, given even reasonable visibility one geographical feature could be identified from great distances. South of Kazan, the Volga formed what was in effect a series of great lakes some 300km long and in places up to 30km wide. With luck, these could supply a useful waypoint before the final leg.

Target selection was relatively easy. Omsk and Novosibirsk were far to the east of the Urals and out of range. The primary targets were tank factories at Magnitogorsk, Chelyabinsk, Nizhniy Tagil and Sverdlovsk. Selected more for their convenient location[11] than for their products, the secondaries were Kuibyshev, Ufa, Kazan and Molotov[12], all of which produced aircraft and aero engines rather than tanks. Chelyabinsk was the primary target for all three Gruppen of KG 5 Hermann Göring; the other three primaries were allocated two Gruppen each.

In the morning of 16 April 1942, airfields in occupied Russia resounded to the thunder of aero engines as nine Gruppen—a total of 261 Do 19s— took off and headed east, forming up as they went. Meanwhile tactical bombers with fighter escort flew diversionary raids to keep the Soviet fighters busy. Forecast conditions were good, with a light crosswind of

MAJOR SOVIET TANK AND AIRCRAFT PLANTS WEST OF THE URALS, 1942

Location	Plants	Product
Gorki	Zavod 112, Krasnoye Sormovo	Tanks
	GAZ 21, Ordzhonikidze	Lavochkin fighters
Kazan	GAZ 22	Pe-2 aircraft
	GAZ 16	Pe-2 engines
Kirov	Zavod 38, Kolomensky Loco	Tanks
Kuibyshev	GAZ 18	Il-2 aircraft
	GAZ 22	Mikulin aero engines
MoscowM'tischi	GAZ 30	Il-2 aircraft
	Zavod 40	Tanks
Saratov	GAZ 292	Yak fighters
Stalingrad	Stalingrad Tractor Works,	
	F. Dzerzhinsky	Tanks

no great significance. Passing well south of Moscow, they were opposed by a handful of MiG-1s, but suffered no losses:

> We were going to attack Ivan in his lair! In Asia no less! It was a great adventure! But hour after hour passed, and still the dark and brooding forests stretched to the horizon. The Volga came and went. Was there no end to this vast country? Gradually our mood changed. We grew silent. Could we really conquer a country this large?[13]

Chelyabinsk lay on the eastern slopes of the Urals. Aided by clear visibility over the last 100km, the Kommodore brought KG 5 straight in to bomb. The target was unmistakable—a factory complex several kilometres long, and still under construction. This was Tankograd (Tank City), home of Zavods 75 and 100. So huge was it that the bombers could not miss, and they planted 182 SC 1200 bombs within its perimeter. Then, pursued by moderate anti-aircraft fire, KG 5 turned for home, but two Dorniers had been damaged. One streamed fuel from a holed wing tank; the other had a stationary propeller. With a seven-hour return trip ahead, neither would make it back.

Further south, two Gruppen of the inexperienced KG 2 failed to find Magnitogorsk, which was veiled by low cloud. After some searching, they located Kuibyshev and bombed GAZ 18 (Il-2 attack aircraft) and GAZ 24 (Mikulin aero engines). By now desperately low on fuel, they turned for home. To the north, Zavod 9 (T-34 tanks) at Sverdlovsk was heavily bombed by I. and II./KG 3, who lost three Dorniers to ground fire, while

Zavod 183 (T-34 tanks) at Nizhniy Tagil was raided by I./KG 2 and III./KG 3. Broken cloud hindered the latter attack, and damage to the Zavod was slight.

The return flight was fraught. The Gruppen were scattered across eastern Russia, and the wind had backed and freshened, making fuel critical. Soviet fighters rose to intercept from Kazan, Saratov, Gorki and even Yaroslavl, and ferocious running battles took place in which sixteen Dorniers were lost, three to ramming attacks. Darkness fell as they entered the Moscow air-defence zone, giving them a much-needed respite from the fighters, but this brought its own problems. Unable to fly in close formation at night, the bombers had to split up and make their individual ways home.

One by one, the exhausted Dornier pilots coaxed their machines on to the ground, five being badly damaged in landing accidents. In all, 46 Dorniers were written off, and another eight returned with varying degrees of damage. Worst hit of all was the Magnitogorsk force. Having spent too long searching for the target, they had become critically short on fuel. Five crews baled out over German-held territory and another six crash-landed on forward airfields, while fourteen failed even to reach the front. Having also had three bombers downed by Soviet fighters, their losses were a terrible 51 per cent. In comparison, the other forces had not fared too badly, with a loss rate of just under nine per cent. This was acceptable only if the damage inflicted was severe. It was three days before the results were known. Three out of five production lines at Tankograd had been halted and various storage buildings had been wrecked. Zavod 9 at Sverdlovsk had lost two lines out of three, but damage at Zavod 183 at Nizhniy Nagil was light. At Kuibyshev, both GAZ 18 and GAZ 24 had been hit, but the effect on production was assessed only being as moderate.

What 'Beppo' Schmid's intelligence organization failed to realise was that, while buildings could be wrecked, it was extremely difficult to destroy heavy machinery.[14] The hasty evacuation of factories eastwards had caused considerable disruption. To minimise this, the hardy and primitive Russians had often set up production lines in the open, then built the factories around them. This same principle was applied to damaged factories: once the rubble had been cleared, limited production

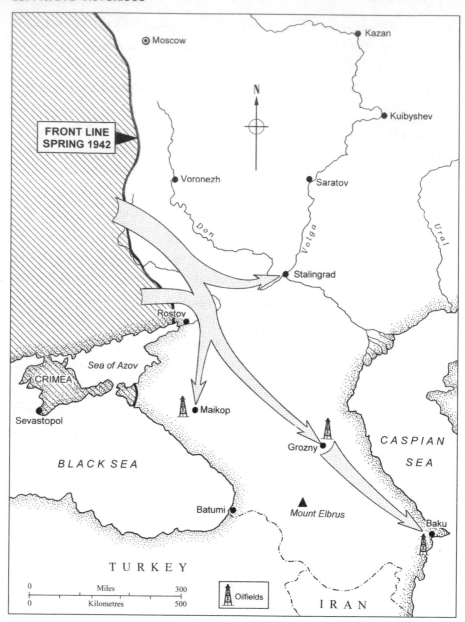

The Caucasus Campaign 1942. The huge peak of Mount Elbrus hampered air operations in the region. Maikop fell on 9 August 1942, but Baku was not reached until early December.

resumed immediately. While there was a loss of efficiency, the process was made easier by the crudity of many products, notably the T-34. The effects of the raid were thus overestimated by Luftwaffe intelligence.

Of the four primaries, the intelligence assessment was that heavy damage had been inflicted on one, moderate to heavy damage on a second and moderate damage on a third, while the fourth had escaped attack altogether. Several conclusions were drawn, not all of them optimistic. First, attacking targets at such extreme range was fraught with risk. On this occasion the weather had been fairly kind; it would often be less so. Secondly, the absence of navigational aids, allied to potentially unreliable compasses, could easily result in disaster. Thirdly, the anti-aircraft defences at such valuable targets would be strengthened, adding to the hazards. Fourthly, after such an exhausting trip, it was important for the bombers to return to base in daylight. Finally, the fierce fighter reaction on the return leg had contained an unwelcome surprise. The Dorniers had been attacked by what appeared to be Petlyakov Pe-2 dive bombers — with a difference. They were in fact Pe-3s, fast, long-ranged and with a fixed armament in a solid nose of two 20mm ShVAK cannon and two 12.7mm UBK machine guns. This was firepower enough to down even the largest bombers.[15] With their performance and range, they were a factor to be reckoned with for the future.

✦ ✦ ✦

It was all of ten days before the Uralbombers were back to full strength. The question of how next to proceed was hotly debated. Overall losses on this single mission exceeded 17½ per cent, which was clearly unaffordable. Dare they be risked again?

To Korten, the answer was clear. It would, he hoped, be another three months before Tankograd could get back to full production, and in the meantime there were several nearer targets to be attacked. If these could be really hard hit, it would make the Soviet Army even more reliant on its plants in the Urals — and they were more than ten days away from the front by rail. In addition to armaments factories, the ramshackle and overloaded Soviet railway network was ripe for destruction.

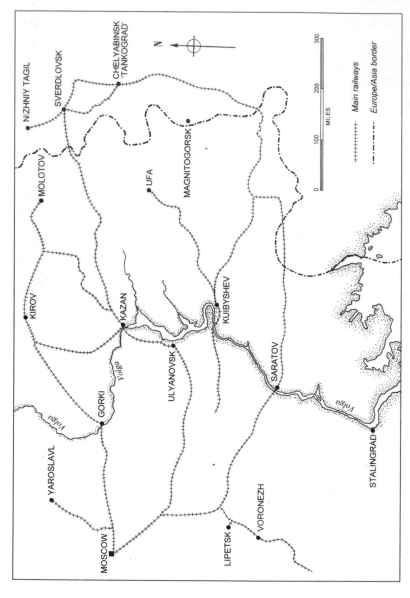

Strategic bombing targets in the Soviet Union. The vast distances told equally against both sides. For the Luftwaffe, the main problem was navigation: the wide Volga river, with its series of lakes, was the most reliable landmark. The delivery of Soviet tanks, guns and munitions from factories in the Urals took up to three weeks because of the inadequate rail system.

Richthofen demurred. The tactical units of the Luftwaffe were tired and overstretched, while the Soviet Air Force was appearing in ever-growing strength. He insisted that least some effort be spared for bombing the aircraft factories, most of which were beyond the range of Pflugbeil's twin-engined force. Korten, aware of the threat posed to his raiders, agreed.

The greatest weakness of the southerly German thrust was that it would leave a long and exposed northern flank. To offset this, Army Groups North and Centre both began limited offensives designed to keep the Soviet armies in play before the two-pronged advance in the south began. Fliegerkorps Ostland interdicted rail and road communications behind the front, while Fernkampfdivision 1 carried out three maximum-strength raids on Stalingrad. The Tractor Factory named after Feliks Dzerzhinsky was laid waste, and the dock area was wrecked from end to end. By this time the Crimea, with the exception of the Maxim Gorki fortress at Sevastopol, had been overrun. This stronghold was attacked by a single Gruppe of Do 19s using PC 1400 Fritz bombs to penetrate hardened targets. Shortly afterwards, the garrison was taken by storm.

During the summer of 1942 Korten's Dorniers raided Kirov, Moscow, Kazan, Gorki, Yaroslavl (the home of the biggest Soviet rubber producer) and Saratov (which had a major oil refinery as well being as a major producer of Yakovlev fighters). They also sought to sever rail links, mainly those across the mighty Volga, at Kazan, Ul'yanovsk, and other places. They found, however, like many airmen before and since, that bridges make exceptionally difficult targets. Be that as it may, the shortfall on Soviet tanks delivered to the front was 22 per cent.[16]

Meanwhile Army Group A swept on. The going through the Caucasus was rough, and the towering presence of Mount Elbrus, 5,642m (18,500ft) high, did not help air operations. The invaders reached Maikop on 9 August, only to find that the well-heads had been sealed with concrete. However, this had been foreseen, and the oil was flowing again by October. Grozny was taken shortly afterwards, although Baku did not fall until early December. With the oilfields secured, Army Group A consolidated its gains. Meanwhile Army Group B pushed towards Stalingrad.

The city was invested from the middle of October by the Sixth Army under Generaloberst Friedrich von Paulus. Soviet resistance was stiff. As the Volga at their backs was three kilometres wide, they had nowhere to go.

By now, however, Army Group B was badly overstretched. The Sixth Army's flanks were held by German allies—Romanians, Italians and Hungarians. Although sadly deficient in tanks and artillery, the Soviets counter-attacked in late November, breaking through the Germans' allies. After just four days, the Sixth Army was encircled.

The Führer was not best pleased. Ordering von Paulus to stand firm, he demanded that the Sixth Army be supplied by air. There was a precedent. At the beginning of the year, cut-off German forces in the Demyansk pocket had been supplied in just this way. At Stalingrad, however, the problems were much greater. With a minimum daily requirement of 600 tonnes, and the Russian winter fast setting in, this was an impossible target, and Kesselring flatly refused to countenance the idea.

Furious, Hitler sacked him, sending him to command in the Mediterranean, which was then a backwater. To replace Kesselring, Hitler chose Wolfram von Richthofen—not that it did him the slightest good. Richthofen was equally adamant that attempting to supply a quarter of a million men by air, in the Russian winter, was complete folly. To Hitler's chagrin, he was forced to accept this. Paulus was ordered to break out, which he did in early December, with relatively few casualties.[17]

The final noteworthy event of 1942 was the re-equipment of I. and II./KG 5 with the Dornier Do 219. Derived from the earlier bomber, it carried the same bomb load some 15 per cent further at an economical cruising speed of 370kph (200 knots). Raids on targets in the Urals would become easier, though not until 1943.

NOTES

1. Historically, Ju 52 losses on top of those sustained in earlier campaigns crippled multi-engine training, leading to a severe shortage of bomber pilots and observers from 1942. However, as noted in Chapter 2, the adoption of the Ju 86 by the schools would have prevented this.

2. Previously EprGr 210, now two Gruppen strong.
3. The assumption here is that a fourth Gruppe of Ju 87s was added to StG 77 while the remaining Stukas, less those detached to form the two carrier air wings, formed an operational reserve of about 60 aircraft. In fact, Luftflotte 2 fielded 170 Ju 87s (103 serviceable) from StG 1 and StG 2; 65 Do 17s of KG 2, of which 47 were serviceable; and 36 Do 17s and 78 Ju 88s of KG 3 (18 and 66 serviceable, respectively). KG 2 is assumed to be equipping with the Do 19A.
3. Korten actually succeeded Jeschonnek as Luftwaffe Chief of Staff in 1943. He was killed in the bomb plot against Hitler in July 1944.
4. Jeschonnek committed suicide in 1943.
5. Harold Faber, (ed.), *Luftwaffe*, p. 117.
6. Hans Kamansky, *Uralbomber Pilot*. Ramming by Soviet fighters was quite common in the early days; about 200 instances of ramming attacks were recorded in 1941 alone. Often the pilot survived. Boris Kobzan accounted for four Luftwaffe bombers by ramming in his total of 28 victories.
7. Lenin's left ear was notorious for coming adrift.
8. Alexander Boyd, *The Soviet Air Force Since 1918*.
9. Jeschonnek remained as Chief of Staff but shot himself in 1943. In this account he only shoots himself in the foot.
10. Mike Spick, *Luftwaffe Bomber Aces*. The suggestion was actually made by General der Flieger Paul Deichmann, but it was not adopted.
11. Fuel constraints dictated that they must be fairly close to their primaries, and close to the direct route home.
12. Now called Perm.
13. Kamansky, op. cit.
14. This was also the case with Allied bombing of German plants.
15. In all, about 500 Pe-3s were built, but had the Luftwaffe possessed the strategic bomber force described it is reasonable to assume that production would have been greater.
16. Historically, Soviet tank production in 1942 barely kept pace with losses. A shortfall of 22 per cent would be very significant.
17. Paulus's Sixth Army proved invaluable in the fighting to come.

9 Night Defence, 1939–43

BEFORE the outbreak of war, the Luftwaffe had not taken night fighting at all seriously. The time-honoured method of air defence was to use searchlights to illuminate raiders so that the anti-aircraft guns could shoot at them. The accuracy of the gunnery was confidently expected to be greatly increased by the introduction of the newly developed radar-tracking. The searchlights and guns were concentrated around cities, ports and production centres. To fill the gaps, and to allow forward defence over the sea, an experimental night-fighter force was formed; after all, Luftstreitkräfte fighters had operated at night in 1918, and, while they achieved little, they had established that night fighting was not totally impossible.

The beginning was modest. In 1939 a mere Staffel, 10./JG 26, was formed at Jever under the command of Oberleutnant Johannes 'Macky' Steinhoff[1]. This unit flew the Messerschmitt Bf 109D, a single-engine, single-seat day fighter, its only modification for night use being the removal of the cockpit canopy. This marginally improved the pilot's view; it also cut down on the annoying reflections caused by the dashboard lights. The blind-flying instruments of the Bf 109D were inadequate, and the aicraft totally lacked night navigation aids. Thus handicapped, it could only operate on clear moonlit nights. However, as these conditions were needed by enemy bombers to find their targets, this was not considered too important. Co-operation with searchlights proved of limited value, especially in cloudy conditions. Ground control often had a fair idea of the whereabouts of enemy bombers, but guiding the fighters to within visual distance was simply not possible.

In the period known as the 'Phoney War', RAF bombers flew over the Reich, dropping leaflets. Luftwaffe Commander-in-Chief Hermann Göring took this as a personal affront. In August 1939 he had declared that if ever an enemy aircraft penetrated the Ruhr, he could be called 'Meier'.[2] It was egg-on-face time.

Late in 1939 Göring convened a meeting to discuss night fighting. Two factors coloured the proceedings: first, the threat was apparently minuscule, and secondly, the problems of bringing a fighter to within visual distance of a bomber at night (typically 200m or less) appeared intractable. As the discussion drifted, Göring sought to inject a little enthusiasm. Launching into Wagnerian mode, he recalled how the Richthofen Geschwader, of which he had been the last commander, operated in the night skies over Flanders in the summer of 1918, and how they had navigated by following the roads, searching the lighter night sky against which an intruder would be silhouetted.

Steinhoff could remain silent no longer. Rising to his feet, he tried to explain that conditions were now different. The cloudy North German skies in winter were a far cry from Flanders in summer, while the greater altitudes made picking out landmarks over the blacked-out countryside all but impossible. This being the case, the pilot rarely knew his own position with any degree of precision. Sightings were purely a matter of chance, and often the bomber was swallowed up in the darkness before an attack could be made. Nor were searchlights of much use. Their beams were diffused by industrial haze from the cities they were protecting, while they were just as likely to dazzle the friendly fighter as illuminate the hostile bomber.

Steinhoff should have known better than to contradict the 'Fat Controller'. Sternly, he was admonished: 'Sit down on your little arse, young man. You've still a long way to go before you can join the discussion here.' Deflated, Steinhoff transferred to day fighters shortly afterwards. However, his words had struck a chord with one person present, and the following day Udet had a quiet word with his commander-in-chief: 'Steinhoff's right, you know. Even if you are told the exact position of an enemy bomber, how can you possibly hope to find it if you don't know precisely where you are to start with? When you have to get within 200m just to see it?'[3] Udet was probably the only man in the Luftwaffe who could talk to Göring like this, and the latter finally conceded the point. What to do about it was another matter entirely. Göring was a technical illiterate, and Udet was little better. Chief of Signals Wolfgang Martini was ordered to seek a solution, but, with more important matters brewing, it was assigned a low priority.

The Luftwaffe took the easy option — more fighters. IV./JG 2 was formed at Jever in February with a complement of Bf 109Ds, but with little success. Having shot down just one bomber, and having lost several fighters in operational accidents, often on landing, it was disbanded in the summer of 1940. The script changed during the night of 15/16 May 1940, when the RAF bombed the Ruhr. The Flakartillerie, still awaiting its radar directors, failed to live up to expectations. Even though little damage was caused, it forced the Luftwaffe to realise that it needed an effective night fighter.

As noted in Chapter 2, the Messerschmitt Bf 110 was proving disappointing by day, and was scheduled for replacement, but as it was available it became the main Luftwaffe night fighter by default. It was fast enough to overhaul the British bombers of the period, and its endurance was sufficient for lengthy patrols. Its firepower was adequate, and it carried a second crewman to assist with navigation and lookout. Most importantly for night operations, its handling was benign and its landing gear rugged.

BIRTH OF THE NACHTJAGDFLIEGER

Gradually a scratch night-fighter force was built up, based on the survivors of Zerstörergruppe I./ZG 1. In July IV./JG 2 traded in its ineffective Bf 109s for Bf 110s, and other units followed to form the first Nachtjagdgeschwader. On 17 July 1940 the first night-fighter division was formed under the command of Oberst Josef Kammhuber. Previously Kommodore of KG 51, Kammhuber had only recently returned from captivity in France. He knew nothing about night fighting, but this allowed him to start without preconceived ideas. A superb organiser, he quickly put night air defence on a sound footing. An abstemious non-smoker and nitpicker, he failed to gain the affection of his men, to whom he was widely and impolitely known as '*Wurzelsepp*'.[4]

Initially the searchlights and guns were grouped around the major target areas, but this meant that the raiders could only be engaged over or near the target. Moreover, the defending fighters were all too often illuminated by the searchlights. Even worse, they were shot at, and sometimes hit, by 'friendly' Flak. The solution adopted was to move the searchlights away from the cities to form an illuminated belt across the line of approach of the bombers, patrolled by night fighters. The guns, with radar-laying now entering service, remained in their original positions.

The problem remained how to bring a fighter consistently to within visual range of a bomber at night. Searchlights were less than effective. A major difficulty was the haphazard nature of the average attack. Guy Gibson, a young Hampden pilot, recalled: 'We could choose our own route; we could bomb from any old height; sometimes we could carry whatever load we wished, we could go off at any time.'[5] The result was dozens of bombers wandering apparently at random through the skies over Germany, searching for their assigned targets. When they reached the searchlight belt, they simply ran the gauntlet: they opened the throttles to cross it as quickly as possible. A night fighter had to be extremely well placed to intercept in the short time available.

German radar development was in many ways advanced, but its application to night fighting had been generally neglected—with one exception. An experimental airborne radar had been flown in a Ju 52 in the summer of 1939; some two years after the RAF had first investigated it. Unfortunately, while the British gave airborne radar top priority neither Göring nor Udet appreciated its import and German airborne radar remained in limbo.

HIMMELBETT

Kammhuber understood that aid from the ground was vital. But with what? The Freya early warning radar had a maximum range of about 120km(75miles), but it could neither discriminate between closely-spaced aircraft, nor determine altitude. The Würzburg gun-laying radar had the required degree of precision, and could determine altitude, but was too short-ranged; just 35km(22miles), and had a very narrow beam, making precision search difficult. But with Freya to provide directional clues, the disadvantages could be overcome. The painstaking Kammhuber made the most of what was available at the time.

The result was Himmelbett, a belt of overlapping areas, or boxes, each containing a Freya, two Würzburgs and a patrolling night fighter. The Freya detected an incoming bomber, then handed it off to one of the Würzburgs while the other Würzburg tracked the fighter. Given fairly accurate positions for both aircraft, the controller could then attempt to steer the fighter to within visual distance of the bomber.

It was a clumsy and overcomplicated system, prodigal of both technical resources and manpower. A handful of gifted crews and controllers demonstrated that it could be made to work, however, and German night-fighter successes commenced. The average time for a single interception was ten minutes but, with the British raids so diffuse, this hardly mattered. Still later, the system was improved when the Würzburg Reise, with a maximum range of more than 65km (40miles), replaced the original model.

This was not enough. Kammhuber, who had been promoted to Generalmajor in October 1940, was thinking ahead. Even though the bombers needed clear visibility to find their targets, faulty weather forecasts often meant that they turned up in less than ideal conditions. In these circumstances, in order to hunt them down he needed an onboard fighter radar.

AIRBORNE RADAR

A year had elapsed since the first trials, but little progress had been made. In 1941 a few experimental 'breadboard' sets were fitted into fighters, and a few victories were claimed. At first, unreliability was a major problem. This was gradually overcome, and in February 1942 the first four radar-equipped production fighters (Ju 88s) reached the Nachtgruppen.

The pilots were far from enamoured with the new system. Many had been strongly opposed to the tight ground control imposed by Himmelbett, feeling that it robbed them of all initiative. Now matters were even worse. They had become mere chauffeurs at the whim of their radar operators, who directed them, often wrongly, from indications given by mysterious 'black boxes', the workings of which they neither understood nor in most cases, wished to understand. To cap it all, performance and handling were reduced by the forest of aerials sprouting from the fighter's nose. Had he lived, the rotund Reichsmarschall would have sympathised.

The Bf 110 also suffered from weight growth. It was not just the 'black boxes': a radar operator was shoe-horned into the already cramped rear cockpit. While the sensible course would have been for him to replace the wireless operator/gunner, permission was refused on the grounds that the 110s might be called upon to operate by day.

The new airborne radar was called Lichtenstein and given the code-name 'Emil-Emil'. Instead of having to guide the fighter to within visual distance of a bomber, it was now enough for the controller to position it within 'Emil-Emil' range, a maximum of about 3,000m. This made the task of both the Flieger and the controllers much easier — at least in theory.

Even when the radar worked as advertised, things were far from simple. The radar indicated the relative position of the bomber at any given moment. Interpreting what it was doing was far more difficult, and to many this smacked of the black arts. In level flight, a contact off to starboard might appear to be at the same altitude, but if the fighter banked towards it the indications changed and it would appear to be higher. Only a handful of gifted operators could manage the mental gymnastics involved. Teamwork was also at a premium, and pilots had to learn to trust their operators.

Teamwork was fortuitously aided by an arbitrary decision by the Führer. Early in 1942 he decided that Kammhuber had enough electronic resources and did not need searchlights. He ordered them redeployed. Kammhuber protested strongly, but to no avail. He later admitted that this had, in fact, been for the best. The Himmelbett boxes had been set up in front of the searchlight belt. To many pilots, the temptation to wait until the bomber emerged into the illuminated zone before attacking was too great, but the removal of the searchlight belt forced pilots to trust their controllers and then, with the introduction of airborne radar, their 'sparkers'. A few gifted crews led the way, proving to the others that the 'magic' really could be made to work. During the first months of 1942 British bomber losses steadily increased, although not to the point where they became prohibitive. Later that year the bombers introduced the first primitive countermeasures. The electronic battle had begun.

INTRUDERS

Himmelbett had not been cobbled together overnight, and, at first, all Kammhuber had was his largely ineffective 'cat's-eye' fighters. However, there was an alternative. Likening the bombers to wasps, he determined to smoke out the nest. Night bombers would be most easily found over or near their airfields, which at night would be lit up when operations were in progress. Visible from miles away, these would be a magnet for intruders, which could patrol the vicinity of known bomber airfields, seeking targets of opportunity.

The Bf 110 was too short-legged for the task, which would require lengthy patrols over enemy territory. Fortunately an alternative was to hand. A number of Junkers Ju 88C-2 and Dornier Do 17Z-10 bombers had been converted to Zerstörer by the introduction of solid noses containing a combined cannon and machine-gun armament, and these had been assigned to the nascent night-fighter force. A further advantage was that they could carry a worthwhile bomb load internally, typically a mix of SC 50s and incendiaries. Based in the Netherlands, these aircraft formed the nucleus of the first Fernnachtjäger (long-range night fighter) unit, NJG 2.

As planned, the intruders would operate in three waves. The first wave would patrol known bomber airfields in time to disrupt take-offs, when, heavily laden and clawing for altitude, the bombers would be at their most vulnerable. The second wave would be timed to intercept bombers returning over the North Sea. The third wave would seek out the airfields to create mayhem during the landing phase. The bomber crews, tired after a long mission, would be less alert because they were nearly home, and, with many bombers returning to the same base, they would switch on their navigation lights to reduce the risk of a collision. This should make them easy pickings. However, such Teutonic precision did not work well against the rather haphazard British methods, and in practice it became catch-as-catch-can! General Martini's signals organisation quickly discovered that, when a raid was planned for that night, the bombers tested their radios during the morning, while the afternoon was quiet. Called the 'Adolf thanks you very much' early warning, the intruders could be brought to readiness in plenty of time.

Intruder missions started cautiously. In July 1940 they were confined to sorties over the North Sea, aimed at catching returning bombers near their own coast. Then, in early August, the Fernnachtjäger began to range inland, probing the defences. As experience was gained, they became more daring.

Successes in 1940 were few. Eighteen victories were claimed, not all of which could be confirmed, for twelve operational losses. Of these, one fell to a fighter and a second to ground fire. Four simply vanished without trace, and four were written off on their return. The final two were wrecked in accidents.

The year 1941 was more successful, with 138 claims for 31 losses,[6] the majority of which occurred in the period of good weather between April and August. However, analysis showed that virtually all the claims were scored in the air. Despite appearances to the contrary, there was little evidence that enemy bombers were being destroyed on the ground. Much of this was due to sheer bombing inaccuracy. When intruders were known to be in the vicinity, all airfield lighting was switched off. Left without a target, and with their night vision impaired, many intruder observers failed to land their bombs within the airfield boundaries. Even those that did rarely caused significant damage. Another factor, which could not possibly have been known to the Fernnachtjäger at the time, was that a proportion of their claims, possibly one quarter, were for training aircraft. While many of these were from operational conversion units (OCUs), this had no immediate impact on the bomber squadrons.

Kammhuber sought a means of increasing the disruption, and he struck lucky. An officer on his staff, visiting his brother in France, discovered that about a million small mortar bombs had fallen into German hands.

They were scheduled for dismantling in order to recover the minuscule quantity of copper in each but, despite the fact that over a year had passed, the process had barely started.[7] As Luftwaffe bomb canisters needed little modification to carry them, Milch agreed to their being requisitioned.

Thus armed, the Fernnachtjäger used them over England from September 1941. Released from a height of 1,000m, four canisters each with 200 bomblets, would cover an area of about two hectares (roughly four football pitches). Even if they hit nothing of note, the disruption they caused was huge. After a raid, bomblets with delayed-action fuzes (or merely duds) had to be fielded, while those that did detonate spread sharp-edged shrapnel over a wide area. Following such raids, the bombers suffered a spate of punctures which, if they occurred on take-off, could cause serious mishaps. 'Delousing' after a raid was a severe drain on scarce manpower, although this was alleviated by enlisting the aid of the local Home Guard and the Air Training Corps. Whilst the former often suffered from myopia and lumbago, the latter were delighted to help out on operational airfields.

BOMBERS IN DECLINE

By late 1941 the numerical strength of Bomber Command had hardly increased from its pre-war level. The reasons were fourfold. Operational losses to all causes were rising. The Manchester, one of the new breed of heavy bombers, was a failure. Then, with the Battle of the Atlantic going badly, all too many bomber squadrons were being diverted to Coastal Command. Finally, the Middle East constantly demanded bombers to interdict Rommel's supply lines.

Night after night, British bombers set off for the Third Reich, but, propaganda aside, how much damage were they actually doing? To answer this, crews were required to photograph their aiming points. The results were appalling: only one crew in every three was managing to place its bombs within five miles of the target. In the haze and smoke-shrouded Ruhr, this figure dropped to barely one in ten. This finding caused members of the British War Cabinet to question whether Bomber Command should be disbanded, and its assets used elsewhere. After all, there was little point in exporting bombs to Germany if no significant damage was caused. However, aware that Bomber Command was the only force able to strike directly at Germany, Prime Minister Churchill kept faith, subject to improvements being made.

The bombing failure lay in the extreme difficulty of navigating over the vast area of Occupied Europe. Once the enemy coast had been crossed, the bombers often flew for two hours or more without once seeing a recognisable landmark. Unpredictable changes of wind and weather often meant that they could be 50 miles adrift, and, moreover, the Germans, like the British before them, grew adept at providing decoy targets to draw the bombs.

Only the best and most experienced crews consistently arrived in the target areas. Once there, blinded by searchlights and unable to see the ground, their bombing was inaccurate. Radio navigation and blind-bombing aids such as the Kampfflieger possessed in 1940 were unworkable over the great distances involved. Distance also played a part in loss rates: RAF bombers over the Reich were at risk for far longer than their Luftwaffe counterparts had been over England. Luftwaffe intelligence naturally knew that British bombing was very inaccurate, and in part attributed it to the efficiency of the night defences. With his night fighters accounting for the majority of bombers shot down, Kammhuber took much of the credit, reinforcing his favourable view of the complex and wasteful Himmelbett system. He could not have guessed what was in store.

A DESPERATE MEASURE

On 22 February 1942 Kammhuber was given a new adversary when Air Marshal Arthur ('Bert') Harris replaced Richard Peirse at the head of Bomber Command. With hindsight, it was no contest. Defensively, the German commander was resting on his laurels, secure in the knowledge that Himmelbett could not be bettered. By contrast, Harris knew that his Command was ineffective. His task was to turn it round and carry the fight to Germany.

A careful study of the German night defence system revealed its Achilles' heel. The allocation of night fighters to specific 'boxes' meant that, typically, a single fighter patrolled an area some 30km (20 miles) wide. While bombers flew widely scattered in space and time, the fighters and ground-control system in each box could cope with the occasional bomber that entered it. Nor were the Flak defences around major targets overstretched. Rarely were more than a handful of bombers overhead at any given moment.

Kammhuber was blinkered by his own bombing background, in which a mid-air collision is the night bomber pilot's nightmare. Over England, Luftwaffe night bombers flew in a 'Krokodil', spaced four minutes apart. Kammhuber assumed this to be the greatest concentration achievable if the risk of collision were to be reduced to acceptable levels. Tailored to this 'worst-case scenario', his Himmelbett boxes could reasonably be expected to engage a maximum of one in every three bombers passing through them. If just one in every three engagements resulted in a victory, British bomber losses would be nudging the unacceptable; and Flak, plus the inevitable operational wastage, would tip them over the edge.

What Kammhuber failed to see, but Harris saw clearly, was that the risk of collision could be allowed to mount appreciably if losses to fighters and Flak could be reduced. The Luftwaffe night-fighter defences relied heavily on technology, but the technology was designed to cope with a numerically limited threat, and if this could be significantly increased Himmelbett would very quickly unravel. The same reasoning applied to Flak in the target area. The gunlaying radars could engage only one target at a time, and although this was unfortunate for the designated target, many other raiders would pass unmolested.[8]

Little changed during the first months of Harris's tenure. The Nachtjagd-flieger defending the north were kept busy, as raids continued on the U-boat yards at Bremen, Hamburg and Kiel. Close to or on the coast, these were relatively easy for the British to locate at night. A rather more difficult problem was the minelayers, which, in addition to the North Sea, penetrated to the Baltic training areas at low level. The most destructive raid at this time was made on the old Hanseatic port of Lübeck in March.

The shock came during the night of 30/31 May, when Harris launched over a thousand bombers against Cologne. Concentrated in three streams, they smashed through the Himmelbett belt at the rate of six aircraft a minute. Only a small proportion of the night fighters available were able to make contact, while the Cologne Flak defence was degraded, apparently confused by sheer numbers. Bomber losses were comparatively light.

Harris had solved the problem. By attacking on a narrow frontage, concentrated in time, his bombers had comprehensively defeated the Himmelbett system. Only a few boxes had engaged, and these had far more targets than they could possibly cope with. The rest of the Nacht-jagdflieger had been left impotent, circling their beacons, while the Cologne Flak had been swamped. As young Halifax pilot Leonard Cheshire put it: 'Here at last is the first bomber battle, and the bombers are winning.'[9] Bf 110 pilot Wilhelm Johnen saw things differently: the bombers 'flew at short intervals, almost goose-stepping towards the weakest night fighter areas; then they crashed by sheer weight through this area like a broad stream driven through a narrow channel.'[10]

To Kammhuber, this was totally unexpected. Previous British raids had been perhaps 250-strong, as had that on Lübeck. Josef 'Beppo' Schmid of Luftwaffe Intelligence, by now a Generalmajor, later confirmed that a thousand bombers had indeed taken part in the attack on Cologne. Disbelieved, he was accused of defeatism. How on earth, argued OKL, could the enemy apparently quadruple their striking force overnight?

Faced with the probable disbandment of Bomber Command, Harris had seized upon the idea of a thousand-bomber raid to impress the War Cabinet. It was touch and go: his first-line strength was less than half this. He had scraped together every last bomber and pilot—instructors, advanced pupils, training aircraft—and to make up the magic number had borrowed back several Coastal Command squadrons.[11] The stakes were high: failure would have meant the end of Bomber Command.

Why Cologne? The city was chosen for two reasons, first because it was within range of 'Gee', a radio navigation aid carried by the leading bombers, and secondly because the bends of the Rhine would show up clearly by moonlight. Afterwards, the results were there for all to see. Appalled by the devastation,[12] Goebbels imposed a news blackout—a measure only possible in a totalitarian state.

Having gone to such lengths to gather his force, Harris was reluctant to disperse it, but the First Sea Lord insisted on the immediate return of the Coastal Command squadrons. Even without them, Harris still managed to launch two massive raids of about seven hundred bombers during June, against Essen and Bremen.[13] However, cloud covered both targets and the bombing was scattered. Bomber Command's training assets were then released from the front line.

HIMMELBETT DEFEATED

In July, Harris switched from infrequent but huge raids to unrelenting pressure; three or four raids a week, typically 150 or more strong. The now proven bomber stream was retained, and it was concentrated on a narrow frontage. On each occasion more than 150 German night fighters were airborne, patrolling their boxes, but, despite the fact that the bombers had to cross the Himmelbett belt twice, barely one-sixth of the fighters available were called into action, and rarely were more than six victories claimed.

Kammhuber was slow to recognise that his clever but cumbersome defensive system was now of limited use. His immediate and impetuous reaction was to increase its depth to two or even three boxes. However, while night victories rose, this was due more to the greater familiarity of the night fighter crews with 'Emil-Emil' than to the increased depth of the Himmelbett defences.

A BETTER WAY

The Staff of Fliegerkorps XII set to work to analyse the new British bombing tactics. One thing was soon apparent: the bomber stream was vulnerable. At take-off, six or more airfields needed to launch up to 30 bombers each. As this was time-critical, laden bombers would be queueing nose-tail round the perimeter track. After take-off, they had to climb out and join up with aircraft from other bases, at a predetermined location. At this point, the night sky was crowded and, to avoid collisions, the bombers were forced to burn their navigation lights. Only when they set course did they switch their lights off.

Right, upper: The prototype Dornier Do 19 in flight, showing the position of the dorsal gunner. Initially regarded as an interim type, the Do 19 was surprisingly successful, giving the Luftwaffe a strategic bombing capability that it would otherwise have lacked.

Right, lower: 'Somewhere in France': an elderly Hurricane Mk I with a two-bladed, fixed-pitch propeller. Luftwaffe Experte Werner Mölders, who flew a captured example, described it as 'decidedly inferior to the Bf 109'.

Below: The best British bomber of the early war years, the Wellington suffered heavy losses to Luftwaffe fighters in daylight, forcing the RAF to revert to night bombing. Fitted with a dorsal antenna, a Wellington later became the world's first airborne warning and control system (AWACS) aircraft.

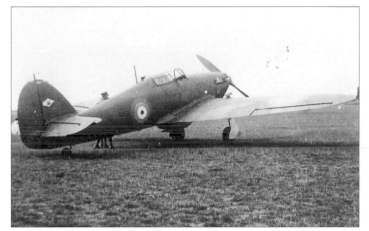

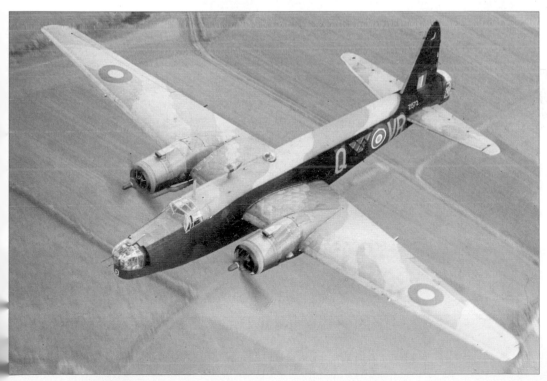

Left, upper: 'Now chaps, if only you had done this . . .' A former RAF Fighter Controller replays the raid in which Reichsmarschall Göring was killed to an audience of former Luftwaffe flyers in 1978.
Left, lower: Faulty intelligence brought about the myth that the RAF was down to its 'last fifty Spitfires'. The myth was exploded on 15 September 1940 when the 'Big Wing' from Duxford—five squadrons led by Douglas Bader (centre)—intercepted a huge German raid on London.
Above: Used as a bomber in the Spanish Civil War, and to a lesser degree over Poland, the Ju 52 ('Tante Ju'), became the mainstay of the Luftwaffe's transport force.

Below left: In 1918 Hermann Göring was the final commander of the Richthofen Geschwader, in which Ernst Udet commanded a Jagdstaffel. Twenty years later they were, respectively, Commander-in-Chief and a subordinate general This picture is unusual in that Göring's Blue Max, which he was even rumoured to wear in bed, is not blatantly on display.
Below right: Generalfeldmarschall Erhard Milch, a superb administrator, had before the war made Lufthansa into the world's pre-eminent airline. Göring's deputy at the outbreak of war, he was twice bypassed for the top job.

Left: Although he was a disaster as Head of the Technical Office, Udet made a considerable contribution to the future of the Luftwaffe by turning a blind eye to the officially forbidden development of German jets. On Göring's death, he was shunted sideways to become General der Jagdflieger—a position he held until his health broke down and he was transferred to the Reserve.

Below left: Generalfeldmarschall Albert Kesselring was arguably the most capable German commander of the war. He was the head of Luftflotte 2 in 1940 before succeeding Göring as Commander-in-Chief of the Luftwaffe, a position he held until the end of 1942. He was then sacked for rightly refusing to attempt air supply to the surrounded Sixth Army at Stalingrad. He saw out the war in overall command of the Mediterranean theatre.

Below right: Generalfeldmarschall Wolfram Freiherr von Richthofen, a cousin of the 'Red Baron', succeeded Kesselring as commander of Luftflotte 2 in 1940, then two years later succeeded him again as Luftwaffe Commander-in-Chief. A worthy successor, he was well able to stand up to the Führer's wilder flights of fancy. Diagnosed as having a brain tumour, he was retired to the Reserve in November 1944.

Above: Armed with four 20mm cannon, the Westland Whirlwind long-range fighter had the speed to catch the Uralbomber and the firepower to destroy it. This aircraft is from No 263 Squadron.
Below: A diesel-engine bomber, the Junkers Ju 86 was unreliable. Once refitted with petrol engines, however, it became the workhorse of the multi-engine operational conversion schools, guaranteeing a continuous supply of trained crews for the bomber units.

Left: His Bf 109E-7 sporting the new overseas paint job, this Jagdwaffe pilot looks worried about the prospect of a long flight to protect Do 19 Ural-bombers. Psychologically, fighter engines always sounded rough on overwater flights.

Below: The FW 190A, 'the rough, tough cavalry horse', seen here in northern France, was in most respects superior to the Spitfire V. In the background is a force-landed Blenheim bomber.

Bottom: The Swordfish, despite its antiquated appearance, was remarkably effective as both a dive- and a torpedo-bomber. Fitted with ASV radar, this 820 NAS aircraft, here above HMS *Ark Royal*, took part in the attack on Schlachtgruppe Lütjens.

Right: Catapult-launched from battleships and cruisers, the cannon-armed Arado Ar 196A-3 was the most potent aircraft flown by the Bordflieger. It was handicappped, however, by its lack of performance.

Below: The OKL failed to appreciate the massive industrial strength of the United States. Seen here is a production line of B-24 Liberators, which played an important part in the Battle of the Atlantic. More than 18,000 were built.

Bottom: Flaps depressed, a Dornier Do 219 takes off bound for Tankograd in the Urals. Luftwaffe strategic bombers made significant inroads into Soviet war production.

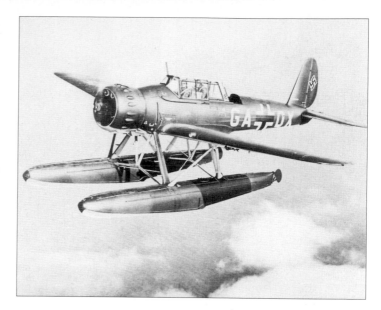

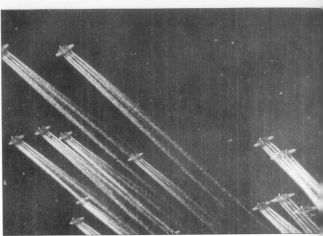

Opposite, top left: A Russian Lavochkin fighter, possibly an La-5FN, makes a steep diving attack on a Uralbomber formation.

Opposite, top right: Tired after the deepest penetration raid ever, and in somewhat ragged formation, Dornier Do 19 Uralbombers of KG 5 return from their first raid against Soviet tank factories in Asia.

Opposite, centre: Underwing drop tanks were used to extend the range of the FW 190G—the Ju 87's replacement—on the Eastern Front. Bomb-carrying slings can be seen beneath the fuselage of this aircraft.

Opposite, bottom: A factory-fresh Bf 110G-4 night fighter awaits its final checks before being cleared as operational. Clearly visible are the drag-inducing radar aerials and the exhaust shrouds. With these handicaps, the Messerschmitt's performance was barely adequate against enemy heavy bombers and by late 1944 the aircraft had been almost completely phased out

Right: Josef Kammhuber cobbled together the Himmelbett system of night fighting using what was available, even though it was not always best suited for the task. His downfall was inflexibility, and when a change in enemy tactics rendered Himmelbett ineffective he was unable to meet the challenge and was replaced. His physical resemblance to the folklore character Wurzelsepp is quite marked.

Below: Josef 'Beppo' Schmid (centre) had an undistinguished career as head of Luftwaffe intelligence. Why he was chosen to command the night fighter arm in succession to Kammhuber remains unclear.

Left, top: The Me 410A-1 was the best Luftwaffe intruder of the war, with a performance close to that of the RAF Mosquito. It often created havoc on English airfields. This view shows the remotely controlled rearward-firing gun barbettes.

Left, centre: The de Havilland Mosquito NF.XII was a superb night fighter, and unsurpassed as an intruder. It gave the Nachtjadgflieger terrible problems.

Left, bottom: The Heinkel He 177 Greif represented an attempt to maximise performance by using coupled engines to give four-engine power with twin-engine drag. While this seemed like a good idea at the time, engine fires and mechanical problems all too often resulted in crashes, as seen in this photograph.

Above: The Heinkel He 277 was a rehash of the deeply flawed He 177, with a revised wing and four separate engines. This revision almost exactly paralled British experience with the Avro Manchester, which was developed into the superb Lancaster, but the change came years too late.

Below: Republic P-47 Thunderbolts were the first American fighters encountered by the Luftwaffe. Introduced as bomber escorts, they were supplanted in this role by the much longer-ranged Mustang. In the final year of the war they were mainly used for strafing.

Left, upper: Separated from its formation, a straggling B-17G Flying Fortress tries vainly to defeat an attack by an Me 262.

Left, lower: This variant of the Grumman F6F Hellcat carrier fighter, armed with 20mm cannon and with radar to track shadowers in cloudy conditions or at night, made convoy attacks by Vultures unprofitable in the final war years.

Below: A Focke-Wulf FW 190G, with an underslung BV 246 glide bomb. These weapons were widely used against shipping during the Normandy invasion.

Right, top: The bi-fuel, rocket-propelled Me 163 was a short-range point-defence interceptor, but the success of the jet-powered Me 262 ensured that it was of little value. More lethal to its pilots than to the enemy, it never became more than an interesting experiment.

Right, centre: An Me 262A-1a of II./JG 7. This unit was just one of many that cut a deadly swathe through USAAF daylight bomber formations.

Right, bottom: The Sturmvogel was the Jabo variant of the Me 262. Penetrating the enemy air umbrella over the invasion area with ease, it continually attacked both the beaches and shipping. So effective was it that the success of the Allied landings was in doubt for many days. Only when its airfields were rendered unusable by bombing and strafing was it pulled back.

eft, top: The conventional Jadgwaffe could not be ntirely denuded of experienced pilots to aid the apid expansion of the jet-fighter force. The two-eater Me 262B was produced to aid the onversion training of newly hatched pilots.

eft, centre: Conventional night fighters were rarely ble to intercept the speedy Mosquito light bomber nd, to overcome this, many Me 262Bs were fitted vith radar. The world's first jet night fighters, they vere too fast to be used against RAF Lancasters.

eft, bottom: The Arado Ar 234B Blitz was the vorld's first jet bomber to enter service. Rather

slower than the Me 262, it was, however, longer-ranged. The odd-looking structure above the cockpit is a periscopic bomb sight used for shallow diving attacks.

Above: The four-engine Arado Ar 234C, built in small numbers, provided sterling service in the reconnaissance role with Kommando Götz, virtually confirming the invasion build-up area.

Below: Gunports blackened, a Lockheed P-80A Shooting Star returns to base after an attempted interception of an Me 262 Jabo over France in the summer of 1945.

Top: The lightly loaded de Havilland Vampire was the first jet able to operate from grass fields. Two squadrons deployed to France from July 1945 but, apart from fleeting skirmishes, their aircraft were never able to bring the Me 262 to battle.
Above: The Amerikabomber—the Messerschmitt Me 264A. This aircraft was intended to bluff the United States into believing that American East Coast cities were vulnerable to nuclear attack.
Below: One of the specially modified Boeing B-29s which in August 1945 dropped 'Little Boy' on Munich and 'Fat Man' on the Wolfsschanze, bringing the war to a swift end.

Once under way, the bomber stream was very concentrated. To many at Fliegerkorps XII, it was a target-rich environment. They reasoned that good results could be obtained by feeding the night fighters into it to hunt autonomously with 'Emil-Emil'. Three main suggestions were presented to Kammhuber. First, intruder activity against the bomber bases should be stepped up to disrupt the take-off phase. Secondly, the join-up phase should be attacked, preferably by radar-equipped fighters, or otherwise by intruders. The greatest difficulty was in finding the location, but powerful, new, long-ranged Mammut and Wassermann early-warning radars, set up on the North Sea coast, could even detect bombers over England as they rose above the radar horizon. Third, autonomous hunting in the bomber stream had the potential to bring far more fighters into contact than could Himmelbett.

Kammhuber understood night fighting under close ground control; after all, he had pioneered it. He also understood intruder operations. However, never having been a fighter pilot, he failed to understand the concept of letting the Nachtjagdflieger off the leash to hunt freely, even though they now had a limited ability to 'see' in the dark. He had two major objections — the difficulty of positive identification was sure to result in 'own goals', and pursuit of the bomber stream would take his fighters far from their bases. Landing away from base would fragment his force, which would spend much of the following day regrouping. Flexibility was not his forte. He once demanded to be given enough Ju 88s to form a second intruder Geschwader, arguing that if raids could be seriously disrupted both the Himmelbett system and the Flak would benefit. With luck, bomber losses would then rise to the point where they became unsustainable. His request was denied.

As Chief of Staff, Richthofen was far more concerned with events on the Eastern Front, which had priority for the Ju 88, with the Mediterranean a close second. Kammhuber then demanded that he be allowed to use 'Emil-Emil' fighters over England. This nearly caused a riot. The Luftwaffe was still reeling from the daring commando raid on Bruneval in February 1942, when the perfidious islanders had purloined enough parts of a Würzburg radar system to compromise its secrets, and OKL really did not want to risk a Lichtenstein falling into British hands.[14] They did, nevertheless, concede that radar fighters could be used to within 30km of the English coast. As a sop, Kammhuber was given priority for the new Messerschmitt Me 410 Hornisse, which was scheduled to enter service in February 1943.[15]

The intruders were supported by the few Luftwaffe bomber units remaining in the West, although these were too weak to be able to mount more than nuisance attacks. Carried out mainly on lightly defended targets on or near the coast, these were the so-called 'Baedeker Raids'.[16] The British controllers soon learned that single contacts heading inland from the East Coast were usually Fernnachtjäger, and intercepting them became a priority.

By 1942, Fighter Command had a sophisticated radar-based ground control system far superior to the German Himmelbett, while its fighter radars were the best in the world. Moreover, from the end of April of that year, the superb Mosquito began to supplement, and then replace, the workmanlike Beaufighter. Thus harassed, intruder losses rose. The German aircraft were forced to fly fast and low to avoid enemy fighters, patrol time was reduced, and navigation became much more difficult. Low flying reduced losses to enemy fighters, but accidents increased. Overall effectiveness declined.

Attempts to disrupt the bomber stream at the rendezvous were at first moderately successful, but when the British realised what was happening they threw out barrier patrols ahead of the bombers. Night fighter fought night fighter in bitter but usually inconclusive skirmishes, while the bombers remained largely untouched.

As 1942 drew to a close, the partisans of autonomous night fighting prevailed. On 17 November Operation 'Adler' was launched. Forewarned, the Nachtjagdflieger assembled in Staffel strength over beacons near the projected track of the bomber stream, whence they were vectored into it. Although several victories were claimed, 'Würzelsepp' remained unconvinced. 'Adler' threatened his carefully nurtured Himmelbett, which he still refused to see as being now obsolete. At his insistence, 'Adler' was discontinued.

BOMBERS RESURGENT

The build-up of the British strategic bombing force had been seriously delayed by events in the Battle of the Atlantic. With the U-boat force apparently on the brink of a famous victory, the needs of Coastal Command took precedence. In 1943, however, the pendulum swung violently in the opposite direction. The cause was a combination of Allied air and sea power, backed by advanced detection technology and new weapons such as the homing torpedo.

The Luftwaffe was powerless to intervene. As seen in Chapter 5, the Vultures of KG 40 had been reduced to relative impotence, and it was therefore suggested that Schlachtgruppe Ciliax, centred on the aircraft carrier *Peter Strasser*, should be revived, but events moved too rapidly for this to be an option. From early 1943, heavy-bomber units assigned to RAF Coastal Command started to revert to Bomber Command, which gained strength more rapidly than 'Beppo' Schmid would ever have believed possible. Raids of between 400 and 700 aircraft now became commonplace.

The British seemed to have at least partially solved the problem of target-finding. At the head of the bomber stream flew crews specifically tasked to mark the target with coloured lights and coloured flares.[17] A few of these had been shot down, and Luftwaffe investigators reported that they carried previously unknown radio aids which, German scientists were appalled to discover, were far beyond their own current technology. The British could now accurately navigate long distances without ever seeing the ground, and bomb targets through solid cloud. This was a disturbing development.

INTRUDER RENAISSANCE

Almost completely defeated by winter 1942, the intruders took on a new lease of life when NJG 2 started to re-equip with the Hornisse. Longer-legged than the Ju 88, it was also much faster — fast enough, indeed, to give even the superlative Mosquito problems. By Easter 1943 the intruders had once more become a viable force, and by midsummer individual Hornisses were, time and time again, attacking British bomber airfields, disrupting stream take-offs and destroying aircraft on the ground. Nor were the night fighter airfields spared. Fernnachtjäger losses were light, and they even had the capacity to make an occasional attack on the crowded airfields of the US Eighth Air Force. The British, of course, retaliated, using their own intruders to patrol Hornisse bases, though to little effect. The truth was that fighters were far more vulnerable on the ground than in the air, and catching them there was difficult.

One thing Kammhuber badly wanted to use was Düppel.[18] Developed in 1942, this consisted of metallic strips which could produce a radar echo similar to that of an aircraft; used by his Hornissen, it would throw British night defences into disarray. This was a hot potato: such a simple jamming method could easily be copied, and the thought of the British using such a countermeasure caused many a German sphincter muscle to tighten.[19] Permission to use it was strictly *verboten*.

Shortly after midnight on 24/25 July 1943 the blow fell. Having largely evaded the attentions of the Hornissen, several hundred bombers raided Hamburg, dropping 'Window' (Düppel) as they came, to jam the Würzburg and Lichtenstein radars. Electronically blind, the fighters and the Flak were impotent. The dozen bombers (1.6 per cent) shot down were hit entirely by chance. Other raids followed in quick succession, and Hamburg was laid waste. For Kammhuber, it was the end. Shortly afterwards he was replaced, amazingly, by Schmid.

The overall commander of Reich air defence was Generaloberst Hubert Weisse. He took immediate steps to redress the situation. Former bomber pilot Oberst Viktor von Lossberg had been one of the main protagonists of 'Adler'. A protégé of Erhard Milch and a night-fighter expert, he advocated the introduction of a loose form of ground control, with greater autonomy given to the fighters. This was code-named 'Zahme Sau'. By now the Bf 110 carried long-range under-wing tanks. Once vectored into the bomber stream from its beacon, it would continue until low on fuel or ammunition, after which it would land at the nearest airfield to replenish. Often it would not return to base until the next day. The other method proposed was the brainchild of former bomber pilot Major Hajo Herrmann. In this, single-engine fighters would fly over the target areas, searching visually. Often bombers would be silhouetted against the fires below. It was called 'Wilde Sau'. One result of the destruction of Hamburg was that the Führer demanded reprisals. Former Inspector of Bombers Generalmajor Dietrich Pelz was appointed Angriffsführer England.[20] In addition to units already in place, Pelz received the intruder force, while the Vultures of II./KG 40 were redeployed from Norway to Northern France.

NOTES

1. 'Macky' Steinhoff became one of the highest-scoring fighter aces of the war, with 176 victories. He became Chief of Staff in the post-war Luftwaffe.
2. Hans Kamansky recorded in *Uralbomber Pilot* that KG 5 Hermann Göring was scurrilously known as the 'Meier Geschwader'. When the Führer found out, the Kommodore was relieved of his command.
3. Ernst Udet, *Film Pilot to Fighter General*.
4. Kammhuber's gnomic features and pointed ears gave him a supposed resemblance to this figure from German folklore. The division expanded and in August 1941 became Fliegerkorps XII.
5. Guy Gibson, *Enemy Coast Ahead*.
6. The actual figures were 123 claims for 28 losses. Historically. Hitler halted intruder operations in October 1941, allegedly because he wanted the bombers shot down over Germany 'where the people could see them'.
7. Copper was a scarce strategic material in Germany, and in fact the bombs were all dismantled, fortunately for those who might have been on the receiving end.
8. Some four decades later, target priority was still a problem.
9. Leonard Cheshire, *Bomber Pilot*.
10. Wilhelm Johnen, *Duel Under the Stars*. While not actually the Cologne raid, it was a typical night fighter pilot's impression.
11. This was part of Harris's original plan, but it was blocked by the Admiralty. Given the revised scenario, it seemed reasonable to reinstate it, with the assumption that Churchill would have overruled the First Sea Lord. Harris had managed to scrape together more than a thousand bombers from his own resources.
12. Concerned at the survival of the cathedral, Harris made it the aiming point for inexperienced crews. His faith in their inaccuracy was not misplaced!
13. In reality these were also 'thousand' bomber raids'.
14. British analysis had more or less deduced how Lichtenstein worked, and countermeasures were in hand. This was confirmed in May 1943 when Herbert Schmidt and Paul Rosenberger defected to Scotland with their Ju 88.
15. Ordered by Hitler, these were reprisals for a devastating attack on the old Hanseatic city of Lübeck in March 1942.
16. Actually a little later, but we have to allow the alleged Teutonic efficiency to work sometimes.
17. The Pathfinder Force was now up and running.

18. 'Window' to the British, 'chaff' to the Americans.
19. The British had already thought of it, but held it back until such time as a resistant radar could be developed.
20. This appointment was actually made earlier, in March 1943.

10 War in the West: The Middle Years

WHEN, in 1941, the bulk of the Luftwaffe moved east for 'Barbarossa', a rump of Luftflotte 3 remained in the west. Apart from units such as KG 40 and KGr 606, which were assigned to supporting the Kriegsmarine, its effectives were just two Jagdgeschwader, JG 2 and JG 26, with a nominal strength of 240 Bf 109 fighters, and four medium bomber Gruppen with a mere 105 He 111s, including the understrength KGr 100, the only Luftwaffe Pathfinder unit. The function of Luftflotte 3 was to keep the British in play until the conquest of the Soviet Union had been completed, after which the Luftwaffe would return to the west in overwhelming strength. As this was confidently expected to occur at the end of 1941, the strength of Sperrle's emasculated air fleet was judged to be sufficient.

On the far side of the Channel, RAF Fighter Command was undergoing a massive expansion. As the Luftwaffe's offensive action tailed off, so the British became increasingly aggressive, mounting huge fighter sweeps over northern France. With nothing to gain by opposing them, the heavily outnumbered Jagdflieger often refused battle. The British countered by sending a few bombers with the fighters to act as bait.

From 21 June 1941 the campaign intensified. Two sweeps were launched, and bitter fighting took place. In return for five RAF fighters and one bomber shot down, the Jagdflieger lost nine Bf 109s and six pilots. From then on, the defenders became more circumspect. As they were not defending their homeland, they had no need to become involved in desperate defensive actions, but could use hit-and-run tactics to erode the enemy's strength. The pendulum thereby swung the other way.

Operating on the principle 'maximum harm for minimum risk', the Jagdflieger interspersed hit-and-run attacks with 'nibbles' at the fringes of the British armadas. From this point on, they often achieved victory/ loss ratios in excess of 3:1.

Apart from tactics, many factors contributed to this. The massive British expansion had inevitably resulted in a high proportion of inexperienced pilots, whereas the Jagdflieger had many experienced leaders and, to a degree, better aircraft.[1] In addition, the hordes of British fighters, often more than 200-strong, got in each other's way and created confusion, whereas the numerically small Jagdgruppen were better able to control the local situation. Finally, the Luftwaffe had cobbled together a radar detection and reporting system which offset British radar coverage, which, at high altitude, reached deep into France. This became the first campaign in which ground control was available to both sides. The British were unaware of the adverse victory/loss ratio. The reason was simple: the high confusion levels had resulted in overclaiming, which masked the true figures.

Aircraft quality became a factor. The new Bf 109Fs outclassed the early Spitfires, but in turn could be outfought by the Spitfire Vs. Then, in autumn 1941, the FW 190A entered service. A superb dogfighter, by spring of 1942 it had achieved dominance over the Spitfire V, and only with the arrival of the Spitfire IX in the summer of 1942 was it equalled.

The Jagdflieger paid a heavy price for what was, after all, a sideshow. All too many leading Experten[2] had fallen, Sprick, Balthasar, Pingel and Adolph among them. These men were irreplaceable. Then, on 7 March 1942, the man who many reckoned to be the greatest fighter pilot of them all, was lost.

SPITFIRES GET THE KOMMODORE

Adolf Galland, Kommodore of JG 26 Schlageter, had fought since May 1940, virtually without a break. Shot down several times, including twice in one day on 21 June 1941, he had always returned to the fray, determined to dispel the cloud that had hung over him since the death of Göring. Worse was to come. Peter Göring, the nephew of the late Reichsmarschall, was killed on 13 November while flying as Galland's wingman. Utter exhaustion set in. Werner Mölders, who spent Christmas with JG 26, was shocked by his gaunt appearance and ordered that he be grounded. Galland appealed directly to Hitler, who allowed him to continue flying.

On that fateful March day, Galland led III./JG 26 off from Abbeville-Drucat. Beneath the cockpit his FW 190 carried his personal insigne — Mickey Mouse smoking a cigar and brandishing a six-shooter in one hand and a hatchet in the other. His rudder carried a laurel wreath enclosing the number '100', plus seven single victory bars.[3] He had but one regret about trading in his Bf 109F for the FW 190: the new fighter did not lend itself to his smoking his black cheroots in the cockpit!

The German fighters intercepted the British raid north of Montreuil, when it was already homeward bound, but broken cloud made a planned attack difficult. An inconclusive skirmish resulted, before ground control reported that the raiders were crossing out south of Le Touquet. Accompanied by the three members of his Stab, Galland set off in pursuit. Out over the Channel, he caught up: there were about a dozen Spitfires, dead ahead and lower. His preferred method was to approach with a full-throttle dive from astern, pulling up hard to dump excess speed, then attacking from the blind spot below his opponent.

It all went horribly wrong. Even as the Kommodore pulled out of his dive he was hit from behind. More Spitfires, previously hidden by broken cloud, were on his tail! Streaming flames and smoke, his wingman spun towards the voracious sea, while his second Rotte broke hard into the attack. And Galland?

Stunned by a glancing blow to the head, he slumped forward over the stick. Obedient to the pressure, his FW 190 nosed over into a shallow dive and began a lazy, irregular roll. By sheer good fortune, this made him a difficult target for the four following Spitfires, all of which were trying to finish him off. Sick and shaken, Galland recovered his senses in time to arrest his dive, only to see the Spitfire leader peering at him curiously from barely 20 metres away. His engine was running roughly; a glance at the instruments showed temperatures off the clock and pressures around zero. It was time to go. Jettisoning the canopy, Galland rolled inverted and fell clear. His parachute barely had time to open before he hit the water. Within minutes he was picked up by an air–sea rescue 'Shagbat' and flown to England.

Only one of the Stab returned to base, badly shot up. He reported seeing the Kommodore and his wingman hit, but, beset by Spitfires, he could tell nothing more. Like the Reichsmarschall before him, Oberstleutnant Galland seemed to have vanished into thin air. It was several days before it was known that he was a prisoner. At this point the Führer relented, and announced the award of the Eichenlaub to Galland's Ritterkreuz.

Galland's reputation had preceded him, mainly via the Swiss magazine *Interavia*, and at first he was treated as an honoured guest. However, his interrogation produced little more than to shed light on the fate of the Reichsmarschall some eighteen months before. A particularly intransigent prisoner, he was packed off to Canada by sea, barely escaping the rampaging U-boats en route.

NUISANCE RAIDS, MARCH–DECEMBER 1942

Offensively, the year was not a good one for Luftflotte 3. The so-called 'Baedeker Raids' were mere pinpricks, costly and of no real military value. Piratenangriffe, or 'pirate attacks', were flown in daylight by single bombers when heavy cloud and poor visibility gave them a fair chance of eluding the defending Spitfires, though only to find radar-equipped Beaufighters waiting. On at least one occasion a He 111 of KGr 100 was outflown by a Beaufighter and crashed without a shot being fired at it.[4]

Then, from August, Ju 86Rs with pressurised cabins began raids on southern England, from altitudes beyond the reach of defending fighters. However, as there were only two of them, as their maximum load was a single SC 250 and as the accuracy if their bombing was almost nil, they achieved little. These few stratospheric raids ceased after nineteen days, when a stripped-down Spitfire managed to intercept and damage one of them.

The two Jagdgeschwader on the Channel coast each had a Staffel of Jabos. At first equipped with Bf 109Fs, able to carry a single SC 250, they made high-speed tip-and-run raids against targets in the south of England.

From midsummer they converted to the FW 190, which carried an SC 500 and four SC 50s on underwing racks. They came in fast and low, beneath the radar, struck, and egressed. Once again, little damage of military significance was caused.

TRENDS AND PORTENTS

The middle of 1942 saw the huge RAF fighter sweeps tail off. Not only had the FW 190 maintained its general superiority over the Spitfire, but the British had found that better results were being achieved with low-level raids by light and medium bombers, which were much more difficult to defend against.

How much more difficult was shown by two daring daylight raids by Lancaster heavy bombers. The first, on 17 April, was against the MAN works at Augsburg, which made diesel engines for U-boats. This was a 2,000km round trip, across France and deep into Germany. Flying low, the Lancasters eluded the Luftwaffe detection and reporting system, and it was only by sheer chance that a Gruppe of JG 2 encountered the first wave, shooting down four out of six. The rest bombed successfully, although ground fire accounted for three more. Then on 17 October, 96 Lancasters attacked the Schneider armaments factory at Le Creusot in south eastern France. They completely eluded the Luftwaffe. Attacking from too low a level, one was blown up by its own bombs, but this was the only loss of the entire raid.

The US Eighth Air Force was committed to a policy of daylight raiding *en masse*. On 17 August it dipped its toes in the water with a raid on Rouen-Sotteville by a dozen B-17s, with a large Spitfire escort. Co-piloting the leading bomber was a Major Paul Tibbets. All returned safely. It was a small but significant start. More raids followed.

The Jagdflieger now encountered the same problems as had their British counterparts against the Do 19. On 9 October, Josef Priller[5] led III./JG 26 against an incoming raid. Misled by their size, three times he failed to gauge the correct altitude and levelled out too low. At his fourth attempt he succeeded, only to have the greatest difficulty in judging range. His pilots opened fire from too far away, and broke off much too early.

187

Many other fighter leaders experienced the same problem, and their complaints reached General der Jagdflieger Werner Mölders. He solved it by the simple expedient of 'borrowing' a Kette of Vultures from I./KG 40 to give his men practice. This did not make him very popular with either the Kriegsmarine or 'Iron Gustav' Harlinghausen, the Fliegerführer Atlantik, and only an appeal to Kesselring had made it possible. Not that 'Vati' was terribly concerned: he was already making himself unpopular in other quarters. Back in 1940, he and Galland had returned to the front from Berlin by train. En route, they had discussed the future — of the Luftwaffe and their own. Perhaps a little tongue-in-cheek, they had agreed that while Galland could be its Richthofen,[6] Mölders aspired to be its Boelcke.[7]

For the General der Jagdflieger, it was crunch time. Like the Red Baron, Galland had gone, if not actually to Valhalla, then to what in 1942 was its earthly equivalent — Bowmanville Camp in Canada. Mölders had long been concerned that his men were being 'flown out', kept on operations until fatigue dulled their senses. Their reflexes became sluggish, and they made fatal errors. Luftwaffe intelligence knew that Allied airmen were rested at intervals, often as instructors. Common sense dictated that his own men should receive at least equal treatment. A devout Christian, Mölders carried an ever-increasing weight of guilt as losses mounted, underlined by the fate of his friend.

Albert Kesselring, always considerate of his underlings, was inclined to agree, but Chief of Staff Richthofen was ruthless. Not an easy man to override, he pointed out that many of his Stuka crews had flown hundreds of sorties without a rest, often eight or ten a day. Then, while his bomber crews had flown fewer sorties, their hours at risk on operations were far greater. Were the Jagdflieger 'Schwuler'[8] that they needed rest? Infuriated, Mölders appealed to Hitler in person, only to be told that dying for the Fatherland was an honour to be sought, not avoided. At this point Heinrich Himmler, former chicken farmer and now Reichsführer SS, intervened. If, he suggested, the Christian God was so important to Mölders, then the General der Jagdflieger should be ranked alongside Pastor Dietrich Niemöller, the First War U-boat commander turned priest, who vehemently opposed the National Socialist regime.

Sacked and disgraced, Mölders considered suicide, but this was against his faith. He also considered defecting to England, but this was not consonant with his honour as a German officer. In the end he accepted martyrdom, and vanished into what the Gestapo called 'Nacht und Nebel' (night and fog). He was replaced as General der Jagdflieger by Gordon Mc Gollob,[9] the first man ever to notch up 150 victories.

Gollob, described as an ambitious and humourless man by Macky Steinhoff, was a Viennese whose unteutonic name was derived from an American friend of his thespian parents. A devotee of Hitler, he subscribed to the view that only total commitment to the cause of National Socialism could bring success. This made him completely ruthless. Flying the Bf 110 over England, his extravagant manoeuvres when attacked had led to the caustic comment: 'Typical Viennois — he even evades in three four time!'[10]

MENDING THE ROOF

Few Germans had any idea of the vast industrial potential of the United States, but one of those who did was the ailing Ernst Udet. Foreseeing a time when vast bomber fleets would attack the Reich, he sought to persuade OKL to step up fighter production, though at first without success. Milch had long been antagonistic to Udet, while the fact that the retired flying ace was now under Gestapo surveillance undermined his credibility with Kesselring and Richthofen.[11]

With no other options, Udet turned secretly to the recently promoted Generalmajor Josef 'Beppo' Schmid. Although initially sceptical, Schmid undertook to investigate. American industrial potential was assessed and the threat extrapolated. The result was horrific: in two years, at most, the USAAF would be able to mount thousand-bomber raids on a regular basis. Combined with the growing night strength of the RAF, this posed a deadly threat.

Schmid was in a quandary. He could not approach OKL with his findings without revealing his contact with Udet, which would not have been a good career move. In desperation, he turned to Albert Speer, Minister for Armament and War Production, and presented him with his projections. This was a masterstroke. Not only was Speer convinced, he had the ear of the Führer, he was widely respected by the military and he worked harmoniously with Milch, who handled aircraft production. To cover Schmid's back, he agreed to present the study as his own idea.

Gradually, plans to strengthen the daylight air defences of the Reich took shape. The first step was to increase the production of conventional fighters, and Richthofen rather grudgingly agreed to form an extra three Jagdgeschwader for home defence, even at the expense of the Russian Front. The Me 262 jet fighter was scheduled to enter service at the end of 1943, and the Ar 234 jet bomber in mid-1944. Jet propulsion was a step into the unknown. While it promised a quantum leap in performance, the engine technology was unproven. New heat-resisting alloys were needed, and these were dependent on adequate supplies of nickel and chromium. While nickel from Finland seemed assured, chromium from neutral Turkey was less so, as the Allies were trying to corner the market.

The Führer may not have been the 'Grösster Feldherr Aller Zeiten' (greatest military commander of all time) but he was a smart diplomatic operator. He suggested that if Turkey committed her entire output of chromium to Germany, he would facilitate her entry into Iraq to seize the northern oilfields of Mosul and Kirkuk. This would not involve Turkey joining the Rome/Berlin Axis; rather it would be presented as a *coup de main* to liberate Iraq from her British oppressors and return it to the benign rule of the old Ottoman Empire.[12] The Turks thought this a excellent idea, and agreed. The supply of chromium to Germany was assured. The British were most unhappy with this turn of events, and declared war on Turkey, but, badly overstretched as they were, they were unable to do much about what was a *fait accompli*.

One final but vital point arose during the development of the Me 262. Its thirsty turbojets meant that its endurance was short, typically well under an hour. In effect this meant that the jet pilot had to start planning his return to base shortly after take-off. This left little time for a leisurely climb-out and form-up, and even less for dodging around clouds under visual flight rules. Therefore Me 262 pilots had to be versed in instrument flying and preferably, in the event of an engine failure, in asymmetric flying as well. Here was an interesting problem. Was it best to take pilots from conventional fighters, teach them instrument flying and then convert them to the jet? Or should they take bomber pilots versed in instrument flying, and teach them to be fighter pilots? The ideal method would have been to convert Zerstörer pilots to the Me 262, but many of these were now with the Nachtjagdflieger.

Common sense prevailed. The main difference between fighter and bomber pilots was one of temperament. It was more difficult to turn a steady and stoical bomber driver into a dashing fighter pilot than it was to teach the latter instrument flying and engine-out asymmetric handling. From mid-1943 experienced fighter pilots were being selected to convert on to jets when the latter became available in the following year.

ALTERNATIVES

Fighter defence was not the only option against the threat posed by USAAF strategic bombers. The key to the situation was supply — the Atlantic convoy routes. As the Luftwaffe was now aware, keeping strategic bombers supplied with fuel, spares and munitions was a major undertaking. How much more so would it be for the USAAF?

As 1942 drew to a close it seemed probable that the U-boats would succeed in closing the North Atlantic to convoys. However, the writing was on the wall for those with eyes to see. Although sinkings were running at record levels, so were losses. Then with little warning, sinkings declined sharply while losses increased to insupportable levels. Dönitz, who early in 1943 succeeded Raeder in command of the Kriegsmarine, had no immediate hope of reversing the situation. What was needed was a fleet of true submarines, fast and with extended endurance underwater. New types were under development, as was a Dutch underwater breathing gadget called the schnorkel, but these were all for the future. In the short term, all Dönitz could do was to order his boats to sea, in a hopeless attempt to keep the pressure on. He also briefly considered using his surface units, of which *Tirpitz* was the most formidable, but the reinforcement of the British Home Fleet by the 16-inch-gun US Navy battleships *Alabama* and *South Dakota*[13] made this a non-starter.

Even before the war, several German companies were engaged in guided weapons research. By sheer good fortune, two of these came to fruition in 1943. The Henschel Hs 293 was basically a miniature aircraft built around an SC 500 light-case warhead, with a rocket motor. Fritz X was an unpowered glide bomb built around an armour-piercing warhead. Both were radio-controlled. What was more, the Vulture was available to carry them, two under the wings in the case of the Hs 293 and up to four Fritz X, two underwing and two internally. A Vulture Erprobungs-kommando had been formed in late 1942 to develop tactics for the new weapons, and in March 1943 it was redesignated I./KG 50[14] and deployed to Mont-de-Marsan. In that same month I./KG 40 was recalled to Bordeaux from Eleusis, allowing 5./KG 40 to return to Stavanger. In 1942 the Vultures had been elbowed out of the skies over the Atlantic by superior numbers of Allied long-range patrol bombers and carrier fighters. It now remained to be seen whether they could attack the convoys without sustaining prohibitive losses. Only time would tell.

Someone at OKL had been reading Douhet. In his book *The Command of the Air*, the Italian general had recommended the use of battleplanes — very heavily armed and armoured aircraft — to escort the bombers. This idea was adopted,[15] and field conversion kits were issued to one Staffel in each Vulture Gruppe. The result was the Do 19D gunship, with eight gun positions, each with either a single 20mm MG FF cannon or two 12.7mm heavy machine guns. The engines and crew positions were heavily armoured. In action, each pair of missile-carriers was accompanied by a gunship, while when they passed within reach of British long-range fighters they were escorted by at least two Schwärme of Ju 88 heavy fighters.

Despite the fact that the Luftwaffe was now obviously the prime mover, operational control of the Vultures remained with the Kriegsmarine. The reason was simple. 'Onkel' Karl's personneal were the experts in cracking British naval codes and monitoring convoy movements, and they still had a handful of U-boats at sea. This made them the obvious choice.

Before the war against the convoys started in earnest, there was a brief diversion. This was the Allied invasion of North Africa in February 1943,[16] coincident with Montgomery's offensive in the Western desert. I./KG 40 mounted several raids against the invasion fleet, but without much success. They did score heavily against Gibraltar at this time, which was packed nose-to-tail with aircraft, although this was not enough seriously to disrupt the Allied landings.

ATLANTIC OFFENSIVE RENEWED

The revitalised Vultures commenced operations with an unexpected success on 5 April 1943. A Kette of aircraft on armed reconnaissance stumbled across an eastbound monster — a large liner sailing independently, relying on sheer speed and erratic changes of course to evade interception by U-boats. This particular vessel was a troopship, and carried an entire US Army Infantry Division, some 14,000 men, complete with their light weapons. Hit by three Fritz X missiles in quick succession, it was torn apart and sank. Barely 300 men survived, and three Vultures had won the equivalent of a major land victory.

A much sterner test presented itself only three days later. A huge convoy of some 86 ships, with fourteen escorts including a light carrier, was located some 400km (250 miles) south of Iceland. The whole of II./KG 40 from Stavanger was sent after it — nine Vultures each with two Fritz Xs and nine more each with two Hs 293s, escorted by the Staffel of Do 19D gunships.

Once within visual distance, the German bombers split up. Closing into tight formation, the gunships headed straight across the convoy at 5,000m (16,400ft) in what appeared to be a bombing run. This drew off the six intercepting Wildcat fighters, while from rather higher and astern the Fritz X Staffel aircraft released the first of their weapons. Meanwhile the Hs 293 Staffel descended to low level, and unseen, attacked from the beam.

The first attack over, the high-level bombers reversed course and again let fly, while those at low level worked their way round to the opposite side before attacking once more. Of the 36 missiles launched, nine found their mark. Four of the five tankers in the convoy were set on fire, while the escort carrier was hit twice and badly damaged. Three freighters were also sunk; others were damaged by near-misses. One of the gunships was lost, although the unit gunners claimed fourteen victories – rather more than double the number of fighters involved. One of the low-level bombers fell to anti-aircraft fire and two more were damaged, but these losses were affordable. In all, it was a very successful operation.

This set the pattern for the months to come, when even larger Vulture formations were used. Tankers and troopships were priority targets; long-range Allied Liberators on anti-submarine patrols were driven off by the gunships. The Luftwaffe was aided by a fortuitous event:yet another 'monster' was sighted and sunk, again with a massive loss of life. This left the Allies in a quandary. Should they continue to route the huge vessels independently, or should they sail in convoy? To this there was no real answer. In convoy they lost their greatest advantage – that of speed – while their great size made them obvious prime targets. If reduced to the average speed of the convoy, they were at risk for four times longer on each crossing; nor, for various reasons, were fast convoys composed entirely of these big, fast ships a practical proposition. With little choice, they continued to sail independently. Once again, the Battle of the Atlantic hung in the balance.

THE REICH DEFENSIVE

The first American daylight incursion over the Reich was to Wilhelms-haven on 27 January 1943. Just three B-17s were shot down; the defending FW 190s of JG 1 lost seven of their number to the crossfire of the bombers.

The two Jagdgeschwader on the Channel coast had already concluded that the traditional attack from astern was far too dangerous and were pioneering the attack from head-on, but this reduced firing time to barely two seconds, and it was quickly apparent that fighter armament was inadequate. Various solutions were sought, including aerial bombing and the 21cm rocket mortar. However, both these were too inaccurate to be really effective. A much heavier gun armament was fitted, typically 30mm MK 108 cannon, an average of three hits from which was enough to down a four-engine bomber. They were often mounted in underwing gondolas, though the weight and drag of these weapons adversely affected performance and manoeuvrability. This did not matter too much: against unescorted bombers firepower was the main priority. The presence of Allied escort fighters was another matter. At first, they could barely reach the German border, allowing the Jagdflieger to delay their attacks until the escorts turned for home. Although the range of American escorts gradually increased during the year, in 1943 there were still many targets beyond their reach.

The 'round-the-clock' bombing campaign against the Reich by the RAF and USAAF could not be as intensive as planned. There were two main causes. The depredations of the Vultures in the Atlantic were causing a severe shortage of aviation fuel, while the activities of the intruders often caused extreme disruption to the Allied bomber airfields. To counter the former, massive B-17 raids were made against the Vulture airfields, albeit with limited success. The intruder bases were hit by tactical bombers in daylight, while RAF Mosquitos and Beaufighters patrolled them at night. The Luftwaffe took the obvious countermeasure, and the big Dorniers and Hornissen were dispersed.

August 17, 1943, was a memorable day for the Jagdwaffe. Some 363 B-17 Fortresses set off in two waves to raid the German ball-bearing industry at Schweinfurt and the Messerschmitt aircraft works at Regensburg. Their losses were appalling — 60 bombers shot down and a further 58 written off. The Jagdflieger lost a mere 25 fighters. That same night RAF heavy bombers raided the research facility at Peenemünde. Their way was cleared by a diversionary attack by just eight Mosquitos, which successfully misled the Luftwaffe ground controllers. British losses were moderate.

In late August the British attempted to raid Berlin in strength, but, warned by the monitoring service, the Luftwaffe was ready. Shortly after dusk some 50 Me 410s of the Fernnachtjäger thundered in over the coast at low level, dropping Düppel. Twelve airfields were attacked, halting take-offs completely on two and causing considerable delays on the others. Fourteen bombers were destroyed during this phase. British night fighters hastened to the scene, but the combination of hundreds of bombers already aloft, intruders and Düppel resulted in total confusion and two collisions.

Recalling so many heavily laden bombers was not a practical proposition. With insufficient time to improvise, the raid was allowed to proceed.

With the schedule for the assembly of the bomber stream completely disrupted, the latter became diffuse, which in turn rendered its counter-measures less effective. Once over Europe, nearly 200 night fighters rose to oppose it. Of these, more than 140 made contact, claiming 68 victories. The bombing was scattered, and the overall loss rate of 17 pe cent was unsustainable.

The Fernnachtjäger, aware that surprise would not be obtained twice, did not attempt to repeat the raid. The British, uncertain, shut the stable door with barrier patrols of night fighters over the North Sea when large raids were due, albeit to little effect for the horse had bolted. Following this success, the Fernnachtjäger had resumed their normal harassing activities, only to fall foul of the British barrier patrols. In September they stood down to re-train for a different mission.

Since the Schweinfurt débâcle American deep-penetration raids had virtually ceased, but it was only a question of time before they were resumed. The Luftwaffe was ready, with a daylight variation on the previous theme. Shortly before 0900 hours on 14 October, German early-warning radar started to pick up contacts inland from the East Anglian coast. The Fernnachtjäger, who had been on 30 minutes' standby since dawn, were brought to cockpit readiness. When after half an hour it became clear that a massive raid was building, two Gruppen of Me 410s were scrambled. Heading out over the unfriendly North Sea, they flew low to avoid detection. Under each wing they carried two 21cm air-to-air rockets. While not the most accurate weapons, these were effective in sowing alarm and despondency among packed bomber formations. At a command from Ground Control, the Hornisse pilots opened their throttles wide in order to gain maximum speed. Then almost as one, each pilot eased back on his stick and rocketed skywards. There, ahead and above, were the leading Fortresses, barely 20km from the English shore and still climbing.

The climb seemed to last forever; in fact, it was barely four minutes before the aircraft levelled out, their previous high speed spent by the battle climb. So far, all had gone according to plan. The first Gruppe was close to head-on with about two kilometres to run, with the second Gruppe following at about the same distance. Each Schwarm of four Messerschmitts selected a box of bombers as its target and accelerated. So far the Americans had not reacted: at this distance the Hornisse looked much like a Mosquito. Then as the range closed, 96 rockets were salvoed almost as one, and pandemonium reigned. Caught totally unprepared, many Fortresses broke formation, narrowly avoiding collisions with their neighbours. The leading Gruppe bored straight on for a gun attack on the following formation before breaking steeply down. The second Gruppe selected individual targets for its weapons, salvoed its rockets, fired its guns and then dived for the relative safety of the sea.

High above, they left mayhem. Eight 'Forts' were going down and others were streaming smoke. Surprise had been total and return fire minimal. One Hornisse had collided with a bomber; another had an engine stopped. Had they stayed they could have inflicted much more damage, but of one thing the German pilots were certain: somewhere not too far behind them would be between 50 and 100 angry P-47 Thunderbolts. Firewalling their throttles, they fled!

They were right. In hot pursuit were two Fighter Groups — 102 P-47s. They quickly finished off the damaged 410 and were fast overhauling the rest as they neared the Dutch coast. At this point they encountered 28 FW 190s of I./JG 1, which intervened as planned. A massive but largely inconclusive dogfight took place, the upshot of which was that the P-47s had to return low on fuel, leaving the raid short of escort fighters.

Meanwhile, although shaken, the bombers had managed to sort themselves out and came on, while another fighter group was detailed to meet them at the coast of Holland. This also had been anticipated by the Luftwaffe, which engaged it with II./JG 1. Forced to drop their tanks, the P-47s had to return early. As the force crossed into Germany, the mission was a disaster in the making. Assailed all the way to Schweinfurt, shotdown bombers littered the route. Of the 320 bombers dispatched, 84 were written off.[19] Such losses could not be borne. It was the last deep penetration made without a fighter escort all the way.

NOTES

1. Given the huge expansion of Fighter Command, a very high proportion of inexperienced pilots was an inevitability.
2. The Luftwaffe did not use the term 'ace'.
3. Galland was withdrawn from JG 26 in November 1941 to replace Mölders as General of the Fighters. His score was then 94. Too iconic a figure to kill off, he has been removed from the scene to explore the difference that the less ruthless and more cerebral Mölders might have made.
4. A Beaufighter of No 604 Squadron, flown by John Cunningham and 'Jimmy' Rawnsley, 23 May 1942.
5. Known as 'Pips', Josef Priller had succeeded Gerd Schöpfel as Kommandeur of III./JG 26 and later succeeded him as Geschwader Kommodore. He survived the war with a total of 101 victories, all in the West.
6. Manfred von Richthofen, the 'Red Baron', ranking Oberkanone of the First World War and not to be confused with his cousin Wolfram.
7. Oswald Boelcke, a tactical thinker and strategist widely regarded as the 'father of air fighting'.
8. The nearest English equivalent is 'poofters'.
9. Six victories with the Bf 110, the rest with Bf 109s in the East. His 150th victory came on 29 August 1942. Historically he succeeded Galland as General der Jagdflieger in January 1945.
10. Just fun!
11. Gestapo surveillance commenced shortly after the defection of Hitler's deputy Rudolf Hess in May 1941.
12. An uprising against the British in May 1941 had failed.
13. They arrived at Scapa Flow in May 1943 to neutralise *Tirpitz* and her friends while elements of the Home Fleet supported the Allied landings in Sicily. They returned to the United States in August. Given the changed scenario, they have been considered as straight reinforcements.
14. In reality I./KG 50 was equipped with missile-carrying Do 217s and was redesignated III./KG 40.
15. The USAAF also tried it. The result was the YB-40.
16. Operation 'Torch' actually took place in October 1942, but see Chapter 5.
17. The true figure was 67.

11 Victory in Sight?

AT the beginning of 1944 the German High Command could look back on the previous year with a degree of satisfaction. The intruder campaign had not only succeeded in disrupting enemy night bombing, it had also forced the British to allocate scarce resources to defence, with a consequent reduction in offensive capability. At home, the Nachtjagdflieger had recovered well from the shock of Düppel over Hamburg. By using more flexible tactics, aided by new electronic devices, night victories were once more beginning to increase. By day the fighters had inflicted heavy defeats on the USAAF bombers, and unescorted deep penetrations appeared to have ceased. Even better, the potent new Me 262 jet fighter, of which great things were expected, was on the point of entering service. At sea, the Vulture/guided weapon combination had cut a deadly swathe through the Atlantic convoys, causing extreme fuel shortages and delaying the twin Allied build-ups in Britain and North Africa. While this could not be expected to continue, the fast new electro-boats ordered by Dönitz would start to contest the North Atlantic late in 1944.

By contrast, the North African campaign had been a relative failure. As related in Chapter 5, interdiction of his supply routes had forced Montgomery to delay his assault at El Alamein, and not until February 1943 was he ready to take the offensive. Never a man to cede the initiative, and judging his moment carefully, Rommel struck first. Heavily outnumbered both on the ground and in the air, he commenced a series of spoiling attacks, switching rapidly from one place to another. Although his planned offensive was thrown into disarray, Montgomery was not stampeded into precipitate action. He pulled Rommel into a battle of attrition which the latter, his logistics too heavily stretched, could not win. Finally forced to admit defeat, Rommel withdrew the battered remains of his army, harried from the air as it went. Although victorious, the British could at first only mount a token pursuit. In the expectation of victory at El Alamein, strong Allied forces landed in Algeria, some 2,400km (1,500 miles) to the west. Having overcome initial opposition from the local Vichy French, they debouched cautiously eastward.

What to do next? In OKW, opinions varied. To capture the Suez Canal and open a gateway to the oilfields of the Middle East now seemed impossible. Some were for evacuating Rommel and the Deutsche Afrika Korps, leaving the Italians to defend their Libyan colony as best they could. After all, Luftflotte 2 in Sicily could keep the Mediterranean closed to British sea traffic.

Wiser counsels prevailed. Abandoning North Africa would have two possible results. First, it would leave the Allies free to invade Sicily, from where the Italian mainland was just a short hop. If this happened, Italy might sue for a separate peace. This could not be allowed to happen. Secondly, it would free large and well-equipped British forces for further adventures in the Middle East, possibly Iraq. Having first bolstered the garrison, they could then forcibly eject the Turks from the north of the country, before attacking the German-held Caucasus oilfields. The general consensus was that it was better to hazard, and possibly sacrifice, troops in North Africa than to risk the loss of the vital oilfields. Reinforcements were at once sent to Tunisia, while Rommel commenced his long fighting retreat westwards. By the end of the year, large Axis forces, now under the command of Generaloberst Jurgen von Arnim,[1] were still holding out around Tunis, supplied mainly by air.

On the Eastern Front the war had gone well, even though it had as yet failed to bring about the long-awaited collapse of the Soviet Union. However, at the beginning of 1943 the German front appeared dangerously over-extended. The Russians sought to exploit this by launching a massive two-pronged thrust towards Rostov, aimed at cutting off Army Group A in the Caucasus. After hard fighting, in which Fliegerkorps Ostland distinguished itself, this was halted near the confluence of the Don and Donetz rivers, then forced to retreat. In the north, the Heer suffered its only reverse of the year when Soviet armies raised the siege of Leningrad. The Führer now wanted to reduce the city named after Stalin as a matter of prestige. This was potentially disastrous: once involved in house-to-house fighting, the Germans would see their superiority in manoeuvre and training largely lost.[2] The day was saved only when Richthofen offered to bomb it into submission.

His offer accepted, the full might of Ferndivision 1 and Fliegerkorps Ostland was turned against the unfortunate city. After eight days of unremitting bombardment, a shortage of bombs caused the pressure to be eased. The centre of Stalingrad was almost totally destroyed. Occupation proved easy, the few dazed survivors putting up little resistance, and the city's capture was announced by Propaganda Minister Josef Goebbels. This was not entirely the case: Stalingrad straggled along the west bank of the Volga for some 20km, and Russian pockets held out in these suburbs. However, Goebbels argued, the suburbs were not really Stalingrad proper . . . ! The unfortunate Romanians were given the task of winkling them out.

The German offensive of 1943 commenced in May, following an early thaw. By the end of the year Saratov had been taken and Kuibyshev was being threatened. This last was where Stalin had established his new headquarters. He quickly decamped to parts further east. The front now ran from Penza to Ryazan, threatening Moscow with encirclement, but a northern thrust aimed at Yaroslavl had failed and had bogged down at Kalinin.

While the lack of progress was disappointing, it was hardly surprising. German lines of communication and supply were stretched to their limits, and only a generous supply of fuel from the Caucasus had enabled them to get as far as they had. Still the Soviets managed to put new and reconstituted armies into the field. Their resources still seemed endless, even though the German strategic bombers struck deep into the Urals time and time again, wrecking the tank and aircraft factories while medium bombers constantly attacked the rail links.

THE SCHWALBE HATCHES

The first production Me 262 jet fighter arrived at Lechfeld in October 1943 for operational evaluation. This would be carried out by a dedicated new unit, EprKdo 262. To lead it, General der Jagdflieger Gollob selected a fellow Austrian, Walter Nowotny. It was an easy choice: on 14 October 1943 'Nowi' Nowotny had become the first man to score 250 victories. He was therefore considered the most likely to do well with the new machine. Six weeks later 'Nowi' took a detachment, Kommando Nowotny, to Achmer, near Osnabrück, for its combat debut. His idea was to engage the American escort fighters and force them to drop their long-range tanks, leaving the bombers vulnerable to the conventional fighters. However, he had not thought the idea through carefully enough. Plagued by the unserviceability inevitable with the introduction of a new type, Kommando Nowotny was never able to put up more than ten fighters at a time, and, based so far forward, these were swamped by the numerous escorts. In its first month nineteen victories were claimed, for the loss of thirteen Me 262s in combat or in accidents. One of these was Nowotny himself, shot down by American P-51B Mustangs.[3]

Meanwhile the first jet Jagdgeschwader, JG 7, was being formed, commanded by the vastly experienced Major Johannes 'Macky' Steinhoff. Before the war he had flown biplanes earmarked for the new aircraft carriers, then in 1939 had commanded the Bf 109D night fighter Staffel 10./JG 26. Having transferred to day fighters, he led 4./JG 52 against Britain in the summer of 1940, then flew with this Geschwader against Russia, where he gained his 150th victory in February 1943. Shortly afterwards, he was appointed Kommodore of JG 77 in Tunisia.[4] On his arrival at III./JG 7 (the first jet Gruppe to be formed), he was promoted to Oberstleutnant.

The main advantage of the new jet was its overwhelming speed, some 160kph (100mph) better than the latest conventional fighters. Steinhoff's primary task was to evolve tactics to minimise its many limitations. Briefly, these were very poor acceleration, engines sensitive to surging and compressor stalling if the throttles were mishandled, limited endurance, poor manoeuvrability as a result of the high wing loading, a complete inability to operate from anything other than a lengthy hard runway and, finally, its heavy but short-ranged armament. Even in combat certain restrictions applied. Hard turns were to be avoided as they bled off speed at an alarming rate, and this could only slowly be regained. Even the traditional diving attack had to be employed sparingly: the Me 262 quickly reached its compressibility limit, at that time an incompletely understood phenomenon which often resulted in loss of control.

Steinhoff swiftly addressed the problems. He 'borrowed' two Bf 110s and a Kette of Dornier 19s, the former to give his pilots 'engine-out' experience in a benign environment and the latter—since many of the pilots came from the Russian Front—to give them practice in judging distance when attacking very large bombers. Flight restrictions, and 'flying' the engines as much as the aircraft, were simply a matter of training and experience.

More serious was the lack of endurance—an hour at most, and often rather less—while the need for permanent airfields with long runways limited deployment options. All jet pilots had undergone a course in blind flying before reaching JG 7, so diversions to avoid weather were minimised. The problem then became how quickly they could get off the ground and form up.

An original thinker, Steinhoff abandoned the standard Schwarm of four in favour of the Kette of three. His logic was impeccable. The hard runways essential for Me 262 operations were just wide enough to allow three jets to take off in formation. Once at cruising speed, which, in contrast to conventional fighters, was only a little less than maximum, the Me 262 was almost impossible to bounce from astern, making the cross-cover provided by the Schwarm less necessary. There was a drawback. The permanent runways that he needed made Me 262 bases readily identifiable, and therefore targets. Once Kommando Nowotny's base at Achmer had been spotted, it had been intensively patrolled by USAAF escort fighters, making take-off and landing hazardous undertakings. Nowotny himself had been shot down within sight of his own field. Steinhoff's solution was to recommend a strategy of the central position. By basing all jet fighter Gruppen well inland, they could range out in all directions.[5]

Moreover, the extra distance would reduce the time that the marauding Mustangs could spend on patrol. During Me 262 operations, airfield approaches would be defended by conventional fighters, allowing the jets to land in relative safety.

A believer in forward defence, and imbued with National Socialist doctrine, Gollob strongly disagreed. On meeting implacable opposition from Steinhoff, he sacked the Kommodore, only to find that he had a near-mutiny on his hands. Senior fighter commanders banded together and sent a deputation to Richthofen.[6] The latter, doubtful that quotations from *Mein Kampf* made a man a better warrior, removed Gollob. In his place he installed Oberst 'Franzl' Lützow.[7] It was an inspired choice. Son of the famous Admiral who for years had commented on the war at sea for German radio, veteran and leading tactician of the Condor Legion in Spain, Kommodore JG 3 from August 1940 and only the second man (after Werner Mölders) to reach 100 victories, he was universally admired and respected by the Jagdflieger. His first act was to rehabilitate Steinhoff, appointing him Inspector of Jet Fighters. Steinhoff's replacement as Kommodore JG 7 was the high-scoring Theodor Weissenberger,[8] who had accumulated 23 victories as a Zerstörer pilot before switching to single-engine fighters.

INTO ACTION

On 24 February, 21 Me 262s of III./JG 7 intercepted a large raid heading for the Heinkel factory at Rostock. In a determined attack, they pulled the escorting Mustangs out of position, allowing more than 120 conventional fighters to get at the bombers. USAAF losses amounted to 78 bombers and ten escort fighters shot down, and more than 50 bombers badly damaged. The Jagdflieger lost 25 fighters, of which three were jets, but only nine pilots. This was a promising start.

Further actions followed, with broadly similar results. Concerned, the USAAF analysed the situation. Whilst it had become obvious that their escort fighters could handily out-turn the German jets, this was of little use if they could not be caught. However, they had alternatives. They could increase the escort-to-bomber ratio, and hope to disrupt the jet attacks; they could bomb the jet bases to render the runways unusable; and, as they had done at Achmer, they could send Mustangs to patrol known Me 262 airfields, hoping to catch them flying low and slow.

In practice the sheer speed of the jets allowed them to penetrate the escort screen with relative ease, regardless of how many US fighters were present. Few Me 262s fell to fighters, most losses being caused by the massed guns of the bombers. Bombing fared little better: masters of rapid repair and camouflage, the Luftwaffe filled in the holes, then painted realistic dummy craters on the runways. To overcome the jets' vulnerability during take-off and landing, lanes of light Flak covered the approaches, while the locality was defended by conventional fighters. Ferocious dogfights took place when Mustangs tried to hunt down jets near their airfields.

As spring gave way to summer, I. and II./JG 7 were declared operational, while two Gruppen of JG 1 were converting on to type. It looked as though it would be a thin summer for the US 'heavies'. Nor was that all. In 1943 the Führer had declared that the Me 262 was exactly what was needed to halt the Allies if they ever had the temerity to invade his Festung Europa.[9] On 20 December he stated: 'The most important thing is that they get some bombs on top of them just as they try to invade. That will force them to take cover, and waste hour after hour! But after half a day our reserves will already be on their way. So if we can pin them down on the beaches for just six or eight hours . . . !'[10]

At first Hitler insisted that all Me 262s should be Jabos (fighter-bombers), but shortly after this two of his increasingly rare broadcasts were interrupted by daylight raids on Berlin carried out by a couple of Mosquitos.[11] A furious Führer demanded to know why these fast, light bombers had not been intercepted. In the absence of Gollob, in hospital with politically inspired jaundice, his wrath fell upon Günther Korten, the new Luftwaffe Chief of Staff. In a misguided attempt to avert an infantry posting to the East, Korten pointed out that the Me 262 was the only fighter fast enough to reliably catch the 'wooden wonder'. This was not what Adolf wanted to hear. The day was saved by strong support from Richthofen, who was quick to seize the opportunity of establishing a jet fighter force. Hitler finally relented, and ordered Me 262 production to be split equally between Jagd and Jabo units.

By May 1944 all four Gruppen of KG(J) 51 had been declared operational, while two more from KG(J) 53 were working up. These were flown by former bomber pilots. Also converting to jets at this time was III./KG 76, with the Arado Ar 234 Blitz single-seat jet bomber. Only slightly larger than the Me 262, it carried a greater bomb load for double the distance, albeit externally. Although rather slower, its greatest advantage over the Me 262 was that it was fitted with bomb sights, allowing both shallow-dive and high altitude-attacks. By contrast, the Me 262 Sturm-vogel, as the Jabo variant was known, could only aim its bombs in a shallow dive by using the gun sight. Not only was this far from accurate, the heavily laden jet accelerated much too quickly in the dive. Moreover, in a low-level attack its bombs, typically two SC 250s, had to be released by eye. During trials the average miss distance had been about one kilometre. This was far from promising.

Hard pressed, Stalin had made appeal after appeal to his Western allies to relieve the pressure by opening a second front, and Hitler himself had been concerned by the possibility ever since the Dieppe raid in August 1942.[12] Despite serious losses in the Atlantic, Allied forces were inexorably if slowly building up in England. It seemed that a cross-Channel invasion could not long be delayed.

With the bulk of the Heer committed in the east, there was little spare capacity to meet it. Generalfeldmarschall Erwin Rommel, now in charge of the Atlantic Wall defences, agreed with Hitler that the landings had to be delayed for as long as possible to allow reserves to be brought up. Equally, the Me 262 Jabos were best able to penetrate the fighter umbrella that the enemy was sure to put up. The question was: lacking even a modest level of accuracy, could these new aircraft really delay the landings to any significant degree?

As is so often the case, the solution was already to hand. Rather than use conventional bombs, with their limited blast and shrapnel radii, both of which would be attenuated on a sandy beach, cluster bombs — bomblets scattered from dispensers — would give much better results. The spread of these would largely compensate for the lack of accuracy, while the beaches themselves would be packed with 'soft' targets, that is, men and matériel. The Luftwaffe had used these weapons extensively against the Soviet hordes, and they would be equally effective against the new enemy. A Staffel of Me 262s, each with two dispensers, could seed an area of about 12 hectares with some 2,400 bomblets. While not all would find immediate targets, delay fuzes and anti-handling devices would severely hamper troop movements. And from May 1944, twelve Staffeln were available, plus the Geschwader and Gruppe Stabs, with another six working up.

THEY'RE COMING!

For the Reich, matters took an ominous turn in the spring of 1944, when much of the Allied air power switched from bombing Germany to a blatant attempt at cutting communications in France. The two resident Jagd-geschwader, JG 2 and JG 26, were heavily outnumbered. In a long-planned move, two Gruppen of JG 77 from Italy and the four Gruppen of JG 27 from Germany were flown in to reinforce them.

Where would the blow fall? To find out, the Luftwaffe deployed a detachment of Ar 234s modified for reconnaissance. With just four aircraft, this unit, Kommando Götz, ranged over southern England from early May, cameras clicking industriously. A combination of speed and altitude enabled them to evade what the Allies had thought was an impenetrable fighter screen and bring back vital intelligence.

Supreme Allied Commander General Dwight D. Eisenhower had set up a sophisticated deception operation to mislead OKW into thinking that the invasion would come by the shortest route, the Pas-de-Calais, with a possible diversion to Scandinavia. In the main, it used a huge volume of bogus radio traffic, designed to indicate the presence of whole armies in Kent and East Anglia. It was not, however, proof against aerial reconnaissance. The Arados detected nothing of significance in these areas, but they did photograph armadas of tanks moving south through Hamp-shire, the gathering of shipping in south coast ports and masses of gliders and their tugs in central southern England.

The knee-jerk reaction of OKL was to hurl every available bomber against the British embarkation ports, but these were so far-flung that concentration could not have been achieved. Wiser counsels prevailed: let the enemy land, then throw everything against their lines of supply. Just one exception was made. The Arados of III./KG 76 raided known army encampments, notably Bordon and Longmoor, and the glider fields near Andover, with bomblets. These caused little damage and few casualties, but a great deal of consternation. Two Ar 234s were lost: one succumbed to a night fighter, the other simply failed to return.

Eisenhower was in a quandary. Thanks to the losses in the Atlantic, he did not have the troops he felt were needed for a successful landing. The decision was, however, political, as Churchill and Roosevelt were adamant that pressure on the Russians must be relieved at any cost. If the Soviet Union collapsed at this point, huge German forces could be switched to the west, and if this happened the war in Europe would become a stalemate. With great misgivings, he gave the order to go.

OVERLORD

When, over a period of several days, the German coastal defences were subjected to a massive but fairly ineffective aerial bombardment, the invasion was known to be imminent, although not until paratroop landings were reported in the wee small hours of 6 June was it certain that the enemy was on his way. Units of the Nachtjagdflieger hastened to the scene, only to catch a few straggling glider tugs on their way home. In fact, the airborne assault had gone badly wrong, mainly due to Rommel's Finger-spitzengefühl,[13] which had enabled him to predict correctly most of the drop zones.

As dawn broke, the Vultures of I./KG 40 sought targets for their anti-shipping missiles, but for the most part they were thwarted by low cloud and poor visibility. However, the conditions largely protected them from the swarming Allied fighters. Ju 88 torpedo-bombers attacked from the west but lost heavily to fighters, for little return.

An hour after dawn the jet Jabos made their first appearance. Flying just below the overcast and parallel to the shore, they streaked across the beaches scattering bomblets in their wake, before making good their escape into the murk, leaving the sky dotted with the puffs of anti-aircraft shells. With the defenders distracted, two more Staffeln appeared, low over the water, and headed for the ships. Their pilots trained in skip-bombing techniques, these aircraft each carried two semi-armour piercing SD 250s. The effect was devastating. They sank a cruiser, two destroyers and five tank landing ships. Others were damaged. The Sturmvögel flew 1,120 sorties that day, losing just 21 of their number. Of these, fourteen fell to anti-aircraft fire, one was shot down by fighters, three either flew into the sea or collided with ships they were attacking and three were lost in accidents.

Rommel's ambition of throwing the invaders back into the sea was nearly, but not quite, achieved. The Americans established a bridgehead at 'Utah' beach on the neck of the Cotentin peninsula but, to the east, 'Omaha' beach had been a major disaster. Stopped dead, the survivors were evacuated at nightfall. Elsewhere the British and Canadians were in trouble. They had penetrated a few miles inland from 'Gold' and 'Juno' beaches, but were then held by ferocious German counterattacks. On the eastern flank, the troops on 'Sword' beach had been pushed back almost to Juno.

On D-Day the jets had just tipped the scales in favour of Germany. Forewarned by the Arados of Kommando Götz, Rommel had been able to position his forces and deploy his reserves remarkably well. Then the ability of the Sturmvögel to elude enemy fighters had allowed the beachheads to be attacked at will, delaying the Allied breakout as Hitler had forecast. If Rommel, the master of manoeuvre, had been given adequate forces, a German victory would have been assured.

Appalled by the near-disaster, the Allies turned the full might of their air power against the Sturmvögel. Their bases, located by D+3, were bombed and strafed incessantly. Decimated on the ground, within ten days the Geschwader were pulled back to reform and re-equip. They were replaced by FW 190Fs of SG 4 and SG 10, which operated from well-camouflaged grass fields.

By night the offensive was kept up by Me 410s, and by the Do 219 Fafnirs of KG 2, which had arrived post-haste from Russia. While the inaccuracy of night bombing was legendary, the Allied bridgeheads were so densely packed that it was difficult not to hit something. So crowded were the night skies over Normandy that the Allied night-fighter controllers were unable to keep track of events and 'own goals' were, perhaps, inevitable.[14] Given the confused situation, Luftwaffe bomber losses were bearable.

With the enemy established ashore, German priorities became twofold. On land the bridgeheads had to be contained; at sea the supply routes had to be interdicted. The former was dependent on the latter. When the Mulberry[15] artificial harbours were set up, they became prime targets for attack by the missiles of KG 40. Despite the presence of a strong fighter escort, the Vultures lost heavily — eighteen out of 58 aircraft in the first attack — but the damage caused was extensive.

The Allies had planned to sail nine supply convoys a day, but, lacking sufficient unloading facilities, this was reduced to five. The Luftwaffe launched a new type of bombardment. This was the Fieseler Fi 103 flying bomb, the forerunner of the cruise missile, and otherwise known as the V1 or Doodlebug. Ground-launched from the Pas-de-Calais, most were aimed at London, but many were air-launched against south-coast ports.

Not only the Luftwaffe tried to disrupt the convoys: the Kriegsmarine threw in schnorkel-fitted U-boats, fast S-boats and midget submarines. While these had some successes, any sinkings were but fleabites to the vast Allied armada. The critical point was unloading capacity at the beachheads. In the air, the Jagdwaffe was outnumbered by roughly three to one. While its well-trained pilots and battle-wise leaders inflicted a heavy toll[16] on their less experienced opponents, they were unable to prevent hordes of Allied fighter-bombers from strafing the troops and cutting their supply links. Rommel, the master tactician, was gradually forced to give ground. Then, on 17 July, his staff car was strafed by RAF fighters.[17] Gravely wounded, he was out of the war.

Worried by the failure to throw the invaders back into the sea, in late July the Führer reluctantly authorised the transfer of twelve divisions from the east. This took time. Despite the personal intervention of SS Obergruppenführer 'Sepp' Dietrich, it was eighteen days before the SS

Panzer and Panzergrenadier divisions arrived in France. The remainder, hampered by lack of transport, straggled in more than two weeks later. They were fed into action piecemeal.

Faced with this new accession of strength, the Allied armies ground to a halt. Montgomery's plan had been to draw off the German army around Caen, which he had captured after hard fighting, allowing the Americans to break out and drive south. While at the end of September the Americans held the entire Cotentin peninsula with the exception of Cherbourg, which was under siege, attempts to break out at St-Lô and Coutances had been thwarted. Montgomery then launched a two-pronged thrust towards Lisieux and Villers-Bocage. There the Allied offensive stalled, both sides exhausted.

ELSEWHERE

In the Mediterranean, Sicily was threatened, but Allied landing craft and airborne forces had been withdrawn to take part in 'Overlord'. While an invasion of the island, followed by that of the Italian mainland, looked to be only a matter of time, that time had not yet come. On the other hand, B-24 Liberators based in North Africa had started to raid the Ploesti oilfields in Romania.

In Russia, the Heer's logistics were stretched to the absolute limit. Yaroslavl, north of Moscow and the main Soviet centre of rubber production, had finally been overrun, and Moscow itself had been surrounded. The withdrawal of twelve divisions to France effectively precluded a direct assault on the Soviet capital, and the investing forces halted on the outskirts. On Stalin's orders, it had been provisioned and garrisoned for a lengthy siege.

The situation was ironic. For years the received wisdom had been that when Russia fell, the full might of the Third Reich could be turned against the West. Now, at the end of 1944, the wheel had turned full circle. If the British and Americans could be defeated in the West, the full might of the Third Reich could be turned against the East.

Ferndivision 1 was suffering increasingly heavy losses on its deep penetration raids. Aware that few of their fighters had sufficient hitting power against the German 'heavies', the Russians had dusted off and 'souped up' the elderly RS 82 anti-aircraft rockets. Just one hit gave a high probability of bringing down a bomber; eight salvoed from a single fighter would stand perhaps a five per cent chance of scoring a direct hit. It was, however, often enough if the bombers broke formation, allowing several fighters to concentrate on one bomber.

September 1944 saw the demise of the Ju 87 Stuka. Soviet anti-aircraft fire had taken the measure of this once-feared dive-bomber, and it was phased out in favour of FW 190 Jabos.

Over the Reich, the night battles continued, with the electronic war swinging gradually in favour of the British. From an all-time high of 13.4 per cent on 30/31 March,[18] British bomber attrition had fallen to less than seven percent by December.[19]

By day the fighting was still ferocious. The USAAF raided Berlin for the first time in March 1944. Bomber losses exceeded ten per cent, and even a massive fighter escort failed to keep the Me 262s at bay. Deep penetrations were few and far between for the rest of the year.

The Allied proponents of strategic bombing had suggested many expedients to end the war: ball bearings, the aircraft industry, U-boats, fuel — all had been touted at various times as war-winning targets. As at the end of 1944, none had yet succeeded.[20] Now, as 1944 drew to a close, the schnorkel U-boat had proved itself, while several of the new electro-boats, even faster underwater than they were on the surface, had been commissioned and were working up. The desperate straits in other theatres had so far limited air attacks on U-boat production. Now, in 1945, the Kriegsmarine was about to resume the Battle of the Atlantic.

NOTES

1. Rommel, his health poor, had been recalled.
2. Historically, this is best illustrated by Richthofen's caustic note in his diary that his Stukas were dropping bombs on Russians which German troops could deal with by throwing grenades.
3. This passage mirrors the events in November 1944.
4. In reality, Steinhoff was briefly Kommodore of JG 7 until he fell out with Göring at the time of the so-called 'Fighter Pilots' Mutiny'. The revised timescale has had to eliminate his service in Sicily and Italy.

5. As General der Jagdflieger, Galland proposed this for all defensive fighters, and not just jets.
6. Shades of the 1945 'mutiny' against Göring!
7. Although possessed of a mercurial temperament, Lützow was tough enough to become the spokesman of the 1945 fighter pilots' rebellion against Göring. He was lost in April 1945 while flying an Me 262 with Galland's JV 44.
8. Weissenberger's final total was 208.
9. Fortress Europe.
10. Alfred Price, *The Last Year of the Luftwaffe*.
11. This actually happened to Göring, much to his fury.
12. This was a *ballon d'essai* by the Allies, one purpose of which was to explore the difficulties of capturing a Channel port. It was a costly failure.
13. A sixth sense, which contemporary accounts credit Rommel with possessing in abundance.
14. An American P-61 Black Widow pilot, accused of attacking a British Mosquito, told the court of inquiry that he had mistaken it for a 'little' Ju 88.
15. Mulberry harbours, constructed mainly of concrete caissons, were towed across the Channel and sunk in position. The remains of one can still be seen at Arromanches.
16. In fact, in the post-invasion period the adverse sortie ratio was more than six to one, with losses to match owing to inadequate training.
17. By a strange coincidence, this happened near the hamlet of Ste-Foy-de-Montgomery!
18. The Nuremburg raid.
19. It was actually 0.7 per cent in December 1944, but in this scenario fuel shortages are not grounding the Nachtjagdflieger.
20. In real life, attacks on the oil industry came very close to being decisive. However, in this scenario the Caucasus oilfields are in full production and the Romanian and Hungarian sources have not been lost.

12   The Secret Weapons

A S 1944 drew to a close, the war in the West seemed to be moving towards stalemate. Cherbourg had finally fallen in early November, nearly five months behind schedule. While this gave the Allies access to a permanent port, it took eight weeks to restore the demolished facilities to the point where it reached fifty per cent capacity. The entire Allied campaign was bedevilled by the difficulties of supplying whole armies across the still-contested waters of the English Channel.

Whilst the Heer had failed to repel the invasion, skilled handling of the Panzer and Panzergrenadier divisions, with spirited assistance from the Luftwaffe, had largely contained it. Although heavily outnumbered, the aircraft had prevented British and American tactical air power, much of which, perforce, operated from southern England, from gaining more than localised air superiority. Behind the lines, the Todt Organisation performed near-miracles in its struggle to keep the German supply routes open.

Over the Reich, the USAAF daylight bombing campaign had been blunted by the ever-growing home defence fighter force which, with the jets to the fore, had inflicted heavy losses. A further factor was the frequent need by the Allies to switch the strategic bombers to a role of tactical interdiction against German communication and supply routes.

The night air war was a rather different story. The British had held a commanding lead in electronic warfare throughout, which the best efforts of German scientists had failed to erode. All too often, England-bound intruders were intercepted over the North Sea by RAF Mosquitos. Even risky low night flying often failed to prevent their detection. Like the Americans in the Pacific, the British had introduced radar picket ships in the North Sea to extend their low-level coverage. The Kriegsmarine responded with raids by Schnellboote, only to find that the pickets were protected by motor torpedo boats. The result was fast and furious, if generally inconclusive, small-ship battles.

Another British innovation was the world's first Airborne Warning and Control System (AWACS). This was a Wellington bomber with a 360-degree, dorsally mounted rotating aerial, packed full of black boxes.[1] Flying just 30m (100ft) above the waves, it carried a radio beacon which allowed a few Mosquitos to take station on it at a higher altitude. Although plagued with technical problems, it enjoyed several successes against the Fernnachtjäger.

At home the Nachtjagdflieger were beginning to struggle. The British had also started to use intruders on a large scale, equipped with gadgets that not only enabled them to home on to Luftwaffe fighter radars but also could trigger their IFF.[2] All too often the hunters became the hunted, to the point where the bomber stream—into which the RAF intruders never ventured—was where the German pilots felt safest. Be that as it may, they continued to exact a significant toll of enemy bombers; and, for reasons that they could easily guess, they were ordered to concentrate on defending the U-boat yards.

The British also used the Mosquito bomber for diversionary raids, evading the traditional night fighters by sheer speed. To counter them, Me 262 jets were modified for the night role. At first these did not carry radar, and the Himmelbett system was resurrected to direct them. Still later, two-seat conversion trainers were fitted with radar.

The first jet night-fighter unit was set up by Oberleutnant Kurt Welter, and its pilots were all very experienced in blind flying; before the war many had been airline pilots with Lufthansa. The initial detachment, Kommando Welter, was quickly expanded to a full Staffel, 10,/NJG 11, and then to a Gruppe, IV./NJG 11.[3] The jets could not be used against heavy bombers at night: the high overtaking speeds made a mid-air collision the most likely outcome, but they quickly took the measure of the fast Mosquitos. So the night air battle raged. Although damage to German industry was severe, it was not yet critical.

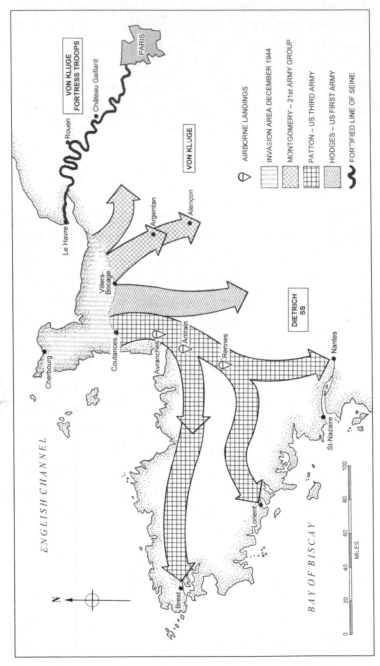

The capture of Cherbourg late in 1944 greatly assisted the Anglo-American build-up in Normandy. Montgomery's 21st Army Group struck south towards Argentan and Alençon, then, days later, Patton's Third Army, preceded by airborne landings at Avranches, Antrain and Rennes, poured south to Nantes before turning west to invest the U-boat bases. Patton's left flank was shielded by Hodges' First Army, which held off counter-attacks by Dietrich's SS divisions. Meanwhile von Kluge had fortified the north bank of the Seine, while keeping his main force south of the river.

COMMAND CHANGE

Late in 1944, the Luftwaffe underwent its final important change in command. In November Commander-in-Chief Wolfram von Richthofen was diagnosed as having a brain tumour[4] and was transferred to the Reserve. This was a heavy blow. His incisive mind had enabled him to cut quickly to the heart of strategic problems, while his doctorate in engineering — a most unusual qualification for a German general officer — allowed him to discuss technical problems with Milch and Speer on terms of equality. Finding a replacement of similar calibre was virtually impossible.

The list of candidates was a short one. Erhard Milch had been passed over once before and could not realistically be considered again. The outstanding diplomatic skills of Günther Korten made him an excellent Chief of Staff but were of little value to a leader, and he lacked charisma. One possibility would have been to bring back the previous incumbent,; the popular and greatly respected Albert Kesselring, from the Mediterranean, but having sacked him almost two years earlier the Führer would not countenance such a climb-down.

As Commander-in-Chief of the Wehrmacht, Adolf Hitler made the final choice. Generaloberst Robert Ritter von Greim[5] had an outstanding track record. As a fighter pilot in the Great War, he was credited with 24 aerial victories and the destruction of one tank, for which he had been awarded Germany's highest decoration, the Pour le Mérite. From 1939 he had commanded Fliegerdivision 5, later expanded to Fliegerkorps 5, which subsequently became Luftflotte 6 in central Russia. His record in both wars had earned him the respect of fighting generals and troops alike. Promoted to Generalfeldmarschall, von Greim became the Luftwaffe's final Commander-in-Chief.

ELSEWHERE

In the Mediterranean, an invasion of Sicily and Italy appeared imminent, but strategically this could be no more than a sideshow designed to draw off reinforcements from other areas. The fear that Italy might make a separate peace had been eased by what was in effect a German occupation,

The limits of the German advance, 1944. As can be seen, the front was perilously overstretched, and, had the Soviet thrusts towards Rostov succeeded, lack of fuel would have resulted in a complete German collapse. As it was, the German capture of the Saratov oilfield spelt disaster for Russian offensives in the area.

albeit with limited forces. Theatre commander Generalfeldmarschall Kesselring was quietly confident that, given the difficult nature of the terrain, he could delay the invaders almost indefinitely.

Since the defeat of the U-boat campaign in the Atlantic in 1943, the enormous industrial capacity of the United States had turned out Liberty ships and tankers far faster than they could be sunk. The all too few Vultures were increasingly opposed by carrier fighters, while 'Monsters' — the huge passenger liners, now bristling with anti-aircraft guns — proved elusive. The handful of U-boats despatched into the Atlantic by Dönitz achieved their aim of tying down the enemy's anti-submarine forces, but at heavy cost. Then, from 1944, schnorkel-equipped U-boats started to enter service. Though much more survivable, these also achieved little.

In the East, matters were more problematic. The Reich had embarked on what was intended to be a short war but now, as it entered its seventh year, the shortage of men of military age had become critical. The days of a cohesive front were long gone; instead, Panzers and other mobile units were concentrated in strongpoints, with a screen of forward troops as a tripwire. Inevitably, the Soviets leaked through the gaps. It was Soviet quantity versus German quality, and the Panzers usually outmanoeuvred and defeated the Russian hordes, but still the latter came — unendingly. The Soviet winter offensive of 1944/45 burst through the iron ring encircling Moscow, and the German armies were forced to fall back to better defensive positions. The major problem for the Germans was logistics: the vast distances made nightmarish demands on the supply echelons that even superhuman efforts could not overcome.

It was much the same in the air. While the German aircraft industry was churning out fighters and Jabos at record levels, the majority of these went to France or to home defence. In the East, the vast distances meant that tactical air units were used as a 'fire brigade', frantically rushing from one conflagration to the next, supplied only by the large force of transport aircraft. By now, experience at home had demonstrated that, even though factories were bombed, their heavy machinery often survived intact. Aerial reconnaissance clearly showed that Russian tank production lines often continued to work amid the wreckage of the buildings around them. To halt them, the Fernkampfflieger started to concentrate on the power stations which supplied the armaments factories rather than the factories themselves. This had mixed results. The stations, which in the Urals were usually hydroelectric, were not only more difficult targets; they were heavily defended. Bomber losses rose.

OKH in Russia was in a quandary. Manpower shortages combined with logistics difficulties prevented them from launching a further offensive. A strategic withdrawal to shorten both the front and the lines of communication had not only been forbidden by the Gröfaz but could all too easily leave the vital Caucasian oilfields vulnerable. They could do little other than sit tight, soak up the Soviet attacks and hope that the bottom of the Russian manpower barrel would soon be reached.

IN SEARCH OF A SOLUTION

The war on two fronts, which had begun so promisingly in 1941, had taken on nightmarish proportions. In another year or so, Germany would bleed to death. The situation could only be saved by the collapse of one of the three main enemies. Was there any means by which this might be brought about?

Had the Soviet Union been a democracy, almost certainly it would have fallen long since, but, held in the iron grip of Stalin and the Communist Party, the Red Army was showing few signs of weakening. There was little hope that the end was in sight there. One of Hitler's greatest weaknesses was his belief in the efficacy of terror against decadent Western democracies, a belief supported by the rapid collapse of France in 1940. From mid-1944 he subjected Britain to a heavy and prolonged robot bombardment, interspersed with bombing raids, totally ignoring the fact that the islanders had withstood the worst that the all-conquering Luftwaffe could throw at them in 1940–41. However, still he hoped.

The first terror weapon was the Fi 103 flying bomb. Crude, unreliable and inaccurate, it was ground-launched from ramps in the Pas de Calais. Only about 75 per cent crossed the English coast, and, of these about a third were shot down by air and ground defences.[6] While Greater London was a huge target, many failed to reach it, and those that did often fell in open spaces. Rarely did the Fi 103 inflict damage greater than its own cost. Its greatest value was the sheer amount of enemy resources it tied down in terms of tactical fighters and anti-aircraft guns.

The next bombardment weapon was the A 4, a theatre ballistic rocket. Unlike the Luftwaffe's Fi 103, it was an Army weapon. Accuracy was poor, and even though it was immune from interception whilst in flight, only about half reached of them the target area. When they did, the one-tonne warheads caused appalling damage, but rarely to anything of military value. It was simply a terror weapon, aimed at forcing the British to rise against their government. Finally there was the V 3, an ultra-long-range 50-barrel gun intended to bombard London from the Pas de Calais. While this was potentially devastating, its great weakness was its total lack of mobility. The French Resistance discovered it before it could be used, and the Allies bombed it out of existence.

What of the United States? It would be greatly to Germany's advantage if this most potent of nations could be forced to withdraw from its alliance with Britain. The main question was how. The Führer took the view that the decadent Americans, sitting in supposed safety behind their ocean barrier, would raise a huge public outcry if New York, the symbol if not the capital of their country, was attacked from the air.

Even before the Americans entered the war, a bomber with the range to attack New York had been proposed. The prototype Messerschmitt Me 264, unofficially known as the Amerikabomber, first flew in December 1942. OKL soon realised that a fleet of these bombers, each carrying a mere 1,800kg (3,969lb) of bombs, would not be able to achieve results which justified the outlay and recommended the aircraft's cancellation. However, designer Willi Messerschmitt, who had the ear of the Führer, was allowed to continue limited development, and a pre-production aircraft, modified to carry three remotely guided bombs, first flew in October 1944.[7]

Ever optimistic where terror raids were concerned, Hitler was fixated on demonstrating that US cities were not beyond reach, even though such attacks could be little more than fleabites. Initial trials of the Me 264 were satisfactory, and top priority was given to the production of six more Amerikabomber. The enormous operational radius[8] of the Me 264B would allow it to attack not only New York but also Boston and Washington, greatly increasing the area that the USAAF would need to defend. However, Kommando Wittmann, as the new unit was named after its new Kommandeur, could not become operational before July. By then, a new and potentially war-winning weapon might be available.

THE GERMAN NUCLEAR WEAPON

The theoretical principles of the atomic bomb were fairly simple, and were widely known before the war. The difficult tasks were collecting enough fissionable material and then turning it into a practical weapon. Then, in 1939, fortune seemed to smile on the Germans: the Czechoslovakian uranium mines fell into their hands when they annexed that country. In that same year, 1939, a nuclear research programme began at the Kaiser Wilhelm Institute for Physics in Berlin.[9]

The most obvious target was London. The destruction of the heart of the British Empire would almost certainly lead to a cessation of hostilities. This in turn would leave the United states without a European base from which to continue the war. With the threats to France and Italy removed, the entire might of the Third Reich could concentrate in the East to achieve the long-deferred 'knock-out blow'.

Should the Americans prove recalcitrant, the Me 264s could raid New York or Washington with conventional bombs, proving that they had the means to deliver a nuclear attack. An alternative was the gigantic two-stage A-9 intercontinental rocket then under development to bombard cities on the US eastern seaboard. The Americans might suspect that the latter could not carry an atomic warhead across the Atlantic, but the element of uncertainty might be enough to force an armistice. If the threat alone did not suffice, the 'worst-case scenario' would be an Me 264 — although, unable to make a two-way trip, its crew would head south and seek sanctuary in Mexico or Venezuela. The alternative was an A-bomb on Moscow, but given Stalin's ruthless disregard for the lives of his countrymen, coupled with the vast size of the area into which he could retreat, Soviet capitulation could not be relied upon.

STARCASTS?

An armistice with the United States would leave the Führer with a tricky diplomatic problem. Should the cease-fire be extended to his Japanese allies? Could he really insist? And, in the long term, what would be the biggest advantage to the Greater Germany? What did Hitler's astrologer say?

His mind was quickly made up. Decadent or not, the USA was an unforgiving nation, as it had shown after Pearl Harbor. Any armistice would be a fragile thing, and there was a fair chance that hostilities with Germany would sooner or later be renewed. He needed time — time to finish off the Soviet Union, then more time to put his defences in order. In the Pacific, the tide of war was flowing strongly the American way. Ally or not, Japan must be thrown to the wolves. The angry giant would be heavily committed for at least two more years, and these were two years that could make all the difference.

The Führer did not shrink from the idea of nuclear war: he was concerned only with getting his strike in first. That meant long-range bombers, flying fast and high enough to be virtually safe from interception. By 1945 German aircraft design offices were littered with futuristic bomber projects — jets, swept wings, forward swept wings, flying wings, stand-off missile carriers.[10] With luck, the first of them could enter service by 1948. What was more, they could be based in England. Let the stubborn islanders take the brunt of any American nuclear riposte!

ATLANTIC REVISITED

The defeat of the traditional U-boat in 1943 had been due to the fact that operationally, it was merely a moderately fast and long-ranged torpedo boat that was able to submerge to avoid detection and evade pursuit. Its weakest point was that it had to spend most of its time on the surface, where it was vulnerable to air attack. Even if all this did was to force it to dive, it was frequently enough. Submerged, it was too slow to keep pace with convoys and quickly lost contact with them. Nor was it fast enough to evade the attentions of the Allied escorts. Maximum submerged speed would quickly exhaust its electric batteries, while when rigged for silent running it took close to a minute to cover its own length.

Long before the war these problems had been addressed by Professor Hellmuth Walter. His solution was closed-circuit propulsion using a turbine driven by high-test hydrogen peroxide (H_2O_2) or HTP. On hitting a catalyst, HTP decomposed into superheated steam and oxygen, with a tremendous increase in volume. At this point, it was brought into contact with fuel oil in a combustion chamber, where ignition was hypergolic. This in turn drove a turbine, which drove the boat. In theory, this gave a true submarine, which not only had to spend little time on the surface but was actually faster submerged than on the surface.

Nothing is ever gained without cost. In this case it was the HTP. It was far more expensive than diesel oil, far more of it was needed, and the technology needed to handle it was complex in the extreme. It was touchy stuff. Dipped in HTP, your finger turns white and starts smoking! Fortunately, water immediately neutralises it. However, so corrosive was it that it had to be delivered in glass-lined railway tank cars.[11]

The result was the Type XVIII. Owing to the need to carry large amounts of HTP, it was enormous — 1,508 tonnes, almost double the displacement of the ocean-going Type VIIC — but once underwater it could attain a speed of 24 knots (44kph) and had a range of 463km (250nm) at 20knots (37kph). This was revolutionary. Submerged, therefore, it could run away from sloops and corvettes with ease. But problems with the closed-circuit propulsion system persisted, while HTP, which reacted instantly with anything of biological origin, was potentially lethal. If accidents were to be avoided, laboratory-style standards of cleanliness had to be observed.[12] The difficulties, and the costs, were simply too great. Reluctantly, work on Walter submarines was abandoned in the spring of 1944.

It was now that someone hit on the idea of the electro-boat. The design of the Type XVIII was hydrodynamically clean for optimum underwater performance, while the hull was large to contain sufficient HTP — large enough, indeed, to permit battery capacity to be tripled. Thus was born the Type XXI, of 1,848 tonnes displacement and capable of maintaining 12–14 knots (22–26kph) submerged for ten hours. Rigged for silent running, it could manage 5 knots (9kph) for 60 hours; fitted with a schnorkel, it could remain submerged almost indefinitely. Just one difficulty remained. The Type XXI was too large to operate in the shallow waters of the North Sea, the Channel and the Mediterranean. Thus a smaller, coastal version was ordered — the Type XXIII of 260 tonnes displacement.

With convoys pouring across the Atlantic, the need for the electro-boats was urgent. Production time was drastically cut by prefabricating the new types in sections, then assembling them on the slipways. Blohm & Voss of Hamburg, A. G. Weser of Bremen and Schichau of Danzig began to mass-produce Type XXIs, while Type XXIIIs were built by Deutsche Werft of Hamburg and Germaniawerft of Kiel.

Secrecy was of the essence. Me 262s endeavoured to keep Allied photo-reconnaissance aircraft away from the slipways, but inevitably a few got through. Further, British Naval Intelligence had got wind of the Walter boats from other sources and were, not unnaturally, extremely worried. The RAF, in particular, repeatedly carried out heavy attacks on U-boat production facilities, and the canal system which transported the larger prefabricated sections to the yards. The latter, notably the Dortmund–Ems Canal, was particularly vulnerable. The Baltic training areas were also heavily mined. Ju 88s and Me 410s of the Nachtjagdflieger fought back hard, with a degree of success. Without the protective umbrella of the Luftwaffe, the rejuvenated U-boat arm might have been stillborn.[13]

The first Type XXI launched was U 2501, on 12 May 1944. It was commissioned just under seven weeks later, and working-up took another sixteen weeks. Production accelerated, and by the end of the year 40 Type XXI electro-boats were ready for action, with another ten or twelve coming on line every week. The temptation to send them out in dribs and drabs had been resisted in accordance with the time-honoured German maxim 'pelt don't piddle!' and all commanders of Type XXI boats were veterans, often recalled from training and staff jobs. By the start of the New Year Dönitz was ready to resume the offensive.

From early January, electro-boats sailed for the North Atlantic convoy routes. Anticipating this, the Allies deployed air patrols over their expected route. It was now that the schnorkel really paid off. Whilst at normal cruising speed it left a 'feather' in the water, this was indistinguishable from the 'white horses' evident in normal sea states. Spotting it was rather like looking for a single button mushroom in a field of white clover! Nor was radar much help; the tiny echo from the schnorkel head was only detectable from very close range. Nor, in such a vast area, were magnetic anomaly detectors much help. Allied anti-submarine aircraft were back where they had been four years earlier.

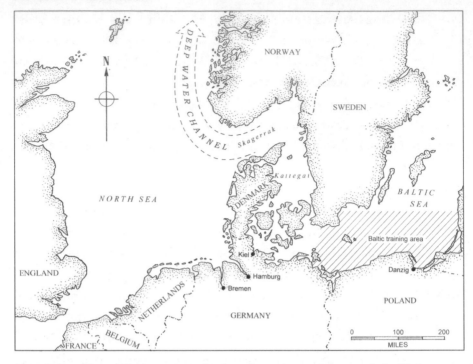

Heavy bombing raids were launched against electro-boat yards in Kiel, Hamburg, Bremen and, to a lesser degree, Danzig. At the same time, intensive mining sorties were carried out in the Baltic training area, the Kattegat, the Skagerrak and the deep-water channel off the Norwegian coast by which the electro-boats reached the open sea. The Nachtjagdflieger played a crucial part in defending against these attacks.

The second Battle of the Atlantic had been carefully planned. Convoys were to be intercepted before they reached a latitude of 35°W, circumstances permitting. The priority was to sink the accompanying escort carriers (at this stage of the war, there were often two carriers, protecting a convoy of 70–80 ships). The effect of this would be twofold. First, the risk to the electro-boats would be considerably reduced, and secondly it would remove the fighter threat to KG 40, making that unit far more effective when the convoy moved within its range. The guided-missile-armed KG 40 had by now re-equipped with the Heinkel He 277, unofficially dubbed 'Vulture II'.

The defeat in 1943 had caused morale in the U-boat arm to slump, and operations since then had done nothing to reverse the trend. Despite the introduction of the schnorkel in 1944, U-boat losses were high and successes minimal. By contrast, Allied anti-submarine units were riding the crest of the wave, bringing overwhelming force to bear on every contact. For this first electro-boat engagement Dönitz badly needed a major victory.

The Kriegsmarine listening service had not been idle, and had detected several convoys in mid-Atlantic. The order went out to all 22 electro-boats in the first wave that a huge eastbound convoy would be the main target. The Allied 'Ultra' service was equally on its toes. The order was intercepted and deciphered and the Allied escort commander alerted. When the electro-boats acknowledged, their transmissions were monitored, their positions were plotted and anti-submarine aircraft headed in their general direction.

While snorkelling allowed a high submerged speed to be maintained, it had one major disadvantage: the diesel engines blotted out all external noise, and the acoustic detection gear could not work in these conditions. The solution was to switch to the electric motors every half-hour or so, dive below the ambient surface noise and listen.

THE BATTLE COMMENCES

The first encounter was with aircraft from the escort carriers. Elderly Swordfish biplanes, they combed the area at slow speed and low altitude, their crews peering intently from open cockpits. Quite by chance, one spotted a schnorkel and attacked, but its depth charges fell wide. Thus warned, the electro-boat dived to safety.

Three hours later a Royal Navy hunter/killer group — eight sloops and corvettes — arrived, but whereas such groups had been successful against conventional U-boats, the two electro-boats in their path on this occasion evaded them with ease, diving to moderate depth and then disengaging, and running submerged at 12 knots (22kph) for the next hour or so. One sloop got a brief asdic contact but, unused to such a speedy opponent, was unable to hold it. The hunter/killer group was left flailing at empty waves.

Gradually the wolf-pack converged to form a 'stripe' across the projected path of the convoy, which, aware that it had been detected, made large and irregular changes of course. Radio communications by both sides betrayed the position of each to the other. By now there were two Allied hunter/killer groups sweeping the area, while air patrols had intensified.

Contact with the convoy was made at dusk on the following day, and the two escort carriers were quickly identified. Radio monitoring quickly established that U-boats were in the vicinity, and the escort group stepped up its search, but in vain. The escorts 'pinged' away with asdic, but, at schnorkel depth, the electro-boats were almost impossible to detect. It was later suggested that the escorts should have relied on passive rather than active sonar, but this probably would not have worked. Relying on their acoustic detection systems to stay out of trouble, once in contact the electro-boats ran on their ample battery power.

Attacked from schnorkel depth, the carriers were quickly sent to the bottom. Counter-attacking escorts were met with Gnat homing torpedoes which, although they failed to score, hampered the enemy. Even when the electro-boats were driven to dive deep, their speed not only made them slippery opponents but allowed them to remain in contact with the convoy. Most remained until they had expended all their torpedoes. Initially the convoy had consisted of 84 ships disposed in eleven columns. Of these, seventeen were tankers and, easily identifiable, fourteen were sent to the bottom. In a three-day battle, they were followed by 43 freighters and three escorts. Sated, the electro-boats, less one of their number, headed for their new bases on the Biscay coast.

Dönitz had his victory. Nor was that all. Thirty Vulture IIs of KG 40 swooped on the remnants of the convoy as it neared the Western Approaches, sinking the remaining three tankers and ten out of 24 freighters. As Silbert Müller recorded, 'For once there was no fighter opposition. As we hove into sight, the demoralised remnants of this once huge convoy fled in all directions. It availed them little. My new observer, Adalbert Fleischer, picked a tanker as his target and released his weapon. His aim was true. As we left the scene, the tanker was ablaze from end to end.'[14]

The Battle of the Atlantic had come full circle. The new generation U-boats had given the anti-shipping units of the Luftwaffe a new lease of life. Meanwhile, a second pack had left Norway for the North Atlantic and a third was forming.

CONSEQUENCES

Appalled, the Allies took measures to ensure that the slaughter would not be repeated. Sloops and corvettes were too slow to be more than marginally effective, but there were not enough fast destroyers available to replace them. There were, however, enough destroyers to screen the carriers, which reduced their vulnerability by maintaining high speeds near, although not actually as part of, the convoys. As time passed, new detection systems and new tactics took an ever-increasing toll of electro-boats, which by midsummer were losing one of their number for every eight merchantman sunk. Although this ratio was higher than the peak of 1942, with barely 100 electro-boats operational it was never enough. To the Allies, however, convoy losses remained unacceptably high.

The initial success of the electro-boats affected other operations. The reinforced U-boat pens on the Biscay coast, for example, became prime targets. By day USAAF B-17s dropped rocket-assisted 'Disney' penetration bombs;[15] by night the RAF dropped 12,000lb 'Tallboys'. While neither penetrated the six-metre-thick concrete roofs of the U-boat pens, near misses by 'Tallboys' falling in the water outside them generated shock waves strong enough to damage the electro-boats, notably the doors to their torpedo tubes. In addition, the Vulture IIs' airfield at Bordeaux/Merignac was heavily bombed and often rendered unusable for days on end. The approaches to Brest and Lorient were heavily mined, and were patrolled by long-range Mosquito fighters armed with six-pounder Molins guns and anti-submarine rockets. The Luftwaffe reacted strongly, with FW 190 fighters by day and Ju 188 fighters by night. Fierce battles were fought over the Bay, the advantage swinging first one way and then the other.

The consequences were by no means confined to the air. In Normandy, Supreme Allied Commander in Europe Dwight D. Eisenhower was under extreme political pressure to end the stalemate with a break-out. Matters were complicated by the fact that 'Ike' had never held a battlefield command but had been selected for his diplomatic skills in reconciling his often unruly subordinates, notably the vastly experienced, if cautious, British Field Marshal Bernard Montgomery, commanding the 21st Army Group, and the hard-charging American General George S. Patton[16], commanding US Third Army. All previous attempts at breaking out had failed, and the arguments had become less about where and when than 'if'.

The deadly threat posed by the electro-boats concentrated Allied minds wonderfully. While a combination of sea and air power had failed to contain it, much of its effectiveness would be lost if its Biscay bases could be overrun. A two-pronged attack was planned. 'Monty' was to make a demonstration in force on a wide front, then launch an armoured thrust south towards Argentan, Alençon and Le Mans to cut German west/east lines of communication. It was hoped that Generalfeldmarschall Gerd von Rundstedt, the German commander in the West, would assume that Monty's thrust would be the main attack and react accordingly. To mislead him even more, the full weight of Allied tactical air power was thrown against the Luftwaffe on Montgomery's front. As predicted, the Heer sought an opening for a counter-attack. Having seized Argentan, the British were halted by a strong Panzer attack on their eastern flank from the direction of Lisieux, threatening their rear. Only with difficulty were the Panzers halted, allowing the advance towards Alençon to continue.

Four days later Patton, with General Hodges' First US Army guarding his flank, struck southwards on the line Avranches–Rennes–St-Nazaire before turning west to invest Brest and Lorient. The Third Army was spearheaded by airborne landings at Avranches, Antrain and Rennes.[17] The Heer was caught flat-footed: not only was the element of surprise absolute, the Luftwaffe Jabos were fighting desperately against heavy odds further east. Never a man to let slip an opportunity, Patton ordered his armour to break through on a narrow front in what German air reconnaissance described as a 'pigpile' formation.

Patton's Third Army reached Rennes on day six. With the First Army providing a thin screen to the east he raced on, bypassing German strongpoints and pausing only to refuel. After an unscheduled change of plan, his advanced units drove into Nantes on day eight, and, with the exception of La Rochelle, all the major U-boat bases in France were now cut off.

The Gröfaz, now aware that the major threat lay in the West, recalled another twelve Panzer divisions from the East, even though he had to authorise a retirement in the northern sector to do so. Also redeployed to the West was Fernkampfdivision 1, which was used against the supply ports in southern England.

After four weeks the new units were in place but, while the enemy advance had been halted, supply lines to the U-boat bases had not been restored. Reluctantly, the electro-boats were pulled back to bases in Norway and the Reich. By the early summer of 1945, the Western Front was again stalemated — as, indeed, was the Eastern.

NOTES

1. This AWACS Wellington was first used operationally off the coast of Norway on 19–20 May 1942. It was also used against V1- carrying Heinkels on 14 January 1945. Like many innovations, it was a solution seeking a problem. Low-flying intruders seem a worthy scenario.
2. 'Serrate' and 'Perfectos', respectively.
3. In reality there was just 10./NJG 11. It was credited with destroying 43 Mosquitos at night in four months.
4. Richthofen died in captivity in June 1945.
5. Von Greim succeeded Göring as Commander-in-Chief in the final weeks of the war.
6. The true figure was slightly more than half, but allowance has been made for the defenders having to deal with bombing and intruder raids at the same time.
7. In reality, Me 264 development never reached this stage.
8. The still-air range of the prototype Me 264 is generally quoted as being 15,000km (8,100nm). It has been presumed that the range of production aircraft would have been rather better.
9. Obstructed at every turn by the scientists involved, it made little progress. Although at times Allied intelligence was very worried by reports filtering through, only after the war was it discovered that Germany had no viable nuclear bomb programme.
10. The Americans were also working on a super-heavy bomber with transcontinental range. This emerged as the B-36 in 1946.
11. After the war, some of these were used by Saunders-Roe to transport HTP for the SR.53 mixed-power fighter.
12. HTP was one of the two exotic fuels used by the Me 163 rocket fighter, which entered service in small numbers as a point-defence interceptor. In our scenario

it would probably have been regarded as no more than an interesting but rather dangerous experiment. A handful of Me 262s were fitted with Walter rocket motors to enable them to catch high-flying Mosquitos.

13. In reality, production was delayed so badly by air attack, and causes indirectly attributable to air attack, that only one electro-boat, a coastal Type XXIII, ever made a war cruise.

14. Silbert Müller, *Vultures of the Atlantic*.

15. First used in March 1945 against E-boat pens.

16. As the invasion of Sicily had not taken place, in our scenario Patton was not in disgrace for his actions there.

17. These airborne forces were those used at Arnhem nearly six months earlier.

13   Endgame

BY August 1945 the war had once again become bogged down. The Germans' failure to halt Patton's headlong rush towards Nantes resulted in the replacement of von Rundstedt by von Kluge, and the SS Divisions were concentrated under Obergruppenführer 'Sepp' Dietrich. Backed by all the tactical aircraft that Luftflotte 3 could muster, Dietrich drove clean through Hodges' screening First Army and reached the sea near Mont St-Michel but then, unable to keep his troops supplied, he was forced to retire. By Easter, Patton's Third Army had invested Brest, Lorient and St-Nazaire[1], forcing the evacuation of most electro-boats to North Sea ports. Only La Rochelle remained in German hands. Although the added distance between their base and their operational area, through heavily mined and patrolled waters, reduced the U-boats' effectiveness, it never became critical. In the Atlantic, the convoy battles continued to rage.

With the Biscay ports safely invested, much of Patton's armour turned east, to help the hard-pressed First Army. As the Panzers under Dietrich fought bitter, fast-moving, but indecisive actions against the Americans, von Kluge was faced with the need to contain Montgomery's 21st Army Group with the few armoured units at his disposal. He also had several low-quality divisions under command, coastal defence troops which had formerly manned the Atlantic Wall. Poorly trained and poorly equipped, and many of them Russian and Ukrainian 'volunteers' from prison camps, they lacked mobility and were no match for the Allies in the open field.

Making the best of what he had, von Kluge fell back on the Seine—a strong, natural barrier with a steep escarpment along much of its north bank, especially prominent east of Rouen. This was quickly fortified, including the dominating ruin of Château Galliard overlooking Les Andelys. This was a massive castle built some eight centuries earlier by the English King Richard I. By a strange twist of fate, it now became a stronghold for his country's enemies.

Held by the coastal defence troops, the escarpment imposed a severe check on the advancing British, while von Kluge's few mobile divisions lurked south of the river, barring the way to Paris. But this situation could not last. Von Kluge's plan was to hang on, giving ground only slowly, until Dietrich proved victorious and returned to aid him. However, in August this had still not happened.

For Italy, the threat of invasion was more imagined than real, thanks to a brilliant Allied deception operation. Secret negotiations were opened in Portugal, and a deal was concluded. Il Duce, Benito Mussolini, was overthrown in a *coup d'état*, and Marshal Badoglio assumed power. Kesselring, knowing nothing of the Italian agreement with the Allies, was caught flat-footed. The need to reinforce other theatres had seen his forces reduced to three under-strength divisions[2] and just eight Gruppen of tactical aircraft, deployed in Sicily and Sardinia as well as on the Italian mainland. His loud protests had gone unheeded by the Führer. Disaster stared him in the face. If the Allies landed in the 'toe' of Italy, sizeable German forces in Sicily would be cut off, and these were forces he could not afford to lose. Grimly, he told Badoglio that he would fight to the bitter end — unless . . .

Badoglio, unwilling to see his country torn from end to end, and aware that the Allies could not reinforce him quickly, agreed to let the Germans evacuate. By air and sea, Sicily was cleared in just three days and the Heer streamed north, though not out of Italy altogether. Instead Kesselring concentrated his forces along the Gothic Line, stretching from La Spezia across the Italian peninsula to just south of Rimini. Having secured the Alpine passes to his rear, he dug in to await events.

In the air, the jets still held sway over the Reich but were gradually being ground down by superior numbers; at night, the advantage was slowly swinging to the RAF by virtue of superior electronic gadgets.

Further west the Allies had also introduced jet fighters — the British Gloster Meteor and de Havilland Vampire and the American Lockheed P-80 Shooting Star — although not in any great numbers. While these posed problems for the Ar 234, they only encountered the Me 262 in its Jabo role over France. When they did meet, exciting but rarely decisive high-speed chases took place at low level.[3]

EASTERN STALEMATE

Weakened by the transfer of many of its best armoured units, the Heer took up a holding position, waiting against the time when the campaign in France could be concluded; only when this happened could they be reinforced for the final, decisive push. Their optimism was not entirely unfounded. After the Soviet winter offensive of 1944/45, major attacks had become smaller in scale and ever more infrequent. Skilled handling of the Panzers beat them off with relative ease.

Deprived of the Caucasian oilfields, the Russians had been forced to draw on sources in Siberia and east of the Urals. At first these had been supplemented from their ample reserves, but now the tank farms were running dry. All fuel supplies now had to be brought vast distances, imposing a tremendous strain on the always inadequate Russian rail system. It was against this weak link that the Luftwaffe concentrated. While the strategic bombers of Fernkampfdivision 1 had been redeployed to the West, the medium bombers of Fliegerkorps Ostland took up the slack.

Back in 1942, the first Eisenbahn Staffeln — units specialising in railway attacks — had been formed; by mid-1944 these had been expanded to full Gruppen, and from the spring of 1945 three in every four Kampfgruppen in Fliegerkorps Ostland had converted. Goods yards and rail junctions were the primary targets, usually bombed from medium or high altitudes. Not surprisingly, bridges were off limits: strong anti-aircraft fire made them too costly as targets, and, moreover, the Russians had a flair for replacing them in hours with temporary structures. Cutting the tracks was slightly better — at least this could be done with minimal risk — while, to delay repair work, the area was seeded with SD 2 delayed-action bomblets.

However, the best results were achieved by attacking the rolling stock. Given that every train contained at least two Flak cars, this was mainly done during the hours of darkness, especially as the Soviet night-fighter force was virtually non-existent. In the light nights of early summer, up to 200 Ju 88s and He 111s, all fitted with 20mm cannon, patrolled the railways, strafing and bombing targets of opportunity. By day they flew at medium altitudes, armed only with bombs and escorted if possible by long-range fighters.

The Soviet rail system never entirely ceased to function, but essential supplies—fuel, ammunition and tanks—slowed to a trickle. Fuel was the most critical. Soviet air regiments were often grounded and armoured offensives were hamstrung. Had OKH realised the severity of the Russian plight, they might well have launched an offensive even with the meagre resources to hand. But they did not. Instead they waited . . . and waited . . .

ARMAGEDDON PLANNED

Meanwhile at the Wolfsschanze, Hitler's headquarters among the Masurian Lakes, the Gröfaz was becoming impatient. It was those *Verdammt* islanders! They had defied his all-conquering Luftwaffe and killed his loyal friend Göring. They had aided his arch-enemy Stalin, and drawn the United States into the war against him. They had defeated the Kriegsmarine at sea. Neither terror raids nor robot bombardment had subdued them. Further, the electro-boats had failed to fulfil his high expectations.

Nevertheless, the end was now in sight. The German atomic bomb would be ready in September, although it had not yet been tested. Obsessed with the idea of ultimate terror, Hitler had decreed that the test would be carried out against London. This would be his revenge against the nation which, more than any other, had turned his plans for a series of short, victorious wars into a lengthy one, which was bleeding white his 'Thousand-Year Reich'.

As for the Americans, he was certain that he could bluff them into accepting an armistice which, in the long term, he had no intention of honouring. President Franklin D. Roosevelt had died of natural causes in the spring. His successor, Harry S. Truman, was an unknown quantity, but was reputed to be a quiet man. Did not quiet indicate inoffensive? Even weak?

As the British capital was destroyed, two Ketten of Me 264 Amerika-bombers would set out to cross the Atlantic, armed with conventional bombs. One Kette would attack New York, the other Washington. Having demonstrated the ability of the Luftwaffe to attack major East Coast US cities, the Führer would then use the nuclear threat to demand an armistice. In the short term this would of course be bluff: in fact, it would take the Germans several more months to produce enough fissile material for another atomic weapon. But Truman could have no means of knowing this. Hitler was confident that his strategy would succeed. And then, in the long term . . . ?

GRAND FINALE

In August 1945 the Jagdflieger of Luftflotte Reich could feel satisfied with their achievements. The massive American daylight raids of the past were fewer now, and smaller in size. Typically they consisted of about three hundred Möbelwagen (removal vans, as the German fighter pilots called the heavy bombers), protected by upwards of a thousand Mustangs operating in relays. Even this was not enough to protect the bombers. German fighter losses were within acceptable limits, though the Mustangs were obviously trying to corral and hunt down the jets with sheer numbers. The Jagdflieger were winning!

For the most part August had started quietly, with no more than a few probing attacks. This was about to change. Early-warning radars picked up large numbers of aircraft assembling over England. As the first of them left the coast, public address systems at Luftwaffe fighter bases began blaring the message: 'Enemy concentrations in map squares Dora-Dora and Dora-Emil, moving east!'

Slowly the German pilots came to fifteen minutes' readiness and then, as the enemy drew nearer, to cockpit readiness. Gradually it became clear that the inbound raid was no ordinary one. As it crossed the Dutch coast, it was judged to consist of at least 800 heavy bombers, with fighters too numerous to count. By recent standards this was enormous. Where was it going? Surely only Berlin could justify a raid this huge, but already it seemed to be heading much too far south.

The first fighters struck as the head of the formation neared Aachen on the German border. Me 262 jets from II. and III./JG 11 streaked past the escorts in threes and sixes, heading for the leading bombers, launching salvos of their R4M unguided rockets at the densely packed formation and then pulling away high in graceful curves, distracting the Mustang top cover. The Mustangs broke, trying to box one of them, but they were not fast enough. More 262s, this time from I./JG 7, arrived, and again came the high-speed approach, brushing aside the escorts with contemptuous ease, again the high disengagement . . . and more jets . . . and yet more . . .

Now the bombers turned south-east over Wiesbaden, the head of the formation in disarray, with huge gaps. But still they came. Now the Bf 109Ks of two Begleitgruppen joined the fray. Light and agile, they tangled with the Mustangs. Then, curving in behind the bombers, was a Sturmgruppe—58 heavily armed and armoured FW 190A Sturmböcke, attacking in arrowhead formation on a broad front. Heavy and unmanoeuvrable, they were normally 'turkeys' against the agile Mustangs, but the Mustangs were already heavily engaged and the Sturmgruppe carved a deadly swathe through the bombers.

Still the identity of the target was a mystery. Würzburg, Nuremberg and Regensburg, where Messerschmitt fighters are built, all lay in the path of the advancing bombers. Then—Regensburg it was. The bombers— what was left of them—shed their loads and their crews steeled themselves to run the gauntlet home. As they left, several German fighter pilots saw a mysterious bright flash, far to the south. They described it as being 'brighter than the sun'.

In the excitement of the huge raid, few German controllers had paid much heed to a few high-flying contacts approaching Munich from the south. They were assumed to be reconnaissance Mosquitos, which would turn back the instant they sighted contrails from an Me 262. A pair of 262s was scrambled from Munich-Riem to investigate. One was flown by the General der Jagdflieger, Günther Lützow, who, it happened, was visiting on that day. Three of the intruders were in fact singleton Mustangs, put up as decoys, and two of them fled as Lützow's Rotte approached. The next one was very different—a four-engined bomber, high above the contrail belt, which Lützow provisionally identified as a Dornier Do 219 Fafnir.

After some delay, ground control advised him that there were no Fafnirs in the area. As he eased the throttles open to take a closer look, the 'bogey' appeared to open its bomb doors, drop something, reef through a 135-degree turn and then 'bug out', nose low, at full throttle. Lützow cut across its turn to intercept. It was his last action on this earth. Left trailing, his Kacmarek reported: 'A glare brighter than the sun. A huge column of purple-grey smoke with a fiery red core, rising fast. At its top a huge mushroom shape about two kilometres wide starts to form. Bubbling like

Munich nuked! A massive conventional bomber raid from England drew off the defenders, allowing a single USAAF B-29 from Castel Benito in Libya to evade the defences and drop an atomic bomb on Munich.

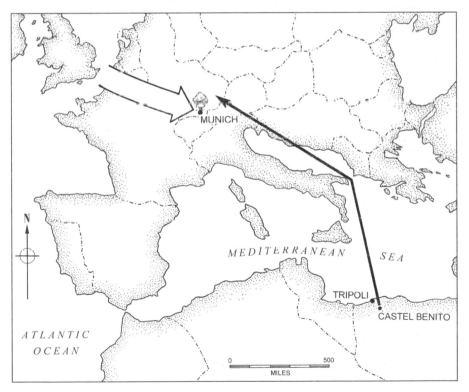

potato soup and shot through with flame, still it rises. Within minutes it reaches a height of 18km.'[4]

The heart of Munich, one of the two places associated with the rise of the Nazi Party, had been gutted. More than 50,000 were dead, and at least as many again would die of radiation sickness.

At first disbelieving, Hitler reverted to the 'carpet diet': as he had done with Hamburg in 1943, he flatly refused to visit the stricken area, ordering Reichsführer SS Heinrich Himmler to impose a news black-out. This proved impossible, even though the electro-magnetic pulse from the explosion had fried radio communications for miles. The local Gestapo had all perished, and although others were rushed to the spot they arrived too late, and were too few, to contain the tens of thousands of refugees, many of them badly burned, who fled the city in all directions.

All attempts to conceal the disaster proved counter-productive. A ban on Luftwaffe flights within 50km of Munich made it all too easy for reconnaissance Mosquitos to slip through and photograph the devastated landscape. The pictures were released to the world's press, while the BBC continually made German-language broadcasts calling for unconditional surrender.

Hitler's instant reaction was revenge. London shall suffer the same fate! His second reaction was that the General der Jagdflieger should be shot for dereliction of duty. He was too late. Lützow had been immolated in the fireball over Munich.[5] The Führer's vaunted intuition told him that, even as Germany had only a single bomb, after which bluff must suffice, the United States must be in like circumstance and the threat of a follow-up attack was hollow. Wrong! The USA had a second bomb — the plutonium-based 'Fat Man'. When after seven days, Hitler made no move to surrender, 'Fat Man' was dropped above the Wolfsschanze by a single B-29 which sneaked past the defences and then low on fuel, recovered to neutral Sweden. The Wolfsschanze was obliterated, and there were no survivors.

The Führer's successor was 'Treuer Heinrich' Himmler, who signed the unconditional surrender document on Lüneberg Heath[6] on 16 August 1945. Arraigned as a war criminal, former chicken-farmer Himmler committed suicide while in captivity.

The war in Europe was now over. Poland, the original *casus belli*, was restored to its pre-war status. The Soviet Union, in recognition of its somewhat dubious efforts as an 'ally' was allowed to returned to her prewar borders, but no more, thus preventing the Cold War. Independence was restored to the Baltic states, and to Czechoslovakia and Yugoslavia, the artificial countries created by the 1919 Treaty of Versailles.

And they all lived happily ever after?

NOTES

1. Historically, Brest was captured but Lorient and St-Nazaire held out until the end of the war.
2. When the *coup* actually took place, almost two years earlier, Kesselring had eight divisions available. Luftflotte 2 had a nominal strength of nearly 1,000 aircraft, about 750 of which were fighters, Jabos or medium bombers.
3. Perhaps fortunately, they never met.
4. Based on an eyewitness description of Hiroshima.
5. The author has assumed that his wingman had a miraculous escape. In reality Lützow was lost while flying an Me 262 during the final days of the war.
6. Hitler's real successor was Grossadmiral Karl Dönitz, but in this revised scenario, given that the electro-boats had failed to deliver the promised victory, it is unlikely that he would have taken over.

Musings

SEPTEMBER 1939 saw a new word enter the military lexicon — Blitz-krieg, or lightning war. In that month, Poland had been overrun by fast-moving Panzers, spearheaded by the mighty Luftwaffe. The following spring saw the process repeated. Denmark and Norway, the Low Countries and even France fell after short campaigns. By July 1940 Britain alone remained unconquered and defiant. Few, however, gave her much chance of survival. The British Expeditionary Force in France had been forced into a humiliating evacuation at Dunkirk, leaving behind its heavy equipment, while the Royal Air Force had sustained heavy losses.

A major key to the brilliant string of German successes was air power. At the outbreak of war, the Luftwaffe was considered by many to be the world's most powerful air force. In a very short space of time it had stormed across Europe, sweeping aside the opposing air forces, including the numerically strong Armée de l'Air, blasting a path for the Panzers and protecting their flanks as they raced for the sea.

Flushed with victory, its formidable reputation apparently justified, the Luftwaffe regrouped in occupied Western Europe for a final show-down with the one remaining enemy. The odds were on its side: it had numerical and qualitative advantages, a well-honed tactical fighter system, the initiative and, above all, supremely confidence. During that blood-stained summer it all started to go wrong. Why? Could things have been done differently?

The Luftwaffe had suffered from its too-rapid formation. In 1939 everything was in the shop window. Although impressive to look at, it had little substance. Reserves were virtually non-existent, while training facilities were inadequate to replace combat losses over an extended period. Two major omissions were a dedicated transport force and a strategic bomber force. Then, for long after the outbreak of war, aircraft production remained at peacetime levels. These shortcomings meant that the Luftwaffe was suited only to fighting short, tactical campaigns. As during the first nine months of the war this was all that it was called upon to do, it acquitted itself well, supporting the advancing German Army. When in the summer of 1940 the Luftwaffe was called upon to fight what was in fact a strategic campaign, it was ill-equipped to do so. Despite protestations to the contrary, it had no real strategic capability.

These deficiencies arose primarily from the fact that the prewar Luftwaffe was an infant service, lacking trained general staff officers with aviation experience and, apart from the Richthofen legend, lacking service traditions. The rot started at the very top. In the Great War, Hermann Göring had been an Oberkanone and Pour Le Mérite holder whose 22 victories placed him fairly low—equal 56th—in the pecking order. His main claim to fame, on which he traded shamelessly, was that he had been the final commander of the Richthofen Geschwader, albeit in the lowly rank of Hauptmann (Captain). Always the opportunist, he had hitched his star to Hitler's bandwagon at an early stage.

Göring's influence during the formative years of the Luftwaffe was largely benign, but, as time passed, his monstrous ego increasingly got in the way. The attainment of power and wealth became his gods, and as both grew he was more and more able to indulge his whims. As delusions of grandeur set in, he became divorced from reality. He failed to recognise that air warfare had changed since 1918. He pampered his young fighter and bomber pilots while expressing open contempt for the vital transport pilots, and electronic warfare remained a closed book to him. Finally, he rejected all criticism. As the mighty Hermann could never be wrong, he sought scapegoats for all failures—with one exception: he could never gainsay Hitler, even on issues of the utmost importance.

It is customary in 'alternate' histories to stick with the actual commanders of the time and simply alter some of their more critical decisions, perhaps with the aid of a change in scenario, but always keeping them in character. Whilst this convention has been largely adhered to, for the Demon King figure of Hermann Göring it simply would not work. Had he succumbed to his wound at the time of the Munich putsch, the Luftwaffe would not have become what it was by 1939. It must not be forgotten that Göring was the 'mover and shaker' who got things done. In this sense it really was 'his' Luftwaffe.

Reversing poor Luftwaffe command decisions was only possible if the Reichsmarschall was removed from the scene, but how to do so realistically was a major problem. The solution adopted has been to use his vanity to manoeuvre him into a combat scenario in which he could be 'bumped off'. September 7, 1940, provided an ideal opportunity, and allowed him to exit the stage in character, larger than life and with his personal courage unquestioned. This would leave the field clear for the vacancy to be filled by a highly respected, professionally trained officer, in this case Albert Kesselring, who would not, however, remain the incumbent for the remainder of the war. Varying scenarios resulted in two more command changes. Let the reader beware: decisions about high-level command changes are far from easy!

Just one further radical command change was needed. One of the greatest of the Luftwaffe's shortcomings was its lack of a strategic bomber force. In reality, this project failed to mature until far too late; in theory, it could have been realised as early as 1940. Its main protagonist was Generalleutnant Walther Wever, the first Luftwaffe Chief of Staff, whose Uralbomber project was initiated in 1934. Wever died in an air crash in 1936. Had he lived, a Luftwaffe strategic bomber force would probably have become a reality and, had it existed, would have impinged on all theatres of war. It would have stretched the RAF's defences in the Battle of Britain. It would have played an important, if not decisive, part in the Battle of the Atlantic. On the Eastern Front, it could have reduced the output of Soviet tanks by a significant margin, making the task of the Heer very much easier. It could also have interdicted British supply routes through the Suez Canal to a considerable degree. As these potential advantages cannot be ignored, Wever has, like a latter-day Lazarus, been resurrected.

In this account, Germany not only suffers far fewer reverses than was historically the case, but often seems on the very brink of winning the war. For the Luftwaffe, this is largely due to the command changes wrought earlier. As an apparently victorious warlord, Hitler would therefore have had less reason to interfere with operational matters.

Two final points. The narrative commences very closely to historical reality. As the effect of every Luftwaffe innovation is cumulative, the narrative gradually diverges. By the same token, for every innovation there is a corresponding counter-measure. It may take a while to develop, or it may be instantly available. In every case, appropriate enemy counters, technical or tactical, are taken into consideration, provided only that they are feasible within the timescale and context.

As the Luftwaffe is the primary subject, the narrative has been constructed from a mainly German viewpoint, varying only when the needs of clarification have so demanded.

CHAPTER 1

The reasons for selecting the Do 19 rather than the Ju 89 as the Uralbomber are clearly stated. When the performances of two aircraft are near enough equal, the two deciding factors are cost-effectiveness and development potential. In both contexts, the Do 19 runs out a clear winner.

The personality of Walther Wever was as described. He was an enthusiastic pilot, but his inexperience was the death of him when he took off from Dresden with the aileron locks of his He 70 still in place. With him died the Luftwaffe's strategic bomber, even though the ill-fated Bomber A project quickly replaced it. His character was such that he might just have kept the procurement programme on an even keel for those vital few years before the war. For the Luftwaffe, his death was a disaster.

In the mid-1930s, an influential group on Luftwaffe General Staff, consisting mainly of engineers but with the tacit backing of Udet, formed what can only be described as a 'Dive-Bomber Mafia'. They led the way in ensuring that the Luftwaffe was mainly a tactical rather than a strategic force. The Ju 87 Stuka had its uses, but it was limited operationally. The most versatile German aircraft of the war was the Ju 88, which excelled as a level and torpedo-bomber, reconnaissance aircraft, heavy fighter and night fighter, would have been even better without the additional weight needed to give it a dive-bombing capability. The attempt to give the four-engine He 177 a dive-bombing capability was the group's most ridiculous decision. This requirement also compromised the twin-engine Bf 210.

CHAPTER 2

This closely follows the historical record. The analysis of the raid on Guernica, and the conclusions drawn therefrom, are based on the best available information, as are the so-called 'terror raids' on Warsaw and Rotterdam — the first of which almost certainly was and the second almost certainly was not. From Poland to France, the greatest advantage the Luftwaffe had was the initiative, and it made this tell. The rapidly following Heer gave rise to the saying that the ultimate in air superiority is a tank in the middle of the runway!

Rather than exulting in the overwhelming victories of 1940, it is probable that the hard-nosed Wever would have been looking to the future. To Göring, his criticisms in the midst of the general euphoria would have made him the spectre at the feast. It was therefore high time for Wever to depart.

CHAPTER 3

It has often been asked why the Germans did not immediately press their advantage after Dunkirk. Hitler's optimism apart, the author believes that they were physically incapable of doing so. Otherwise the events of the Battle of Britain have been followed closely, though with the Luftwaffe's intelligence failures emphasised but not exaggerated. Not until September 7 does the narrative really start to diverge from the historical record. This date sees the combat debut of the Uralbomber, and the death of Göring. Both are landmarks. The former heralds tremendous problems for the British defenders, the latter a sea-change to a far more professional command structure.

In addition, the Bf 109E-7, the first German single-engine fighter to carry plumbing for drop tanks, enters service as a long-range escort for the Uralbomber, whereas in reality it carried bombs as a Jabo. If anyone doubts the severity of the early problems encountered with drop tanks, let them consult the Allied record in this field.

Jamming 'Pip-Squeak' would have made life more difficult for the RAF and easier for the Luftwaffe. While it could hardly have been decisive, it was so simple that it was well worth doing. I am indebted to my good friend Alfred Price for this suggestion. Almost certainly, 'Pip-Squeak' was not jammed because the Luftwaffe's understanding of the RAF command and control system was imperfect.

CHAPTER 4

The overview of the night Blitz, and British interference with Luftwaffe radio bombing aids, follows the historical record. Had the jamming not succeeded, the level of destruction would have been far greater than it was, as evidenced by the Coventry raid, when British jamming was ineffective.

Without Göring's rivalry with Raeder to obstruct matters, the attempt to reduce the British Home Fleet with Uralbombers seems eminently feasible. The results of the raid on Scapa Flow are perhaps over-egged, but they are not beyond the bounds of possibility. The author pleads artistic licence.

The huge size of the Do 19 made judging range extremely difficult for intercepting fighters. Similar problems were experienced by the Jagdflieger against American B-17s some two years later. Nor did machine-gun-armed Spitfires and Hurricanes pack enough punch, even against twin-engine bombers, many of which are recorded as returning safely after sustaining more than 100 hits. For the British it was Hobson's choice. Even though it was plagued by mechanical problems, the Whirlwind was the only high-performance, cannon-armed, long-range fighter immediately available. Therefore it had to be pressed into service regardless.

CHAPTER 5

It is probable that Dönitz was overoptimistic about the advantages of air reconnaissance. The narrative reflects this and assumes more moderate results. However, with Göring removed from the scene, it is likely that the operational control of I./KG 40 would have been retained by the Kriegsmarine. The logical next step would have been to replace the fragile 'this side up' FW 200 Condors, with Do 19s.

The Suez Canal was an obvious chokepoint on the British supply route to North Africa. In reality. the Luftwaffe was only able to mount pinprick raids against it, but a force of strategic bombers would have been potentially devastating. What is more, a slackening of reconnaissance activity over the Atlantic at this time would have made Vultures available, had they existed.

CHAPTER 6

The section on conventional fighters is factual, but it remains to be said that problems with drop tanks were finally resolved, although the tanks were rarely used as intended. More often they were carried to extend range and endurance and retained, notably by night fighters.

In reality, the lack of suitable high-temperature alloys delayed the service entry of German jets to the point where they were too late to make a significant contribution. Had the Me 262 been as successful as the narrative postulates, the He 162 Volksjäger would not have been needed, while the Me 163 Komet rocket fighter would have been no more than an interesting experiment.

The only German strategic bomber to enter service was the ill-fated He 177. It was a victim of all too many poor decisions, and by the time the 'bugs' had been ironed out it was too late. Recent research indicates that Hitler was fixated on bombing New York, which must be the reason why the Me 264 Amerikabomber was allowed to progress as far as it did.

CHAPTER 7

Had, as Hitler once predicted, the war started in 1948, a Kriegsmarine carrier task force might just have been a viable proposition. As it was, the idea was a non-starter. *Graf Zeppelin* class carriers were too small and they carried too few aircraft, of types which were insufficiently specialised and inadequate. The ratio of fighters to attack aircraft was too low, ignoring the fact that security of base is a cardinal rule of warfare. Then, without a body of peacetime experience to draw upon, they would have been committed to learning 'on the job'.

The decision not to proceed with carriers was undoubtedly wise, although their original existence gave the author an unmissable opportunity for a 'what if?' chapter, to explore various possibilities. However, almost certainly, had a Schlachtgruppe put to sea, overwhelming strength would have been brought against it, as in fact happened in the *Bismarck* episode. Even its existence would have posed a deadly threat, as did the presence in Brest of *Scharnhorst*, *Gneisenau* and *Prinz Eugen*. It was a relief to the British when Hitler, acting on intuition, pulled them out, even though the successful 'Channel Dash' in February 1942 was in truth a British defeat. Another threat indication can be inferred by the repeated British attempts to neutralise the battleship *Tirpitz*, even though she rarely strayed from her Norwegian bases.

CHAPTER 8

While the first days of the war against the Soviet Union saw the Luftwaffe gain a great tactical victory, it was ephemeral. However great the Russian losses in *matériel*, they could be replaced from production centres deep into the Soviet hinterland, many of which were in the area where Europe meets Asia. Here they were far beyond the reach of the Luftwaffe. By Herculean efforts, Soviet industry just about managed to keep pace with operational losses, but this chapter explores the potential difference that a Luftwaffe strategic bombing force could have made.

In reality, the lunge for the Caucasus oilfields was unsuccessful. While Maikop was taken, the German advance was halted short of Grozny and Baku was never threatened. In the autumn of 1942 a Soviet counter-attack in the south threatened to cut off Army Group A, and a large-scale German withdrawal took place. It is proposed that the reduction in the number of Soviet tanks reaching the front as the result of strategic bombing would have weakened the Soviets sufficiently to allow the Caucasus oilfields to be taken and held. If so, it would have at a stroke crippled all Soviet offensives in the area while significantly easing German logistics. Not the least effect of this would be severe operational restrictions on the Red Air Force.

Further north, Hitler had become obsessed with the capture of Stalingrad (Stalin's City), to provide him with a major propaganda triumph over the Soviet leader. This was a major error. The German Sixth Army under General von Paulus quickly became bogged down in street fighting, where it lost most of its advantages. Then, when the Red Army counterattacked, it became encircled. Using the Demyansk airlift as a precedent, Hitler demanded that the Sixth Army, some 250,000 men, be supplied by air. With the Russian winter fast setting in, Kesselring was not stupid enough to agree, even though his transport force was more numerous than would in fact have been the case. Never a man to be contradicted lightly, the Führer would certainly have sacked him.

Kesselring's obvious successor was Luftwaffe Chief of Staff Wolfram von Richthofen, who if anything was even more hard-nosed than his predecessor. With no more malleable replacement in sight, it seems probable that Hitler would have conceded the point. Having allowed the Sixth Army to break out, it would play a vital part in subsequent campaigns on the Eastern Front. In reality, in a moment of monumental folly, Göring agreed to the airlift. In what must rank as one of the greatest military disasters ever, the Sixth Army was annihilated. Luftwaffe transport and bomber losses (bombers had been pressed into service to ferry supplies) were prohibitive. It was a blow from which the Wehrmacht never fully recovered.

CHAPTER 9

Dedicated almost entirely to offensive action, the Luftwaffe neglected the development of radar-aided night-fighting, giving the British a lead of about three years. This lead was never seriously eroded; nor, as the Luftwaffe was committed to offensive action, does it appear feasible for the Reich to have made any headway in this field in any significant manner.

With the exception of the continued use of intruders after Hitler's ban of October 1941, together with the use of bomblets and a little discreet juggling of events and statistics, this chapter follows the historical record fairly closely.

CHAPTER 10

A fairly lengthy period is covered here in which many strands, both factual and fictional, come together. The air campaign in the West was much as described. However, the charismatic figure of Adolf Galland is impossible to ignore. In reality, he succeeded Mölders as the General der Jagdflieger, a position he held until he was sacked by Göring in late 1944. He then commanded the elite jet-fighter unit JV 44 until the end of the war. In the narrative, however, this cannot happen. As Udet does not commit suicide, Mölders is not killed while flying to Udet's state funeral, so Galland cannot be promoted to fill the vacancy. So what do we do with him?

Galland's status is rather less here than it became in real life. For failing to protect the Reichsmarschall in 1940, it is probable that he was doomed by Hitler to remain as Kommodore of JG 26 until he was killed or severely wounded, or until his health gave way. One simply does not do this to an iconic figure like Galland: the only honourable option was to have him survive as a prisoner of war.

As General der Jagdflieger, Galland was a hard taskmaster, as 'Macky' Steinhoff relates.[1] Werner Mölders was a much more thoughtful man, and this aspect of his character has been explored. Inevitably, he fell foul of Nazi doctrine and was then removed from the scene.

The scenario leading to the strengthening of the Reich's air defence is entirely fictional, as is the means of assuring the supply of chromium from Turkey. In reality, the Me 262 entered service much later, and its engines were much less reliable. It was, in the event, overwhelmed by superior numbers.

As noted previously, huge British and American bomber raids were very vulnerable to interference on take-off and while forming up. Instances of the possible effects of intruder action are given, and of the possible retribution that followed.

CHAPTER 11

The cumulative effects of events related in previous chapters have by now taken the narrative a long way from reality. At the end of 1944 the campaign in North Africa had been roundly defeated, although the remnants of the Axis armies were still holding out around Tunis. On the Eastern Front, Stalingrad was bombed into submission, while further advances were made into the Russian heartland. In reality, the German retreat was nearing the homeland.

At home the Me 262 jet fighter entered service. As experience was gained, it took an increasing toll of the American heavy bombers. Ar 234 jet reconnaissance aircraft had established the main thrust of the invasion; when it was launched, Me 262 Jabos nearly, but not quite, turned the tide. By the end of 1944 the invasion force was confined to a relatively small beach-head.

In reality, Anglo-American armies had reached the borders of the Third Reich by the end of 1944. Sicily and much of Italy had fallen, while German industry was being relentlessly destroyed from the air. A shortage of fuel had largely grounded the Luftwaffe and had hamstrung land operations. Defeat stared the Third Reich in the face.

ENDGAME

At sea, the vaunted electro-boats had been successful, but not successful enough to turn the tide of war. In France the Allies were fighting their way out of the pocket and had overrun much of Brittany. Allied jets had now entered the fray and were pursuing Me 262 Jabos through the skies of France. On the Eastern Front it was stalemate: German logistics were stretched to their limits, while the shortage of fuel severely restricted their opponents.

Hitler, always a believer in terror, had tried to cow the British with a robot bombardment of V-1s and V-2s. It had not worked. Now he was waiting for news that the German A-bomb was ready. This, he was convinced, would bring the war to a swift and victorious conclusion. It was like giving a pig a pill. Insert the pill into a tube, insert the tube into the pig's mouth, and blow. Unfortunately for him, the pig blew first!

The 1942 agreement between Britain and the United States had been 'Germany First'. As the Americans had beaten the Germans to develop a nuclear weapon, Germany was the obvious recipient. Japan was second-ary. Several problems had first to be resolved, however. What should be the target? Ideally it should be a major city which had not already suffered too much bomb damage. It should also be somewhere with strong Nazi connections. Only two German cities met these criteria in full — Nuremburg and Munich. Munich was chosen, mainly because, close to the southern border, it involved the shortest penetration of German air space.

The next problem was how to get the bomb there without being intercepted. After all, the Allies only had two, and if the bomb carriers were shot down before reaching the target . . . ! The answer adopted was to mount a huge diversionary raid from England. While this would inevitably be costly, the fact that it might bring the war to an abrupt conclusion was judged worthwhile.

The final problem was a suitable base for the raid. It needed to be a long way from civilisation, for security purposes. Another factor was that if the overloaded bomber crashed on takeoff, might it not trigger the nuclear explosion?[2] The one British base considered was Macrihanish, in the wilds of Scotland, but this was a considerable way from Munich and involved a long overflight of German territory. For this reason it was rejected. The base chosen was Castel Benito, about 24km (15 miles) south of Tripoli. The course of the adapted B-29 bomber took it across Italy, up the Adriatic and across Austria. The diversionary raid drew the Luftwaffe fighters to the north, giving the solitary B-29 a clear run. The first-ever nuclear raid was successful, and the centre of Munich was devastated.

Even now, the Führer failed to acknowledge defeat. A second B-29 set forth from Macrihanish, skirted Norway and overflew Sweden to bomb Hitler's headquarters, the Wolfschanze, in the Masurian lakes. Adolf, now able to glow in the dark, never surrendered. It was done for him by Reichsführer-SS Himmler. In reality, of course, Germany had surrendered in May 1945, making Japan the unwilling recipient of 'Little Boy' and 'Fat Man'.

NOTES

1. Johannes Steinhoff, *The Straits of Messina*.
2. The raids on Hiroshima and Nagasaki were launched from the small Pacific island of Tinian. At the time it was feared that an accident would totally destroy the USAAF base there.

Bibliography

Anon., *The Rise and Fall of the German Air Force, 1933–1945*, Arms & Armour Press (London, 1983).

Barker, Ralph, *The Thousand Plan*, Chatto & Windus (London, 1965).

Becker, Cajus D., *The Luftwaffe War Diaries*, Macdonald (London, 1967).

Boyd, Alexander, *The Soviet Air Force since 1918*, Macdonald and Jane's (London, 1977).

Cheshire, Leonard, *Bomber Pilot*, Hutchinson & Co. (London, 1943).

Deichmann, General der Flieger Paul, (ed.), *Spearhead for Blitzkrieg: Luftwaffe Operations in Support of the Army*, Greenhill Books (London, 1996).

Edwards, Bernard, *Dönitz and the Wolf Packs*, Arms & Armour Press (London, 1996).

Faber, Harold, (ed.), *Luftwaffe: An Analysis by Former Luftwaffe Generals*, Times Books (New York, 1977) and Sidgwick & Jackson (London, 1979).

Galland, Adolf, *The First and the Last: The German Fighter Force in WW 2*, Methuen (London, 1955). Original Edition: *Der Ersten und die Letzen: Die Jagdflieger im Zweiten Weltkrieg*, Franz Schneekluth (Darmstadt, 1953).

Gibson, Guy, *Enemy Coast Ahead*, Michael Joseph (London, 1946).

Green, William, *Famous Fighters of the Second World War*, Macdonald & Jane's (London, 1975).

Green, William, *Famous Bombers of the Second World War*, Macdonald & Jane's (London, 1975).

Hermann, Hajo, *Eagle's Wings*, Airlife (Shrewsbury, 1991).

Hogg, Ian V., *Anti-Aircraft: A History of Air Defence*, Macdonald & Jane's (London, 1978).

Hooton, E. R., *Phoenix Triumphant*, Arms & Armour Press (London, 1994).

Hooton, E. R., *Eagle in Flames*, Arms & Armour Press (London, 1997).

Johnen, Wilhelm, *Duel under the Stars*, William Kimber (London, 1957).

Kamansky, Hans, *Uralbomber Pilot*, Grünberg Löwebuch (Stuttgart, 1986).*

Klessen-Wartmann, Egbert, *Kriegsmarine Luft*, Grünberg Löwebuch (Stuttgart 1974).*

Liddell Hart, B. H., *History of the Second World War*, Cassell & Co. (London, 1970).

Mellinthin, F. W. von, *Panzer Battles*, Cassell & Co. (London, 1955).

Müller, Silbert, *Vultures of the Atlantic*, Grünberg Löwebuch (Stuttgart, 1991).*

Parry, Simon W., *Intruders over Britain*, Air Research Publications (London, 1992).

Poolman, Kenneth, *Scourge of the Atlantic*, Macdonald & Jane's (London, 1978).

Price, Alfred, *Aircraft versus Submarine*, William Kimber (London, 1973).

———, *Instruments of Darkness*, Macdonald & Jane's (London, 1977).

———, 'The Jet Fighter Menace', in Macksey, Kenneth, (ed.), *The Hitler Options*, Greenhill Books (London, 1998).

———, *The Last Year of the Luftwaffe*, Arms & Armour Press (London, 1991).

———, *The Luftwaffe Data Book*, Greenhill Books (London, 1997).

Ramsey, (ed.), *The Battle of Britain Then and Now*, Book 5, After the Battle Magazine (London, 1982).

Showell, Jak P. Mallmann, *German Navy Handbook 1939–1945*, Sutton (Stroud, 1999).

Smith, John R., and Kay, Antony, *German Aircraft of the Second World War*, Putnam (London, 1972).

Spick, Mike, *All Weather Warriors*, Arms & Armour Press (London 1994).

———, *Luftwaffe Bomber Aces*, Greenhill Books (London, 2001).

———, *Luftwaffe Fighter Aces*, Greenhill Books (London, 1996).

Stahl, Peter, *The Diving Eagle*, William Kimber (London, 1984).

Steinhoff, Johannes, *The Last Chance*, Hutchinson (London, 1977).

Tarrant, V. E., *The Last Year of the Kriegsmarine, May 1944–May 1945*, Arms & Armour Press (London, 1994).

Udet, Ernst, *Film Pilot to Fighter General*, Schlabedissen (Munich, 1958).*

Wagner, Ray, (ed.), trans. Leland Fetzer, *Soviet Air Force in World War II: The Official History*, Doubleday (New York, 1963) and David & Charles (Newton Abbot, 1974).

Wakefield, Kenneth, *The First Pathfinders*, William Kimber (London, 1981).

Winton, John, *Air Power at Sea 1939–45*, Sidgwick & Jackson, (London, 1976).

Zaloga, Steven J., and Grandsen, James, *Soviet Tanks and Combat Vehicles of World War Two*, Arms & Armour Press (London, 1984).

*Note: Books marked thus * are fictitious titles which might have appeared had the scenario outlined been historically correct.*